GW00322507

RICHARD
BRANSON

REACH FOR THE SKIES

By the Same Author

Losing My Virginity: The Autobiography

Screw It, Let's Do It: Lessons in Life and Business

Business Stipped Bare: Adventures of a Global Entrepeneur

RICHARD BRANSON

REACH FOR THE SKIES

BALLOONING, BIRDMEN
AND BLASTING INTO SPACE

2 4 6 8 10 9 7 5 3 1

Published in 2010 by Virgin Books, an imprint of Ebury Publishing
A Random House Group Company

Copyright © Richard Branson 2010

For legal purposes the copyright acknowledgements and picture credits
serve as a continuation of this page

Richard Branson has asserted his right under the Copyright, Designs and Patents Act 1988
to be identified as the author of this work

All rights reserved. No part of this publication may be reproduced, stored in a retrieval
system, or transmitted in any form or by any means, electronic, mechanical, photocopying,
recording or otherwise, without the prior permission of the copyright owner

The Random House Group Limited Reg. No. 954009

Addresses for companies within the Random House Group can be found at
www.randomhouse.co.uk

A CIP catalogue record for this book is available from the British Library

The Random House Group Limited supports The Forest Stewardship Council [FSC],
the leading international forest certification organisation. All our titles that are printed
on Greenpeace-approved FSC-certified paper carry the FSC logo.
Our paper procurement policy can be found at www.rbooks.co.uk/environment

Mixed Sources
Product group from well-managed
forests and other controlled sources
www.fsc.org   Cert no. TT-COC-2139
© 1996 Forest Stewardship Council

Design & layout: www.carrstudio.co.uk
Printed in Great Britain by Clays Ltd, St Ives plc

Hardback ISBN 9781905264919
Trade paperback ISBN 9780753519868

To buy books by your favourite authors and register for offers visit
www.rbooks.co.uk

This book is dedicated to lost friends and vanished

acquaintances: to the aviators and adventurers whose

friendship enriched my life, and who later paid

the ultimate price for their dreams.

CONTENTS

Prologue

When I was a young boy we used to spend our summer holidays staying with my Aunt Clare in Norfolk. She was a close friend of Douglas Bader, the second World War fighter ace who had lost both his legs in a plane crash. We would often go swimming in the millpond at the bottom of her garden. Douglas would unstrap his legs and haul himself into the water. Seizing my chance, I used to run off with these tin legs and hide them in the rushes by the water's edge.

There are few things more thrilling for a small boy than to be chased by a decorated war hero. Even better, I knew I could not be caught – or so I thought. I was about to learn that years of combat experience are a powerful weapon against horrid little boys. Legs or no legs, victory comes to the pilot who tumbles out of the sun upon his enemy, holding his fire until the last possible second. I ran round the corner of my aunt's mill house – and stopped dead, horrified, as this great barrel of a man, growling and gnashing his teeth, bounded towards me on powerful arms. I screamed for help.

From her deckchair, Aunt Clare shot me a look that, had it been directed at an aeroplane, would have seen it plummeting into the ground. 'Good God Richard! Would you give Douglas back his legs!'

If in my life I have associated ideas about ambition and achievement with dreams of flight, it is thanks to Douglas Bader, who used to take my aunt out flying and, true to form, would hurl their plane through all these daring aerobatic manoeuvres. (I think he fancied her.) With his example before me – one of the great flying aces of the Second World War – was it any wonder that I turned out the way I did, always reaching for the skies? I wasn't the only child of my generation to be inspired by his example and his story (Paul Brickhill's biography of him *Reach for the Sky*, later to become a film starring Kenneth More, is the classic to which this book pays homage). 'Don't listen to anyone who tells you that you can't do this or that,' he once said. 'That's nonsense.'

As far back as stories go, pioneers have reached for the skies. In the last two hundred years, they have mastered the air and made the modern world possible. Today they are bringing outer space within our reach. They're inventors and toymakers, amateurs and adventurers, visionaries, dreamers and, yes, crackpots. Some have called them irresponsible, even dangerous. But I have met many of them. I have worked with them, and funded them, and flown with them. I admire them, and trust them, and I think they and their kind are our future.

Some paid the ultimate price for their efforts. Richard Ellis taught me to fly, or tried to. Alex Ritchie, a brilliant engineer, and Steve Fossett, an aviation pioneer, were friends. Fumio Nima was a gallant and charming rival as we strove to balloon across the Pacific. In 2006 I climbed aboard an English Electric Lightning supersonic jet with the South African pilot Dave Stock. We were attempting to break the world vertical speed record, rising from a standstill on the runway to an altitude of 29,000 feet in under 102 seconds. We missed the record by only two seconds, and Dave went on pushing the boundaries. In November 2009, at the Overberg Air Show in South Africa, Dave's Lightning failed.

'Hydraulic malfunction,' he announced, cool and professional to the last. 'I'm bailing out.' A second later he said: 'I have ejector seat failure.' Dave died with his plane as it crashed to the ground. He was in his forties, and had two children. Dave and the others were all my inspiration as I assembled this history. In these pages you will find tales of heroic rescues; of records made and broken; of incredible feats of endurance and survival, including some of my own adventures, as well as developments in the future of air (and space) travel. It is a story of pioneers, and of course it includes the world-famous Montgolfiers and the Wright brothers, but I also want to describe some of the lesser-known trailblazers – people like Tony Jannus, who in 1914 created the first scheduled commercial flight in the world, flying his passengers over the waters of Tampa Bay at an altitude of just fifty feet; the 'bird man' Leo Valentin, who in the 1950s jumped from 9,000 feet with wooden wings attached to his shoulders; and my friend Steve Fossett, who dedicated his life to breaking records and having adventures.

This is their story. It is also, in a small way, my own.

Introduction

In Memory of Steve Fossett

IT was a freezing January evening in 1997. At the old Busch Stadium in St Louis, Missouri, a man by the name of Steve Fossett was about to attempt a solo circumnavigation of the world by balloon. Since we were competitors, and I had not met him before, I decided to wish him luck and wave him off.

To this day, the newfangled world of extreme aviation is sustained by a very old-fashioned spirit of sportsmanship, and I was looking forward to shaking my rival's hand. When I arrived and saw the balloon, however, incredulity pushed every other thought out of my head: what madman, I wondered, would put their life at risk in this tub? It appeared to me to be one of the most primitive and gimcrack contraptions I had ever seen. This was no jet-stream surfer. This was a balloon built to suffer the outrages of regular, low-altitude weather. He expected to get around the world like this? In this? I got chatting with one of the ground staff and I was just about to comment, not too favourably, on the whole enterprise, when a TV crew approached. Since the cameras were running, I reined myself in a bit.

'You know,' I said, 'this guy must be even madder than me.'

The man nodded. 'Yeah,' he sighed. He reached out his hand. 'I'm Steve Fossett,' he said.

Steve was in his mid-fifties, and had enjoyed a hugely successful career as a floor trader in Chicago, when he decided to see what he was capable of. 'There was a period of time where I wasn't doing anything except working for a living,' he told me: 'I became very frustrated with that and finally made up my mind to start getting back into things.'

Between the mid-1990s and his death in 2007, Steve broke about 130 world records, ninety-three of them in planes, balloons and airships, twenty-three of them in yachts. He climbed most of the world's highest mountains. He swam the English Channel. He learned to glide and, with co-pilot Terry Delore, broke ten of the twenty-one Glider Open Class records. He learned how to fly a balloon, and was the first man to sail one around the world single-handed.

Steve had a hunger for the world and for finding out how the world ticks. His curiosity was insatiable. The technical and theoretical aspects of his adventures consumed him. He understood, and took great pride in, the technical advances his adventures inspired. By 2007 he was looking for ground suitable for his new car: a jet-powered behemoth that he hoped would carry him to a new world land-speed record. The shakedown runs had proven the car's stability. The Target 800 mph team, under project director Eric Ahlstrom, said they were good to go.

'You know,' I said,

'this guy must be even madder than me.'

So, on 3 September 2007, Steve borrowed a plane (a Bellanca Decathlon, a single-engine stunt plane, its fuselage and wings made of wood and stretched fabric – technology as old as manned flight itself) and took off from the Flying-M Ranch in western Nevada on a three-hour scouting flight.

He did not come home.

His disappearance triggered one of the biggest manhunts in history. The Civil Air Patrol, the National Guard, sheriffs' departments and volunteer fleets flying from Minden-Tahoe and the Flying-M Ranch scoured the area for signs of Steve's plane – and after six days with no result, the search effort was extended even further. Peter Cohen of Amazon parcelled out fresh satellite footage to computer users across the Web. Now that Steve had volunteers all over the world looking for him, he was bound to turn up. That was what we thought. Hoped. Prayed for.

We told each other stories of miraculous rescues of the past; of surprising feats of endurance and survival. It would be just

like Steve to walk his way out of the High Sierra. Had he not, as
a student, swum his way to Alcatraz and back? It would be just
like him to survive against all odds, the way he had survived, in
1998, a five-mile drop into the shark-infested Coral Sea.

In the desert, miracles sometimes happen. In 1927, executives
at MGM Studios staged a stunt flight across America for 'Leo',
the lion whose roar opens the company's films. (The lion's actual
name was Slats; it came from Dublin Zoo.) They took a single-
engined Brougham – much the same sort of plane that Charles
Lindbergh flew across the Atlantic – and installed a cage directly
behind the cockpit.

Marty Jensen was hired to ferry Slats from San Diego to New
York. Five hours into the flight, he was lost, grounded, the plane's
wings and landing gear ripped off, trapped inside a ravine with
steep rocky sides and no exit – with a lion.

Jensen gave the lion some milk, water and half his lunch, and
set off on foot for help.

Four days later, nearly dead from exhaustion, he was rescued
by cowboys. As soon as he could, he called the film company.

Their first question was: 'How's the lion?'

We waited, and we told each other stories.

Seventeen thousand square miles.

Slats was rescued unharmed: he carried on touring for a while,
and died in comfortable retirement in 1936.

Forty-four thousand square kilometres.

The desert is big, but it is far from empty. The longer the search
went on, the more wrecks the searchers discovered. Within the
first couple of weeks, rescue teams had identified six crashed
planes. Who had their pilots been? Had they been young or old?
Had they had families? Who had mourned them? What had they
left behind?

We may never know. The desert is riddled with inaccessible canyons. No one who knows the desert is prepared to estimate the number of other wrecks that may be out there.

I suppose this is where the book you're holding was born. It occurred to me that no matter how many books are written, the history of aviation – the real history of aviation – is limitless and, for the most part, unrecorded. In this book I want to tell you my version of the history of flight – the story that matters to me. It's about the people who have inspired me, and says something about what I've done, and what my friends and family have done; about what happened to us, and why. Everything in this book is true enough – but it doesn't try to tell the whole story.

Not every pioneer is a well-funded trailblazer. When the First World War ended, the US found itself with an embarrassing amount of surplus equipment. You could buy a set of flying lessons and they'd throw a plane in for free. Amateur pilots flew from town to town selling five-dollar rides at county fairs. They lived hand-to-mouth, flying so they might eat.

Not every pioneer leaves the ground; they also serve who simply sit and think. The Swedish physicist Svante August Arrhenius published *Worlds in the Making*, the first ever account of the greenhouse effect, in 1906. When SpaceShipTwo takes its first astronauts into space, among them will be James Lovelock, a man who worked out how the Earth's rocks, winds and oceans sustain life on this planet. He did it by studying Mars.

No pioneer works alone. Joseph was a maverick and dreamer; Étienne was severe, and responsible: together, the Montgolfier brothers ushered in the modern history of manned flight. The Wright brothers were equally dissimilar, equally inseparable: together, they invented the moveable wings that made today's planes possible. Today, the Rutan brothers enjoy something of the Wrights' notoriety. Before he turned his attention to spaceships, Burt Rutan wove extraordinary aeroplanes together out of exotic resins; his brother Dick flew them and set world records.

Not every pioneer succeeds. Clément Ader achieved manned heavier-than-air flight well over a decade before the Wright brothers, but his every public demonstration ended in a crash. In the 1990s, Larry Newman spent two solid years running himself ragged – not to mention every backer, volunteer and friend – in his desire to get his radical *Earthwinds* balloon around the world. On its last flight, *Earthwinds* travelled 100 miles.

Most important of all: passengers have been pioneers, too. Explorers, rescue parties, doctors and scientists, geologists and map-makers were among the first passengers to take to the air. But the very first passengers were pleasure-seekers, men and women with an insatiable appetite for seeing the world in a new way. Ultimately, they bankrolled air travel as we know it today, and we have them to thank for the transformation of our world.

I spend a great deal of my life on aeroplanes. I'm sometimes exhausted by the routine, as much as the next business traveller. But there isn't a flight goes by when I don't stare out of the window and thank my stars for what I'm seeing and feeling. I know a lot about air travel, and something about aviation, and because of this, flying fills me with excitement. If this book makes your air journeys just a little bit more magical, just an edge more miraculous, then I will have done my job. The air is full of wonders.

This has been a daunting book to write. As I've gone on, however, I've gained confidence. I've discovered and rediscovered the stories of men and women far more driven,

'There isn't a flight goes by **when I don't stare out of the window and thank my stars** for what I'm seeing and feeling.'

far smarter and far, far braver than I am – and at the end of it all I realise that I am part of this story. I've won more than my fair share of competitions and set a handful of records. Like so many before me, I have plummeted into the sea and been fished, half-frozen, from the water. I know frostbite. I know the wrench you feel in your gut as a balloon rises to where the air is too thin to breathe comfortably. I know what an altimeter needle does when you fall from the sky. I know what it is to take the controls of an untested plane, fly on exotic fuel, and crash a dubious and home-made flying machine.

Best of all, my success in business has given me the chance to help realise the ambitions of adventurers, engineers, scientists and visionaries of every stripe. I have met some remarkable people. None was more remarkable than Steve Fossett. At an age when many people are easing up and looking back on their lives, Steve dedicated himself to breaking records and having adventures. If this is what you make of your life, day in, day out, eventually your luck will run out. Though none of his friends could have predicted the manner of his death, we all assumed Steve would go out in spectacular style, sooner or later. When his luck finally did run out, he was at the controls of a light aeroplane he knew like the back of his hand.

Steve did not have children. He had only his own life to lead, so he led it. Among the projects left unfinished at his death was a submarine. He'd been chasing the world depth record. Steve did not have a death wish. He had the exact opposite. His appetite for life was so strong, it outweighed all fear. So what if his choices shortened his life? His choices filled his life, and enriched the lives of those around him.

In October 2008, in the trackless desert that swallowed him, another adventurer – a weekend hiker – stumbled upon the wreckage of Steve Fossett's plane. The fuselage, wood and canvas, looked little different, after a year in the mountains, from the remains left by pioneers who vanished a century ago.

This book covers more than two hundred years of adventures in the air. Steve is part of that story now. The history of flight is full of remarkable people, and Steve's adventures would have been understood and appreciated by every one of them.

Steve was part of a tradition, and the tradition survives him. It lives on.

Part One

The Rising

Escape plan: Daedalus makes wings for his son Icarus
(frieze *c.* 200AD).

one

Walking on Air

few stories to begin.

The first, from Greek mythology, you probably know already: how Icarus, wearing wings made of feathers and wax, flew too close to the sun; how the wings melted, and he came to a sorry end in the Aegean Sea.

Actually the story, as it grew over the centuries, got better than this. It got more believable. Icarus was the son of Daedalus, a talented but irascible inventor, constantly at odds with his patrons and jealous of anyone with the talent to rival him. Daedalus' sister sent him her son, Perdix, to be his apprentice; but Perdix was too smart for his own good. He was always wandering off, beachcombing, collecting and observing. He studied how nature worked. Inspired by the workings of a snake's jaw, he invented the saw.

Daedalus, whose inventions included the axe, the plumb line, the drill and glue, felt he was being upstaged. He made sure to accompany his nephew on his next walk, led him up a tall tower to catch the view – and pushed him to his death.

He didn't get away with it. Daedalus was exiled to Crete and set to work by King Minos, building a labyrinth for the royal family's least favoured son: the monstrous, half-human, half-bull Minotaur.

Down but not out, Daedalus kept half an eye on his work, the other half on Naucrate, one of Minos' mistresses, and soon enough he had a son, Icarus. Not content with cuckolding his patron, he then gave away the plans of the labyrinth to Minos' daughter, so that she could escape with Theseus, a foreign adventurer and thief imprisoned there. Minos, when he found out, threw Daedalus and his son into the labyrinth themselves.

This is where the wings come in. Daedalus made two pairs: one for himself and one for his son. Together they would fly to Sicily, over the heads of King Minos' soldiers and his fleet of many ships. Like the nephew he murdered, Daedalus took inspiration from nature, tying feathers together in order of size to produce curved flying surfaces, just like the wings of real birds. He secured the larger feathers with thread, the smaller ones with wax, and warned Icarus to keep them out of the water and away from the heat of the sun.

The way we usually hear this story, Icarus is the tragic hero: a romantic figure, overcome with the thrill of flying, who yearned for the sun and died for his trouble. We all too easily forget the upshot of the tale: *his father made it.*

Daedalus flew successfully across the sea and landed in Sicily. There he built a temple to Apollo and secured the patronage of the local king. When Minos finally tracked him down, with his patron's assistance Daedalus murdered him.

Of course, it's just a story. But it comes from somewhere. The people who told and retold it knew something about where ideas come from. They knew the importance of observation and study; when they described Perdix's saw and Daedalus' wings, they showed how engineering takes its inspiration from nature. They knew the kind of ego and self-confidence you need to craft and invent new things, and somehow get paid for your trouble. They knew how easily patrons fall out with their designers and how resentments and broken loyalties can ruin the finest plans.

Another story. On eight or nine occasions between 1630 and 1632, Hezârfen Ahmed Çelebi flew over the pulpit of Okmeydani in Istanbul with eagle wings, 'using the force of the wind'. The sultan, Murad IV, was so impressed he gave Hezârfen a sack of gold coins for his trouble. Then he declared: 'This is a frightening man. He is capable of doing anything he wishes. It is not right to keep such people' – and Çelebi and his new wealth were courteously, but promptly, escorted into exile in Algeria.

History is chock-full of projects for full-scale, people-carrying flying machines, and while none of them ever got off the ground in any meaningful or sustained way, it wasn't for lack of knowledge. Some of Leonardo da Vinci's fifteenth-century flying machines would have flown, had he only had access to lightweight materials. They wouldn't have had to be very sophisticated materials, either: the right varnished silks and papers would have been enough to fill the skies of Renaissance Florence and Milan with hang-gliders and personal flyers.

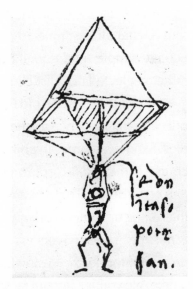

Leonardo da Vinci's designs for flight featured this rather dubious-looking parachute.

They wouldn't have been the first to fly, either: hang-gliding existed in China perhaps by the fourth century AD, and certainly by the time of Emperor Wenxuan of Northern Qi (r. 550–59 AD), who used condemned men as test pilots for his man-flying kites. One startling book, written a good two centuries earlier, even contains a description of a rotary-wing aircraft: 'Some have made flying cars with wood from the inner part of the jujube tree, using ox-leather [straps] fastened to returning blades so as to set the machine in motion.'

Tempting as it is to imagine people riding around in these contraptions, more likely they were models – which brings us to our next story.

'Gentlemen,' Hardy Krüger announces, 'I have been examining this aeroplane.'

Never mind the sterling performances and brilliant cast, headlined by James Stewart and Richard Attenborough, I think *The Flight of the Phoenix* (1965) is one of the most profound and important movies about aviation ever committed to film. No small claim, that. The film is, after all, a simple adventure story, transferring to cinema an equally simple (and equally gripping) novel by the prolific, now rather neglected novelist Elleston Trevor.

It's the mid-1960s. An old Fairchild cargo plane is carrying oilmen out of the Sahara when a sandstorm blows up. One engine clogs and dies. Sand overcomes the other, and the plane comes down, far off course, in the middle of the most arid, inhospitable and unfrequented part of the desert. That's before the credits. What follows is the really interesting bit. A neat early twist means that no one knows the plane is missing. The survivors can't walk out of the desert. All they can do is wait for death. Meanwhile a young, arrogant and thoroughly unlikeable young German (actor Hardy Krüger's finest performance, I reckon) is wandering around the plane, round and round, constantly burning his fingertips on the sun-baked fuselage, stroking, prodding

– he's driving everyone crazy. What is he trying to do? Dorfmann is an aeroplane designer, and he's been dreaming up an escape vehicle. He reckons there are enough serviceable parts left over from the crash to build a new aeroplane. If the effort doesn't kill them all, their gimcrack escape vehicle surely will: but working themselves to death is better than waiting for death, so they begin. Only there's something Dorfmann forgot to mention. He's only ever designed model aeroplanes. He's had no experience of 'the real thing'. Dorfmann's defence, when finally this prickly fact comes to light, is a delight. Sweating and terrified, he delivers a speech – too long and broken to repeat here – which is, in little, a history of aviation. All the great advances in aviation have come from models, he says, and he lists them.

The lovely thing about this speech is that it's true. Model aircraft have been flying for a lot longer than people. Was there ever a time when children did not play with model aircraft? The African-born writer and judge Aulus Gellius, writing in the second century AD, finds several sources to confirm the story of Archytas (428–347 BC), friend of the philosopher Plato and inventor of mathematical engineering: 'For not only many eminent Greeks, but also the philosopher Favorinus, a most diligent searcher of ancient records, have stated most positively that Archytas made a wooden model of a dove with such mechanical ingenuity and art that it flew; so nicely balanced was it, you see, with weights and moved by a current of air enclosed and hidden within it. If true, Archytas's 'pigeon' is the first artificial, self-propelled flying device we know of: a bird-shaped, steam-driven model plane!

In medieval times, the spread of windmills inspired toy pinwheels, and they, in their turn, inspired the kind of toy helicopter first seen in a Flemish manuscript dated to 1325. When the Wright brothers were little, the toyshops were packed

A toy helicopter entertains a child in Pieter Breugel's painting of 1560.

with toy helicopters. Powered by rubber bands, they rose as high as fifty feet into the air. And as we'll see when we meet the spaceship designer Burt Rutan, models are as important today as they always were, and just as inspirational.

Most people hanker for a view of the Earth from space. I should know: I'm one of them. A ticket for a forthcoming Virgin Galactic flight into suborbital space will set you back $200,000. But a sense of the oneness of the Earth and its peoples does not have to come at such expense. I'd love you to join us on Virgin Galactic one day, and we're working hard to make it affordable for everyone; but first, go treat yourself to an £89 balloon ride.

Balloons have been around for a long time, but even when I was a boy, public joyrides were hard to come by. Balloons were the playthings of the rich until around 1960, when an American engineer called Ed Yost found a way to build safe hot-air balloons more cheaply, using nylon fabric for the canopy and propane cooking gas as a heat source. A Bristol Aeroplane Company engineer called Don Cameron brought Yost's ideas to Europe, and his first hot-air balloon, *Bristol Belle*, rose into the air above RAF Weston-on-the-Green on 9 July 1967. Balloons based on those original Yost and Cameron designs are the kind you see floating through summer skies. Ballooning 'fiestas' bring enthusiasts together from miles around. Most are local affairs. The biggest and most famous is at Albuquerque, New Mexico, where several hundred balloonists sink lakes of Budweiser beer and recreate the sort of airborne display that made headlines back in the nineteenth century.

The ballooning fraternity are a proud and close-knit bunch, and they're a bit reticent around the rich adventurers and corporate sponsors that stage major world-record attempts. They take their sport seriously and they don't like being upstaged. Sport ballooning is an absorbing and serious business, and its competitions follow precise, complicated rules. It's no small achievement to fly ten miles in about an hour and pass within a few feet of a predetermined goal, with only the winds at different altitudes to steer you. A handful fly helium-filled balloons in long-distance races. The most famous of these is the Gordon Bennett Cup, started in 1906 by James Gordon Bennett, Jr, the publisher of the *New York Herald* and the man who financed Stanley's search for the explorer Livingstone. Hot-air ballooning and gas ballooning are quite different sports, as we'll see, so each category of ballooning

'Someone bet me that I would not fly across the airfield by the end of the year. They knew I would not be released by the flight surgeon to return to flying status by then. In December I made a makeshift balloon and flew it across the runway.'

Per Lindstrand

sets its own records and salutes its own champions. It can be dizzying for a newcomer.

I came at ballooning from a different angle again. Until the balloon designer Per Lindstrand phoned me up, the nearest I'd ever been to a wicker basket was watching the actor Cantinflas lean out of one to scoop snow from the side of the Matterhorn to ensure that David Niven's champagne was adequately chilled in the film of Jules Verne's *Around the World in Eighty Days*. (In the book, Fogg used every vehicle imaginable to circle the Earth, and his balloon flight was a disaster: they went backwards.)

Per's engineering career took off in the Swedish Air Force, and his first balloon flight – in the early 1970s – lasted just a few seconds. 'I'd been removed from flight status because of a medical condition,' he remembers, interviewed by Tom Hamilton of the journal *Balloon Life* in 1998. 'Someone bet me that I would not fly across the airfield by the end of the year. They knew I would not be released by the flight surgeon to return to flying status by then. In December I made a makeshift balloon and flew it across the runway.'

Per went on to work at Saab and Lockheed. When a neighbour in Sweden bought a state-of-the-art balloon from the UK, Per couldn't believe his eyes. *This* was the state of the art? One look was enough to tell him that he could do better. How much better would reveal itself as the 1980s dawned.

Per's balloons were sophisticated machines, but it was the fabric he used for his envelopes that fascinated me. They were made of this crazy plasticised, metalised stuff – a constantly evolving recipe that he never discussed in public. It was unbelievably thin and light and strong. Given what he wanted to use it for, it would have to be: Per reckoned he could get us both across the Atlantic Ocean by balloon.

He phoned me in 1986, mere days after I'd won the blue riband, propelled across the Atlantic Ocean faster than ever before on *Virgin Atlantic Challenger II* – a boat that was some sort of infernal marriage between speedboat and intercontinental ballistic missile. (Having got away with that, I was still half-inclined to believe that I could get away with anything.)

Before I could fly with Per, I had to get my balloon pilot's licence, so I headed to Spain and placed myself under the watchful (and ever more exasperated) eye of my teacher, Robin Batchelor. I carried two impressions away from that day, both vivid, and each contradicting the other. I was, from the very first, captivated. I was amazed at how peaceful, how natural it was, to rise through the air without motors, without sound. How refreshing, to be able to escape the rigours and irritations of earthbound life and give myself up to the mercy of the winds! Crossing over the Spanish countryside, I found it easy to imagine that the winds were transporting me through time as well as through space, to a gentler, kinder corner of history.

At the very same moment, I was feeling absolutely wretched. *Why was this person shouting at me?* It was like being back at school! Why on earth was I putting myself through this? I had been my own boss since I was fifteen years old, and my whole life to that point had been dedicated to never taking another bloody exam for as long as I lived. And now look where I was: marooned with a teacher! Being shouted at! Again!

I learned ballooning the way I've learned everything else in life: by doing it. Robin Batchelor's lessons got me started, and Per kept a very close eye on me at first. Neither man would ever say that I was a natural in the air. I learned on the job. Most balloonists, and most pilots, acquire their skills by degrees over several years. My story is different. Working with Per, virtually all my experience was gained during epic voyages lasting several days. As a consequence I became, very quickly indeed, one of the world's more experienced balloonists.

I love balloons, and I still have one of my own – just a simple hot-air balloon with a wicker basket. If you want to escape the world entirely, it's all you need. Nobody can trouble you. Nobody can stop you. You can't even give yourself a hard time. You're not in control. You have given yourself up to the air, and the winds are taking you where they will. My world-record attempts were about as choreographed and preplanned as balloon flights ever get, and still, under all that anxiety and effort, I got a tremendous sense of joy from being superbly powerless: human chaff, borne who knows where by the wind.

Today, could you trust me to carry you up, up and away? You might want to remind me of how I'm supposed to talk to traffic control. (I can't for the life of me remember the rigmarole you need to safely overfly an ordinary airport.) Otherwise, you're in safe hands. So let me take you for a ride.

We're standing in a wicker basket, firmly anchored to the ground. Above us, attached to the basket with strong cords, is a gigantic inverted teardrop made of thin fabric. This is our balloon's 'envelope'. The bottom of the teardrop is open, and now and again I fire a burner – a sort of propane stove. This fills the envelope with hot air and is our only means of control during our flight. So how (you may be asking, as the minutes of preparation tick by) are we going to get off the ground?

This was a considerable mystery to the pioneers of flight, who were strapping their balloons together out of whatever they could find or make. Pioneers like the Montgolfier brothers and Jean Pierre Blanchard didn't have clean, safe propane burners. Oh no: these daredevils filled their balloons with air rising from roaring fires of chaff, wool, tinder and even old shoes! If filling one of these early balloons sounds a mucky business – well, it was. Early balloonists weren't entirely sure what it was about heating air that was making their balloons rise. Maybe it was the *smoke* filling their balloons that was making them lighter than air – in which case, the more smoke the better! Only later did people realise that the smoke itself was irrelevant – that it was the *heat of the air* that was making the balloon rise.

Here's why. Gases expand to fill the space they're given, and as they expand, they get thinner and thinner. The air we breathe would go gushing off into outer space for ever, if it weren't for gravity. The Earth's gravity holds the air close to the surface in a thin mantle: this is our atmosphere. 'Air pressure' is simply the total weight of the air above us at any one moment; and the higher we go, the less the pressure of the air. The air pressing on us at ground level weighs a lot: nearly fifteen pounds of air presses against every square inch of our bodies.

There are two basic kinds of balloon: a gas balloon has an envelope filled with a gas (helium, or hydrogen) that is lighter than the surrounding air; a hot-air balloon has an envelope that is filled with ordinary air that has been heated. Air, like any gas, will expand and thin out as it grows warmer. As the air in its envelope warms up, a hot-air balloon will become progressively lighter.

However thin the gas in your balloon, you're eventually going to reach a height where the surrounding air is thinner. At that point, you'll stop rising. The only way to go higher is to lose some weight – in other words, to throw something out of the balloon. That something (sandbags, lead weights, unpopular passengers) is called 'ballast'. To come down again, you need to make your balloon (slightly!) heavier than the surrounding air.

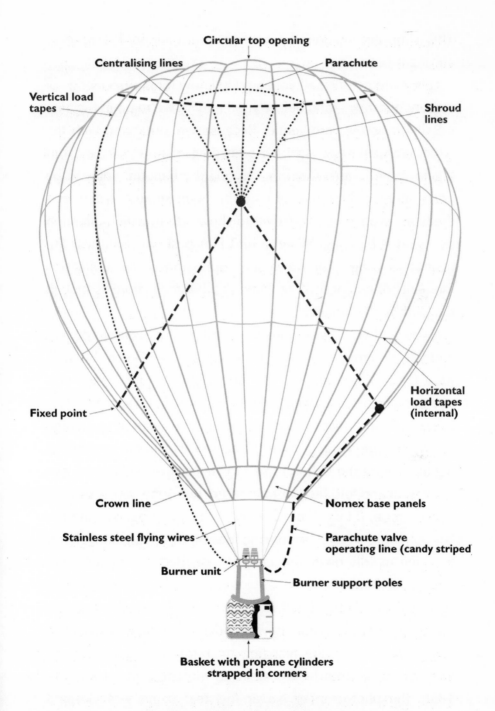

Circular top opening

Centralising lines

Parachute

Vertical load tapes

Shroud lines

Fixed point

Horizontal load tapes (internal)

Crown line

Nomex base panels

Stainless steel flying wires

Parachute valve operating line (candy striped)

Burner unit

Burner support poles

Basket with propane cylinders strapped in corners

Up, up and away: a contemporary hot-air balloon, designed by Don Cameron.

This is most easily done by 'venting' your balloon: letting some air or gas out of it.

This is pretty much all you need to know for now. So let go of that anchor rope – and before you know it, we're up in the air.

Balloon ascents are gentle. Because we're moving with the wind, we won't even feel the breeze against our skin, even in a gale. Even in a snowstorm. On board a balloon, you can be borne along at hundreds of miles an hour, strike a match, and the flame won't even keel over to show you in which direction the wind is blowing. When a bird flies past, you can hear the beat of its wings. The prevailing impression, in these first few moments of ascent, isn't of flying at all: it feels more as though the earth has fallen away.

If you had your eyes closed, you might not even notice you had left the ground. This happened to Charles Green, Britain's most famous balloonist of the nineteenth century. Green was due to make his first ascent from Green Park in London in 1821, as part of the festivities surrounding the coronation of George IV. As the moment of take-off neared, sightseers packed so tightly around the balloon that Green slumped exhausted into the basket and told his assistants to get him some air. They paid out the rope, lifting him a few feet from the ground – and the balloon broke free. Green had no idea he was flying until cheers from the rapidly dwindling crowd persuaded him to peer over the side of the basket.

From the basket of a hot-air balloon, you can really recapture the excitement that must have flooded the minds of the early 'aeronauts', as for the first time in human history they saw their world laid out before them, as though it was a map. In 1858, the photographer Nadar (his real name was Gaspard Felix Tournachon) sailed 258 feet above the valley of Bièvre in

France and captured a daguerreotype – an early photograph – of the earth below, blurred by the vibrations of the balloon. 'We have had bird's-eye views seen by the mind's eye imperfectly,' he wrote. 'Now we will have nothing less than the tracings of nature herself, reflected on the plate.

NADAR élevant la Photographie à la hauteur de l'Art

'Elevating photography to the height of art': Nadar caricatured in 1862.

Of course, map views are a commonplace now. Those of us who lived through the Cold War experienced its most frightening moments almost entirely from the air: aerial images of Cuban missile installations; surveillance satellite photographs; overhead map projections of nuclear-weapon damage; aeroplane views of H-bomb tests.

For me and my generation, I think ballooning is a perfect tonic, a way to discard the paranoia of the Cold War and get back to the sense of wonder enjoyed by Prince Pückler-Muskau as he sailed in a balloon over the city of Berlin in 1817: 'No imagination can paint anything more beautiful than the magnificent scene now disclosed to our enraptured senses: the multitude of human beings, the houses, the squares and streets, the high towers gradually diminishing, while the deafening tumult became a gentle murmur, and finally melted into a deathlike silence.'

People sometimes expect to see the curvature of the earth from the vantage of a hot-air balloon. This isn't possible: the height you normally reach in a hot-air balloon is nowhere near great enough. Few complain. They're too taken up with another strange and very beautiful optical illusion: the earth, far from falling away at the edges, seems to be curving upwards. It looks, as we rise, as though we're contained in a giant bowl.

This illusion, too subtle to be noticed from a plane, is the result of diffraction – the same phenomenon as makes a pencil seem to bend when you dip it into water. The air is thinner now, as we ascend, and we are looking at the ground through air that becomes progressively thicker. Everything seems bent towards us, as though the earth were cupping us in its hands.

Few newcomers to ballooning expect to see outer space, and yet, after a very short period of ascent, the sky does begin to darken. I don't have the words to explain why this should be so moving, but I'm by no means the first balloonist to get a lump in my throat at the sight. The nineteenth-century aviation pundit Monck Mason – never short of a purple phrase or two – writes with genuine passion of the way the balloonist 'obtains . . . unerring tokens of his approach to the nether limits of the void and infinite gulf that lies beyond him; and I have no doubt, could he but continue his course until he had attained the outward margin of the atmosphere, he would . . . behold an impenetrable abyss of perfect blackness, in which every visible source of light would stand like a disk of solid flame.'

The air thins out incredibly quickly, the higher we go. We'll feel the first effects of altitude a mere 9,000 feet above sea level. That persistent headache? That's the low pressure, trying to suck your brains out through your eye sockets. The air here is too thin for most of us to breathe. The people who live at these heights – Himalayan Sherpas, and the folk of remote villages in the Andes – have bred over generations an enviable ability to handle a lower-than-usual level of oxygen.

Let's climb another 9,000 feet. We're less than two-thirds the height of Mount Everest, and already we've left the rest of humanity behind. Nobody lives at this altitude: human lungs just can't cope.

Now let's climb as high as Everest's peak: 29,035 feet. Most untrained people, exposed suddenly to conditions here, fall unconscious within six minutes. Even with oxygen, the low air pressure (one-third earth normal) is sucking blood into our lungs.

Balloons had been around for around twenty years when balloonists began reaching lethal heights. In 1803 Étienne Robertson reached 23,526 feet before he began to choke. A year later, Count Francesco Zambeccari and two passengers were swept up into a rising current over the Adriatic: 'We had difficulty hearing each other – even when shouting at the tops of our voices. I was ill and vomited; Grassetti was bleeding at the nose. We were both breathing short and hard, and felt oppression of the chest.'

In 1862, in an effort to understand the perils of high altitude, the British Association for the Advancement of Science sponsored meteorologist Dr James Glaisher and celebrated balloonist Henry Tracey Coxwell to study the upper atmosphere. Dressed in street clothes, without caps or gloves, they set off from Wolverhampton, in the rain.

At 15,000 feet, the temperature had dropped to minus 8 degrees Celsius, and ice began forming on Glaisher's instruments and around the neck of the balloon. At 25,000 feet, the air temperature had fallen to minus 21 Celsius. Though their hands and lips had turned blue and their eyes bulged grotesquely, Glaisher manfully persevered with his experiments. He had brought pigeons along to see how well they coped with high altitude. At regular intervals, he threw one out of the car. It dropped like a stone. At 28,000 feet it suddenly dawned on Coxwell that he could no longer reach the cord to vent gas from the balloon. He grabbed the iron ring around the base of the balloon to pull himself up – and his hands froze to the metal.

Glaisher convulsed and passed out. Coxwell, vomiting, raised himself up on the iron ring and got the rope between his teeth. He managed eventually to gnaw through it, and lost a tooth for his trouble.

Coxwell and Glaisher topped out at 35,000 feet. Both survived their crash landing.

Higher still. At 39,000 feet, the only reason we're still breathing is because I brought along tanks of 100 per cent pure oxygen.

And higher. Our oxygen masks are tied, screamingly tight, to our faces, and it takes real effort to breathe out. The air in our lungs would much rather escape through our tear ducts. Our eyes are watering constantly, *and it hurts.* Quick, put this pressure jerkin on. It's basically a heavy shirt lined with a bladder that inflates. It makes breathing easier, but now the blood in our bodies is rushing into our arms and legs.

Time for the g-suits. These have bladders to contain abdomen, thighs and calves. Feeling better? Make the most of it. These things were designed for emergencies. Were the cockpit of your military plane to suddenly depressurise, the suit would give you a couple of vital minutes to dive your aircraft down to 38,000 feet. In about two minutes, we will black out, as the blood squeezes out of our veins into the surrounding tissue, expanding to fill unpressurised nooks and crannies.

We are not going to reach outer space, because very soon there's not going to be anything for our balloon to float *through.* How high we can get is hard to say. There is no point at which the Earth's atmosphere obviously stops and space begins. The Hungarian-American engineer Theodore von Kármán drew a line in the sky at 62.1 miles – that's over 327,000 feet. At this height, he said, the air was so thin, you'd have to travel very fast indeed for the wings of your aeroplane to work: so fast, you would put yourself into orbit.

We have risen about a third of the way to the Kármán line; 113,700 feet is the highest ever attained by a human being in a balloon. Of course, Commander Malcolm Ross and Lieutenant Commander Victor Prather, Jr, used a prototype space capsule for their 1961 journey. I haven't given us that luxury.

As far as our bodies are concerned, we're in space. Our saliva starts to bubble. Our skin puffs up in spots. Our stomachs swell and our eyes pop outward. And then – good news! We will not explode! This never happens. Even without a flight suit to contain it, skin is tough, and won't split. Our bodies will simply expand to twice their usual volume, as the water inside us boils and turns to vapour.

But let's look on the bright side (we're only spinning stories, after all). Arthur C Clarke, the space visionary who scripted the movie *2001: A Space Odyssey*, has his astronaut, Bowman, leap unprotected from his space buggy into an airlock, exposing himself to the vacuum of space for about ten seconds. In reality (we know this from a couple of nasty accidents in industrial vacuum chambers) Bowman would have about fifteen seconds before he blacked out. After that, his rescuers would have all of one and a half minutes to revive him.

Unnerved? I certainly am! It's high time we started our descent.

As a child, I was haunted by dreams of being able to fly. I knew that realising my dream was never going to be easy for me. For a start, I'm not great with machinery. I'm dyslexic, and prone to confuse my left and my right. (I'm not alone: the commonest navigational error known to mountain rescuers is an error of 180 degrees. People regularly head off in exactly the wrong direction!) Still, I have the instincts of an engineer. I am fascinated by how things work and how things are done and how things might be done differently.

In the 1980s, if you were as interested as I was then in flight technology and new materials and wild new engineering ideas, Per Lindstrand's was a name that was hard to avoid. Per explained to me that previous record-setting balloons had travelled at about 6,000 or 7,000 feet, buffeted by ever-changing winds, plagued by freezing fogs and not infrequently struck by lightning. Per wanted to take us above the weather, into the jet stream, a river of fast, dry air whose reasonably constant and predictable course would enable us to cross the Atlantic at speeds of up to 130 miles per hour.

He explained that the jet streams that encircle the Earth have an endearing habit of moving especially quickly across oceans – handy for record breakers! – and that the exotic materials he used for his balloon envelopes were the only ones he believed could withstand the stresses the balloon would suffer as we inserted ourselves into the stream.

I asked Per if he had children. Yes, he said: two. This reassured me. I knew then that, however great the risks he would expose us to, they wouldn't be stupid risks. Per had plenty to live for. (This sounds melodramatic, I know, but remember what he was proposing: you don't want to find yourself suspended 38,000 feet above an ocean only to discover your co-pilot has a death wish.)

I've always held to the notion that you only live once, and that if you want your life to have any meaning, you simply have to throw yourself into things. So I agreed to his proposal. I was heading for my mid-thirties – young enough to attempt something crazy, old enough to know that this was a young man's game, and not one I could afford to put off. (Steve Fossett later gave the lie to that idea, becoming an adventurer in his mid-fifties.) I knew, too, that I could put this project to good use, harnessing the publicity from the balloon flight to sell the idea of Virgin Atlantic in America. At the time, our airline was only a couple of years old. We were a tiny company by the standards of the industry, and we didn't have cash to throw around – certainly nowhere near enough to fund the expensive US marketing campaign we desperately needed. Flying in the jet stream with Per would convey, far better than any mere advert, Virgin Atlantic's spirit of innovation and adventure.

I began life as a journalist, and I've always been sensitive to the fact that getting free coverage is one thing; deserving it is quite another. The project had elements of glamour, pleasure and surprise, all of which contributed to the brand. Best of all, it was a real story. What Per was proposing was a genuine adventure, using new materials in an unexpected way to achieve what before had been considered unachievable. Besides, I thought, it's a chance to learn a new sport, it's another step on the way to my pilot's licence – and what could be more restful, more beautiful, than a ride in a balloon?

I had no idea, back then, that only six other teams had ever attempted such a crossing. I didn't know that five had perished in the attempt. Nor did I realise that Per, as well as being the most daring and innovative balloon designer of his generation, was also the most expensive! (I've had more arguments about money with Per than I've had hot dinners on board Virgin Atlantic. Per once proposed coating our inner envelope with *gold*. He used words like 'reflectivity'; I used words like 'no'.) In short, I had no idea – none – what I was letting myself in for. I should have read more history.

At 2.30 p.m. on Friday, 3 July 1987, Per Lindstrand and I reached the coast of Ireland and became the first people ever to cross the Atlantic by hot-air balloon. (You can find the full story of our escapade in my autobiography, *Losing My Virginity*.) The journey had begun badly – two full propane tanks had fallen from our capsule, triggering our rapid ascent! But the flight had been magnificent, and only twenty-nine hours long – far shorter than expected. The winds had worked in our favour, so that by the time we reached Ireland we still had three tanks full of propane attached to the capsule.

We were almost home. Once we had jettisoned our surplus fuel, we were free to land. Per brought the balloon down low, just outside the little village of Limavady. Just as we were preparing to dump the fuel, a savage gust slammed into us, driving us into the ground. Suddenly, we were out of control. Our radio aerials were destroyed, every one of our external fuel tanks was ripped away, and the balloon, free of its burden, rocketed into the air.

Our balloon was now only partly inflated – and the higher we got, the colder the air in the envelope became. Any second now, we would lose our buoyancy and come crashing back to earth. We had one small reserve fuel tank inside the capsule. Per hurried to connect it to the burners. We could still make it.

Then – we couldn't.

When you want to lose height in a hot-air balloon, you simply let some of the air out. A cable hangs down inside the envelope, and pulling it opens a vent at the top. The force of our ascent had flattened the envelope, lowering the cable.

'It's tangled!' Per cried. The cable had snagged on something, and the whole balloon began to corkscrew, closing the mouth of the envelope so that we couldn't heat the air inside.

I opened the hatch, climbed out on top of the capsule and hacked away at the cable with my knife. When it gave, the balloon whipped round and the mouth of the envelope came open. Per ordered me inside, and fired the burners full blast.

We had come within 300 feet of the ground. Per decided we should aim for the beach. We didn't have enough control to chance a landing where there were trees, houses or power lines. I put on my parachute, and when we saw the coastline

Per Lindstrand and I explore the capsule of the Virgin Atlantic Challenger.

approaching, Per vented hot air from the top of the balloon to reduce our height.

Again the wind slammed us, and before we knew what was happening, we were swept out to sea. Heavy fog hung over the ocean. For a moment, we lost all visibility. Then the waves came into view, foaming, rearing – we were going much too fast.

We hit the sea. The balloon dragged us across the surface of the ocean, bouncing us from wave to wave. Per hurtled into me. Winded, I struggled for purchase as Per grabbed the red lever that was now our only hope. Explosive bolts would sever the cables connecting the capsule to the balloon.

Nothing happened. Per yanked the lever up and down but the bolts did not fire.

'Get out!' Per shouted at me. 'Richard, we've got to get out.'

Per braced himself against the hatch and pushed it open. He heaved himself up and climbed through. I lunged after him. We clutched at the steel hawsers and prepared to jump – and another gust of wind caught us.

The balloon rose. Per jumped. I didn't follow him.

I'd been warned about this. My colleague Will Whitehorn, now the president of Virgin Galactic, began his career in the air-sea-rescue business, covering the oil platforms of the North Sea. He wasn't yet working for Virgin but I had bent his ear a few times by phone, getting advice on the sorts of safety procedures we needed for our flight. On one occasion, as we drifted off into general chat, Will said to me, 'You know, it's the weirdest thing. No one ever lets go.' He described his early training sessions to me. One of the first things you learn in air-sea rescue is to resist the urge to cling on to something if it suddenly lifts you off the ground. 'It must be our monkey past or something: you suddenly get it into your head that the trees are safer than the ground, and up you go.'

The urge to cling has killed hundreds over the years, and no matter how hard you train, or how experienced you are, you can never entirely learn your way out of the habit. In 1983 Per dislocated his shoulder after falling thirty feet off a rope he should never have held on to. If even Per can be blindsided by this dangerous urge, then no one is immune. He jumped off the *Virgin Challenger*; I stayed behind.

Per is built like a grizzly bear; with him gone, the balloon was about 200 pounds lighter. Once more, and for the final time, it rocketed into the air. I watched the sea fall away beneath me; seconds later, fog enveloped everything.

'The last time I had jumped, I had pulled **the wrong release tag** and jettisoned my parachute.'

I was as good as dead.

Alone in charge of the balloon, I fought down my mounting panic. I figured, if I could only get to 8,000 feet, I could parachute off the capsule. Then it occurred to me: if I came down with the capsule, I would have a better chance of being spotted. My parachuting technique wasn't faultless. The last time I had jumped, I had pulled the wrong release tag and jettisoned my parachute, and the skydivers around me had had to help me activate my reserve. (They later presented me with a Wally of the Year award. I accepted with a grin, thankful still to be alive.)

No: better to stay with the capsule, bring it down as slowly as I could and jump off at the last moment. Looking back, this was one of the best decisions I've ever made. I was lucky, too, of course: as I came out through the bottom of the clouds, I saw the grey sea below me – and I also saw an RAF helicopter!

I waited until I was just above the sea. I pulled my life-jacket ripcord and hurled myself into the water. It was like diving into knives, it was so cold. The life jacket brought me back to the surface and righted me. I turned and watched the balloon. Without my weight, it soared back up like a magnificent spaceship and vanished in the cloud.

Incredibly, Per survived. He was picked up by a dinghy two hours after jumping into the ocean without his life vest. He was airlifted to the same ship as I was and when I saw him his face was as white as flour and he couldn't stop his teeth chattering.

I think of that moment, and I think of all the pioneers who came before us and who came so near to perishing. I think of Jean Pierre Blanchard, the first man to cross the Channel by air, hurling his trousers into the sea in a frantic attempt to arrest the descent of his balloon. I think of the passengers on board *Le Géant*, the largest balloon ever constructed, clinging for dear life to the furniture aboard a gondola so grand and heavy it smashed down trees during its forced descent.

Researching these stories, I've noticed something disturbing: the earlier the exploit, the more cartoon-like it appears. The passage of time has robbed these adventures of their reality. The terror and horror of these incidents has leached away until, in many cases, only the absurdity is left. Will our own desperate dunking in the Atlantic one day seem like Blanchard's – merely quaint? Merely amusing? Probably.

That may be why we regard the prehistory of flight with such incredulity. We just can't believe so many people would risk their necks in projects that, with hindsight, were so obviously doomed to failure. Still, the many accounts that exist worldwide of prodigious flights from mountain heights, minarets and belfries speak for themselves. No doubt these stories are seriously exaggerated, but there are too many for us to dismiss them altogether. Long before the Montgolfiers built their first balloon, people risked their lives in pursuit of the dream of flight.

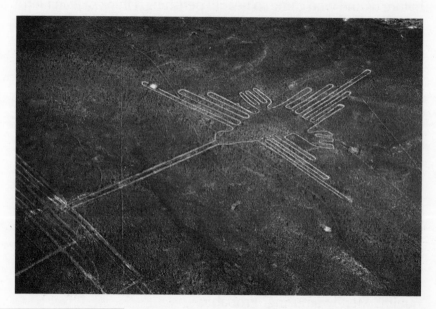

Peru's ancient 'Nazca lines' only make sense from the air – so who were they for?

two

Lighter than Air

Scratched upon Peru's vast, barren Nazca Plains are hundreds of long, ruler-straight lines: the work of people who lived about 1,500 years ago. From the ground, Nazca is totally incomprehensible. From the air, it's the world's most astonishing and haunting art gallery – a surreal collection of huge geometric symbols and giant drawings of birds and animals.

In 1973, an American called Jim Woodman visited the site. Woodman had a theory. Quecha – a language spoken in the Nazca area – has a word for 'balloon maker'. A pottery shard discovered on the site contains a design remarkably like a balloon. In Gautemala, village rituals included the construction and launch of small, smoke-filled balloons. South American balloons have been around for a long time. Were they ever big enough to carry people? Were they big enough and controllable enough to allow the Nazca people to map out their extraordinary art from the air?

It all came down to materials. The Montgolfiers succeeded where their precursors had failed because, as paper-makers, they had access to the finest papers, linens and varnishes. Did the Nazca Indians boast any remotely airtight materials?

Jim Woodman's researches led him to the village of Cahuachi, not far from Nazca. There, the ancient dead of the village are wrapped in burial shrouds, some of them 1,500 years old – and the older the shroud, the finer the weave! In 1975 the International Explorers' Society of Miami, using only traditional tools, wove a gondola out of reeds from Lake Titicaca, and an enormous tetrahedron balloon made from fabric virtually identical to that used to make ancient burial shrouds. On a clear spring day in 1975, *Condor One* was prepared for launch.

To pilot the craft, Jim Woodman was joined by Englishman Julian Nott, a professional balloonist who's since amassed seventy-nine world ballooning records and ninety-six British aviation records. The trouble was that Nott, like Woodman, was over six feet tall, so they had to straddle the gondola rather than sit inside it. Neither wore a parachute. A tar fire was used to fill the envelope with hot smoke, and when the safety lines were released, the balloon rocketed up at around eighteen feet per second. *Condor One* reached 380 feet above the Nazca Plains, and drifted for a good minute and a half.

Afterwards, Julian Nott was careful not to claim too much for the experiment, but his account is inspiring:

> [W]hile I do not see any evidence that the Nazca civilisation did fly, it is beyond any doubt that they could have. And so could the ancient Egyptians, the Romans, the Vikings, any civilisation. With just a loom and fire you can fly! This raises intriguing questions about the development of science and, most of all, the intellectual courage to dare to fly, to dare to invade the territory of the Angels.

Of the sixteen children born to the Mongolfier family, Joseph-Michel and Jacques-Étienne made unlikely business partners. Joseph was a maverick and dreamer, hopeless in business. Étienne was severe, dapper, responsible, and a bit dull.

One night in 1777, as his laundry dried over a fire, Joseph noticed pockets forming under the material. The next day (this, anyway, is the story) he set about building a box out of very thin wood. He covered the sides and top with lightweight taffeta cloth and under the bottom of the box he lit some crumpled paper. The contraption lifted off its stand and collided with the ceiling.

He wrote to his brother: 'Get in a supply of taffeta and of cordage, quickly, and you will see one of the most astonishing sights in the world.'

The mental leap from laundry to ballooning was not a large one. The Montgolfier family had been making paper since the fourteenth century, and Joseph and Étienne had learned their trade well. They knew about advances in paper and fabric production. They had an intimate working knowledge of new coatings and resins and finishes. And they had nearly a century of aeronautical designs and experiments to draw from – projects, mainly French and Italian, that had been nudging ever more closely towards achieving manned flight by balloon.

Perhaps it occurred to Joseph as he watched his laundry billowing that, after centuries of waiting, the materials necessary to manned flight were at last available. Whether of silk and paper, envelope materials could now be made that were light, strong and relatively leakproof. What used to be toys could now be scaled up.

And how! The first (unmanned) balloon the brothers made was so buoyant they lost control of it on its very first test flight.

Their next model, which weighed about a quarter of a ton, took to the air on 4 June 1783. While it was filling with smoke it 'seemed only a covering of cloth, lined with paper, a sort of sack thirty-five feet high', wrote Fulgence Marion in 1874. ('Fulgence Marion' is the none-too-cryptic pseudonym for Nicolas Camille Flammarion, the celebrated French astronomer and spiritualist. Flammarion researched his short, popular history of early flight well; it would go on to feed the imaginations of writers from Mark Twain to Edgar Rice Burroughs.)

As it inflated, however, the brothers' balloon 'grew large even under the eyes of the spectator, took consistence, assumed a beautiful form, stretched itself on all sides, and struggled to escape. Meanwhile, strong arms were holding it down until the signal was given, when it loosened itself, and with a rush rose to the height of 1,000 fathoms in less than ten minutes.'

Seeing the thing cover two kilometres and reach about the same height, official onlookers quickly passed the word to Paris.

Meanwhile, amid the hubbub generated by these unmanned balloon launches, and with the promise of a manned flight just a few weeks away, the French physicist Louis-Sébastien Lenormand was working on a different but closely related problem: assuming you could get up in the air, how exactly were you going to get down again?

The history of modern parachuting is exactly as long as the history of modern ballooning, and for the obvious reason. Balloons do not 'land'; they crash. Half the art of ballooning is to make your crashes so gentle you can fool yourself into calling them landings. In any event, you have no fine control over the process. Designing a reliable escape vehicle was essential, and work began on the task even before manned balloons left the ground.

Lenormand's first experiment was not calculated to win any science prizes. He simply jumped out of a tree clutching two umbrellas. When that did not kill him, he went on to build a fourteen-foot parachute with a rigid wooden frame. On 26 December 1783, he jumped from the tower of the Montpellier observatory. He landed uninjured. Among the cheering crowds was Joseph Montgolfier: the balloon pioneer had come along to judge this interesting bit of safety equipment for himself!

Lenormand's rigid parachute: a promising safety feature for pioneering balloonists!

On their arrival in Paris, the Montgolfier brothers set about their next unmanned balloon demonstration. They collaborated with wallpaper manufacturer Jean-Baptiste Réveillon to build an envelope of fireproofed taffeta to carry three animals aloft: a sheep, a duck and a rooster. (The sheep was thought to have a roughly human physiology. The duck, unlikely to be harmed by altitude, would only come to harm if something about the balloon flight itself proved dangerous. The rooster – a bird that spends its life on the ground – was included as a further control.)

On 19 September, before a huge crowd at the royal palace in Versailles, including Queen Marie Antoinette and King Louis XVI of France (who couldn't see the point of the animals and had wanted to send condemned criminals up instead) the flight was a barnstorming success. It covered two miles at an altitude of about 1,500 feet and landed safely.

Following the successful demonstration at Versailles came several tethered manned flights. By the end of October, three passengers had been lifted up to ninety-nine metres into the air: the physics and chemistry teacher Jean-François Pilâtre de Rozier, the wallpaper magnate Jean-Baptiste Réveillon, and Giroud de Villette, another wallpaper manufacturer from Madrid.

Now Étienne started construction of a truly monstrous envelope – nearly two cubic kilometres in size, painted and gilded and decorated with streamers – to carry people into the air in free flight. Even as the brothers prepared for their first untethered manned launch, a significant rival was snapping at their heels. His name was Jacques Charles, a bureaucrat who, inspired by the writings of American inventor and statesman Benjamin Franklin, had thrown in his civil-service career to pursue a scientific one.

Charles was no mere also-ran. He had a wholly different way of getting balloons into the air. Rather than filling his balloon with hot air, he planned to fill it with a rare and expensive gas. Hydrogen, sixteen times lighter than air, was discovered seven years before by the British scientist Henry Cavendish. Charles – a firm favourite on the Paris lecture circuit – delighted in filling soap bubbles with hydrogen, watching them rise, and then setting a match to them, causing small explosions. There was a serious point to these demonstrations: Charles believed that hydrogen gas would one day lift people into the skies – and he was determined to be the first passenger. His first task was to create a balloon envelope capable of holding hydrogen for any length of time. The Montgolfiers' varnished taffeta balloons were not especially airtight, and a lighter gas like hydrogen would escape even faster than ordinary air would, making flight impossible. If you've filled regular balloons with helium for a children's party, you'll probably have noticed that they shrink and shrivel after just a few hours. That's because atoms of helium are lighter than the atoms that make up the air, and work their way through the rubber much more easily. Hydrogen atoms are lighter still.

Charles joined forces with the brothers Anne-Jean and Marie-Noël Robert, who had found a way to coat fabric with natural rubber. A couple of months before the Montgolfier balloon's first manned voyage, Charles and his assistants constructed a balloon of rubber-coated taffeta, twelve feet in diameter, and set about filling it with hydrogen. Now this was the hard part. Hydrogen was so expensive to make, a public subscription was started in Paris to help the team afford the 1,125 pounds of iron and 560 pounds of sulphuric acid they needed – all to inflate a balloon that could lift barely twenty-two pounds. The filling took four hours!

On the morning of 26 August 1783, a day before the launch, workmen manoëuvred the balloon out of the Robert brothers' workshop and secured it to a wagon, 'surrounded on all sides by eager multitudes,' so that 'the night-patrols, both of horse and foot, which were set to guard the avenues leading to where it lay, were quite unable to stem the tide of human beings that poured along to get a glimpse of it.' Marion's account gives a great sense of the occasion: 'A vanguard, with lighted torches, preceded it; it was surrounded by special attendants, and was followed by detachments of night-patrols on foot and mounted. The size and shape of this structure, which was escorted with such pomp and precaution – the silence that prevailed – the unearthly hour, all helped to give an air of mystery to the proceedings.'

Troops were stationed around the Champ de Mars and, as the day wore on:

an immense crowd covered the open space, and every advantageous spot in the neighbourhood was crowded with people. At five o'clock the report of a cannon announced to the multitudes, and to scientific men who were posted on elevations to make observations of the great event, that the grand moment had come. The cords were withdrawn, and, to the vast delight and wonder of the crowd assembled, the balloon shot up with such rapidity that in two minutes it had ascended 488 fathoms [over 890 metres]. At this height it was lost in a cloud for an instant, and, reappearing, rose to a great height, and was again lost in higher clouds.

And there the story might have ended, had the team not made a crucial error: they had sealed the bottom of their balloon.

They must have imagined that their expensive hydrogen gas would somehow have escaped from the balloon had they left the bottom open. But since hydrogen is so much lighter than air, this was never going to happen. In sealing the envelope, Charles and the brothers Robert had in fact guaranteed a rather spectacular end to their balloon's maiden flight. The higher it rose, the smaller the pressure exerted by the surrounding air, and this drop in pressure allowed the gas inside the balloon to expand. Had the balloon been left open at the bottom, the rapidly expanding gas could simply have vented out of the bottom. As it was, the envelope stretched, and stretched . . .

Having swept virtually unnoticed over the French countryside, the balloon burst right over the heads of 'a number of peasants, whose terror at the sight and the sound of this strange monster

Shock of the new: fearful peasants tore the world's first gas balloon to shreds.

from the skies was beyond description.' A couple of local monks hurried to the scene to make things worse, telling the startled crowd that had gathered around the wreckage that it was the hide of a monstrous animal, at which point 'they immediately began to assail it vigorously with stones, flails, and pitchforks . . . They finally attached the burst envelope to a horse's tail, and dragged it far across the fields.'

The King, who'd been following Charles's experiment closely, rushed through a proclamation explaining the experiments. It was headed: 'Warning to the People on Kidnapping Air-Balloons'.

On 21 November 1783, dressed in blue velvet suits and wearing plumed hats, Pilâtre de Rozier and the soldier François Laurent, the Marquis d'Arlandes, became the first men ever to ascend to the skies in untethered flight. Their vehicle was a hot-air balloon constructed by Étienne Montgolfier: the brothers had won the race to build the first manned aircraft.

It was quite a sight. The upper part of their balloon was embroidered with fleurs-de-lis and the signs of the zodiac. The design around the middle alternated the King's monogram with images of the sun. The lower part was a chaos of masks, garlands and spread eagles. A circular gallery 'made of osiers and festooned with draperies and other ornaments', hung off the bottom of the balloon.

Most balloons these days carry their passengers in a gondola or a basket, suspended directly below the open mouth of the balloon. Rozier and d'Arlandes, however, had much more room to move around. Their three-foot-wide circular gallery ran around the mouth of the balloon and was protected on the outside by a parapet over three feet high. Below the gallery, and directly under the mouth of the balloon, there hung an iron grating. The balloon had been inflated by smoke from a fire pit on the ground. The fire had heated the iron grating to the point where, once up in the air, it would set light to any fuel dropped upon it. By throwing dried straw and wool on to the grating, the men could keep their machine afloat. That, at any rate, was the theory.

'I was surprised at the silence and the absence of movement which our departure caused among the spectators,' wrote d'Arlandes later. 'I was still gazing, when M. Rozier cried to me, "You are doing nothing, and the balloon is scarcely rising a fathom."

'"Pardon me," I answered, as I placed a bundle of straw upon the fire and slightly stirred it.'

Try as he might, Rozier just couldn't get d'Arlandes to concentrate. Halfway through the marquis's spellbound recitation of all the bends of the Seine laid out below him ('Passy, St Germain, St Denis, Sèvres . . .') Rozier snapped, 'If you look at the river in that fashion you will be likely to bathe in it soon. Some fire, my dear friend, some fire!'

After twenty-five minutes the machine landed among windmills, outside the city walls.

The Montgolfiers had won, beating Charles's team to the launchpad – but only by a hair's breadth. A mere ten days after Rozier and d'Arlandes made their first manned flight, Charles and Marie-Noël Robert ascended to a height of about 1,800 feet (550 metres) in his hydrogen balloon, *La Charlière*, 'its beautiful emerald colour showing to fine effect in the sun.'

Coming second did not do Charles any real harm. His balloon designs came to dominate the field. Most contemporary engravings, ornaments and decorations commemorate not the Montgolfiers' balloon but Charles's. Model *charlières* filled the Paris skies, the envelopes made of a very thin parchment called goldbeater's skin. 'The whole of Paris amused itself with them, repeating in little the phenomenon of the great ascent,' writes Marion. 'The sky of the capital found itself all at once traversed by a multitude of small rosy clouds, formed by the hand of man.' So many people were injured trying to make hydrogen for these toys that in the end the government stepped in and banned them.

Charles and the Montgolfiers became the toast of France. Their pioneering balloon projects were a sensation. Along with the engravings commemorating the event, chairs with balloon backs, balloon-shaped mantel clocks and balloon-painted crockery filled the interiors of Europe. There were commemorative knick-knacks to suit every pocket. Balloons found their way into everything, from cuisine to coiffure. The hairstyles had great names: you could walk out of the salon '*à la Montgolfier*', '*au globe volant*', '*au demi-ballon*', or '*à l'air inflammable*'!

In 1784, the year following these two epoch-making launches, fifty-two balloon ascents were made.

Drunk on their first victory over gravity, pioneers raced to haul heavier and heavier contraptions into the air. On 19 January 1784, Joseph Montgolfier took seven people up in a real monster. *Le Flesselles* boasted a gallery seventy-two feet in circumference. Its seats were four feet wide and eight apart. Its furnace, twenty feet in diameter, burned faggots of wood and straw. It was so big, and there were so many people crawling over and around the thing, that when it launched, a young man called Fontaine was accidentally included in the party.

Incredibly, it did manage to get off the ground, and rose to a very creditable 3,000 feet, before the envelope tore and the whole lot came down, none too gently, less than a quarter of a mile from its starting point.

A healthy rivalry persisted between Charles and the Montgolfiers. The teams were rivals, but there was never any animosity. They publicly complimented each other's efforts, and sometimes shared technical information.

One of the Montgolfier brothers' balloonists, Jean-François Pilâtre de Rozier was, like Charles, a physics teacher who gave private lectures about the new field of gases. It was while studying Charles's system, and comparing it to the one he had already flown, that Rozier was seized by an idea. Here were two kinds of balloon, one filled with hot air, the other with an inflammable gas. *Why not combine the two?*

Charles warned Rozier that he was simply 'putting fire beside powder', but Rozier would not listen. The royal court had given Rozier funds to develop his own balloon system, and had begun to press him for results.

Rozier's system consisted of two balloons, one inside the other. The bigger, outer balloon was filled with hydrogen. The inner envelope was a hot-air balloon (or *'montgolfière'*). The outer hydrogen balloon provided most of the lift. The hot-air 'core' was used to control the altitude of the flight. Stoking the fire under the hot-air balloon would increase the amount of hot air in the balloon, swelling it and making it rise. As the balloon rose, the fall in air pressure and warmth of the sun would make the hydrogen in the outer envelope expand, increasing the balloon's rate of climb. At this point, the fire could be damped down, reducing the speed of ascent. Damping the fire even further would cause it to descend. 'It is probable', writes Marion, 'that, by the addition of a *montgolfière*, [Rozier] wished to free himself from the necessity of having to throw over ballast when he wished to ascend and to let off this gas when he wished to descend. The fire of the *montgolfière* might, he probably supposed, be so regulated as to enable him to rise or fall at will.'

Staying in the air for a long time was important to de Rozier, because he was interested in setting endurance records. For starters, he wanted to be the first to cross the English Channel. Rozier and his companion Pierre Romain were ready to make the attempt by the autumn of 1784, but technical difficulties and bad weather delayed by almost a year, by which time another Frenchman, Jean Pierre Blanchard, and his American companion, Dr John Jeffries, had already crossed the Channel in a hydrogen-gas balloon.

Pilâtre de Rozier and his brother Pierre Romain pressed ahead, convinced that their design would eventually revolutionise ballooning. They set off from Boulogne-sur-Mer on 15 June 1785.

'The theory,' Monck Mason comments, dryly, 'was correct; the error lay in the application.' After about half an hour – and with the wind obstinately forcing the balloon back to shore – the watching crowd noticed that Rozier and his brother were showing 'signs of alarm'. They quickly lowered the lid over their brazier; but it was too late.

Rozier had underestimated his hydrogen's rate of expansion as the balloon rose and the surrounding air pressure dropped: 'The inflammable contents of the larger sphere soon filled the vacant portions of the silk, and pouring down the tube which formed the neck of his balloon speedily reached the furnace, which was disposed at its lower extremity, and became ignited.'

The result: an almighty bang. Rozier and Romain fell on to rocks at a spot between Calais and Boulogne. 'The dead body of Rozier was found burnt in the gallery, many of the bones being broken. His brother was still breathing, but he was not able to speak, and in a few minutes he expired.'

Rozier died 200 years before his radical balloon designs came of age.

The first balloonist to cross the Channel, Jean Pierre Blanchard, was one of those people who likes to know where he's going. Though celebrated today for his Channel crossing, Blanchard had his sights set much higher. He wanted to invent the world's first truly practical flying machine, and devoted his long and colourful ballooning career to the problem of motive power. He dreamed of airships – and they were all extraordinarily silly.

Blanchard was born on 4 July 1753 in Petit Andelys, near Paris. Fleeing his poverty-stricken home while still a teenager, he tinkered his way to the top. His youthful inventions included a rat trap with a pistol, and a primitive bicycle. He was not a natural balloonist. He was much more interested in heavier-than-air flight, and struggled for a long time with designs for a manually powered aeroplane and helicopter. By 1782 he was exhibiting a sort of *flying boat* – 'a machine furnished with oars and rigging, with which he managed to sustain himself some moments in the air at the height of eighty feet'.

Still, like everyone else, Blanchard was bowled over by the Montgolfier brothers' 1783 demonstrations of hot-air ballooning in their home town of Annonay, and it occurred to him that balloon technology might help him develop the power systems he needed for his aircraft. Blanchard's appetite for forward motion blinded him to virtually every other consideration. Though in other respects a gifted engineer, he showed a remarkable lack of sense when it came to handling air. He thought he could *row* through it!

Some ideas only seem crazy to later, better-informed generations. Others are just plain stupid. When, towards the end of 1783, Étienne began toying with the idea, Joseph wrote: 'For my sake, my good friend, reflect; calculate well before you employ oars. Oars must either be great or small; if great, they will be heavy; if small, it will be necessary to move them with great rapidity.' Already, Joseph understood the cardinal rule of ballooning: the only way you can steer is by controlling your height, catching different winds at different altitudes.

On 2 March 1784, Pierre Blanchard and his companion, Pesch, a Benedictine priest, prepared to launch their *charlière* (a hydrogen-gas balloon) from the Champ de Mars in Paris. Pesch had escaped from prison to be on the flight, having defied a formal instruction from his order forbidding travel on this 'Devil's invention'. Sad to say, he never got to fly. The launch was disrupted and almost cancelled because of the actions of a disturbed young man, for years supposed to be the young Napoleon Bonaparte. (The rumour proved so persistent and annoying, Napoleon mentions it in his memoirs, declaring once and for all that it *wasn't* him: merely an old school chum of his, Dupont de Chambon.)

De Chambon demanded to ride in Blanchard's balloon, and when the pilots refused, he drew his sword and leaped into the basket. He sliced open Blanchard's hand, cut the rigging, and before the police managed to drag him away, he broke Blanchard's taffeta-bladed 'oars'. The balloon was quickly refitted, and the launch went ahead the same day – but with only Blanchard on board. (When Pesch's order caught up with him, they exiled him to the remotest monastery they had.)

Blanchard's own account of his flight is a calculated and vivid bit of self-promotion. (He had, after all, to attract sponsors if he was ever to fly again. Gas balloons were far from cheap.) His wilder claims include improvising a sail in mid-flight to propel his balloon through the air! This is pure nonsense since, as Fulgence Marion points out, 'the whole machine, globes and sails, being freely thrown into the air, would infallibly follow the direction of the wind, whatever that might be'.

Whether or not he really did try to rig a sail, Blanchard soon had other things to worry about: 'The rays of the sun had so heated and rarefied the inflammable air that soon I forgot my rigging in thinking of the terrible danger that threatened me.' Now this bit is certainly true: Blanchard had, like Charles before him, sealed the bottom of his balloon! And as he rose, so the atmospheric pressure dropped, causing his balloon to swell to bursting point. (There is, as I explained a few pages back, no need to seal the bottom of a hydrogen or helium balloon. Those gases are lighter than air, so they're never going to spill out of the bottom. Blanchard picked one hell of a moment to find this out.)

Once he'd resolved this problem, Blanchard 'mounted perpendicularly'.

> The cold became excessive . . . The silence became appalling, and to add to my alarm I began to lose consciousness. I now wished to take snuff, but found I had left my box behind me. I changed my seat many times; I went from prow to stern, but the drowsiness only ceased to assail me when I was struck by two furious winds, which compressed my balloon to such an extent that its size became sensibly diminished to the eye. I was not sorry when I began to descend rapidly upon the river.

Blanchard's faculties returned to him: in particular, his ability to spin yarns. Never mind that the lunatic de Chambon had destroyed them, he insisted that 'the fear that I should have to descend into [a river] made me agitate the oars very rapidly.

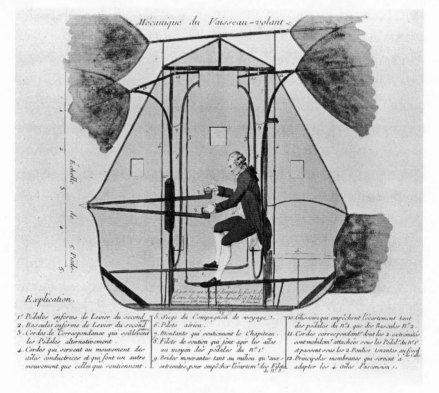

Jean-Pierre Blanchard seeks sponsorship for his self-propelled balloon.

I believe that it is to these movements that I owe my being able to cross the river transversely, and get above dry land.'

Blanchard's first voyage lasted seventy-five minutes. It was a considerable achievement – but Blanchard *would* keep banging on about those oars! It made his contemporaries wince. The physicist Jean-Baptiste Biot, who had watched the whole thing, quickly and loudly contradicted Blanchard's claim that he had in any way sailed or rowed through the air. Blanchard stuck to his guns. He knew that whoever came up with a way of directing balloons from point to point would clean up in the sponsorship stakes and the European after-dinner circuit. In Paris, however, the competition for sponsors was intense. The solution: move to London. That great capital had yet to launch a manned flight. There was his opportunity!

On 15 September 1784, just a few weeks after Blanchard stepped off the ferry, the Italian Vincenzo Lunardi flew from London to Ware in Hertfordshire, a total distance of nearly twenty-five miles, and the first air voyage of any great distance. Overnight, Lunardi became the darling of London, his name splashed across the front pages, his courage extolled in popular song. Worse still, Lunardi had equipped himself with oars!

Luckily, however, he had dropped one oar as he took off, so Blanchard's own tales of rowing and sailing through the air still met with enthusiasm in the drawing rooms of London. For British sponsors, Blanchard represented an excellent catch-up opportunity: the first self-propelled balloons would be British!

I suspect that by now, Blanchard was falling victim to his own wishful thinking. Of his first (solo) flight in the UK he insists that he had to row his way back to earth, 'and in fifteen to twenty minutes I arrived . . . after much fatigue, my strength being nearly exhausted'. Flying alone, I suppose it would be possible to convince yourself of all manner of things. With passengers, however, it's a different story. Imagine rowing your way to earth in front of a keen witness – or, even more challenging, a sceptical sponsor!

Blanchard went to considerable effort never to carry anyone else on his flights. On 16 October 1784, he was due to fly with a celebrated and eccentric anatomist called John Sheldon. To the wicker car of his balloon Blanchard 'had fitted a sort of ventilator, which he was able to move about by means of a winch. This ventilator, together with the wings and the helm, were to serve especially the purpose of steering at will, which he had often said was quite practicable as soon as a certain elevation had been reached.'

All this, not to mention 'a number of scientific and musical instruments, some refreshments, ballast, &c.', kept the balloon stubbornly earthbound until, finally, Sheldon disembarked. At last, the balloon had enough buoyancy to rise. 'After many vicissitudes,' writes Marion, '[Blanchard] landed upon a plain in Hampshire, about seventy-five miles from the point of departure. It was observed that, so long as he could be clearly seen, he executed none of the feats with his wings, ventilator, &c., which he had promised to exhibit.'

At the time, no one read too much into Sheldon's disappointed ejection from the balloon. By the time Blanchard was preparing to 'row' across the English Channel, however, the penny was beginning to drop.

Dr John Jeffries, a Bostonian living in England, put up the money for this project – easily the most exciting of the year – on condition that he came along for the ride. Blanchard did everything he could to put his sponsor off. He even drew up a contract stating that Jeffries agreed to throw himself overboard 'if necessary for the success of the flight'.

Jeffries called Blanchard's bluff, and signed. After that the men's relationship deteriorated into open warfare. Blanchard, who was preparing his balloon at Dover Castle on the Kent coast, barricaded the camp. In response, Jeffries hired a party of sailors to storm the fortress.

On 7 January 1785, the balloon was carried to the edge of the cliffs at Dover, and Blanchard let Jeffries into the car. Lo and behold, the balloon refused to lift. Blanchard announced that they were carrying too much weight: Jeffries would have to go. Jeffries examined the vehicle. Then he examined his co-pilot.

Blanchard was wearing a lead belt.

With that disposed of, the balloon rose into the air over the cliffs of Dover: a small, black, boat-shaped gondola complete with rudder, four wings and bright, silk-covered oars. Silence reigned. For hours, the men barely spoke to one another.

They weren't halfway across the Channel when the balloon began to lose height. This didn't seem a problem at first. They had, after all, plenty to throw away: a telescope, a clock, a small scientific library, musical instruments, works of art . . . By the time they were three-quarters of the way across, they were throwing out letters, life jackets and ropes. Blanchard decided to row for it. He grabbed the gondola's silken oars and flailed at the air. Jeffries attempted to steer with the rudder. We don't know which of them first suggested dismantling this rubbish and throwing it into the ocean, but over it went.

The balloon kept on sinking. Now the car was skipping across the waves. They threw their coats away. They threw away the letters they were carrying. They threw away their trousers. They took turns to piss into an empty bottle and threw it overboard. And, with painful slowness, the balloon began to rise.

Half-frozen and clad only in their underwear, Blanchard and Jeffries landed in a forest near Ardres, not far outside Calais. When they got to town, Jeffries reached into his underpants and pulled out a crumpled letter addressed to Temple Franklin, Benjamin Franklin's grandson. It was the first ever airmail.

That same year – and inspired, perhaps, by his terrifying Channel crossing, Jean Pierre Blanchard conducted his own parachute experiments. He took his dog for a balloon flight, attached it to a canopy of his own invention and threw it out of the basket. The dog made a perfect four-point landing, ran for the trees and was never seen again.

Delighted, Blanchard turned the routine into a public attraction; but after dropping a dog and a sheep to their deaths, he had to abandon the idea. Instead he offered to make a parachute descent himself, playing the violin. Spectators flocked to see Blanchard jump, and so he did – from a height of about ten feet. The disappointed spectators rioted and Blanchard's equipment was destroyed.

André-Jacques Garnerin was the first to dream up the first frameless, fabric chute. The former physics student had learned ballooning in the French Army. On 22 October 1797, he demonstrated his new invention in spectacular style. Riding a smoke-filled balloon 3,200 feet above Paris, he then ordered his brother to cut the cords holding his gondola to the balloon. For a few heart-stopping moments, the chute secured to the gondola stayed furled. 'All of a sudden, however, it burst into its proper shape, and the downward progress of the adventurer appeared at once to have been arrested.'

Garnerin's descent was far from smooth. The small gondola began to pendulum wildly. At one point it swung *above* the canopy, and spectators feared for Garnerin's life. After twelve minutes of drunken, spinning descent, the gondola landed, and Garnerin staggered out, as sick as a dog.

Air trapped inside Garnerin's fabric parachute had to spill out at some point along the parachute's edge, and it was this that had set the parachute and its passenger swinging to and fro. The French astronomer Jérôme Lalande hit upon a solution: cut a hole in the top of the parachute. The hole would reduce its effectiveness a little, but by giving the air inside the dome somewhere sensible from which to escape, it would stabilise the ride. With that small but essential modification made, Garnerin was set: he toured the world, making numerous exhibition jumps, many of them with his wife and niece.

For most people today, ballooning seems a gentle, contemplative pastime. Nineteenth-century pioneers had other ideas. Some were clearly determined to make it as hair-raising as possible. How many swigs of laudanum does it take, I wonder, before flying among the clouds on a pony seems like a good idea? Charles Green, a London-fruiterer-turned-Britain's-most-celebrated-balloonist, did exactly that on 29 July 1827 – all the while assuring fearful onlookers that the animal had been 'especially trained for the purpose'. It must have been quite a training programme, because the pony wasn't the least bit put out by its journey 'and ate freely of a quantity of beans, with which his gallant rider from time to time supplied him, from his hand.'

Nine years later Green graduated from showman to pioneer, setting a major distance record in the balloon *Royal Vauxhall*. Flying overnight from Vauxhall Gardens in London to Weilburg in Germany, Green, his sponsor Robert Hollond and the balloonist Monck Mason covered a distance of 480 miles – a record that stayed unbroken until 1907. They travelled in style, too: Mason's 1838 account mentions cloaks, carpet bags, barrels, speaking-trumpets, barometers, telescopes, lamps, wine jars, spirit flasks and 'many other articles, designed to serve the purposes of a voyage to regions where, once forgotten, nothing could again be supplied'.

The journey was inspirational. Monck Mason wrote: 'In [Green's] view, the Atlantic is no more than a simple canal: three days might suffice to effect its passage.' (Green was right: Per and I proved his point in 1987. I'm not sure we ever considered the Atlantic a 'simple canal', though!) Mason goes on: 'The very circumference of the globe is not beyond the scope of his expectations: in fifteen days and fifteen nights, transported by the trade winds, he does not despair to accomplish in his progress the great circle of the earth itself. Who now can fix a limit to his career?'

Without a doubt, the most grandiloquent early long-distance flight of the nineteenth century was accomplished by the aptly named *Géant* – the brainchild of the French photographer Gaspard-Félix Tournachon, who went by the pseudonym Nadar. Not content with a wicker basket, *Le Géant*'s passenger car was a wickerwork two-storey house, eight feet high and thirteen feet long, containing a small printing office, a photographic department, a refreshment room and a lavatory. On 18 October 1863, half a million people cheered as it rose from the Champ de Mars in Paris, with thirteen people on board.

Le Géant proved such a hit with European sightseers that Nadar had to use wooden trestles to keep gawping crowds from the launch site. (To this day, the Belgians call crowd-control barriers *nadars*.) Sadly, the balloon failed in its main purpose: to raise funds for a society researching (wait for it) heavier-than-air flight.

Jules Verne was the society's secretary; his book *Five Weeks in a Balloon* was inspired by *Le Géant*'s adventures. Nothing in that book equals the drama that unfolded for real, just a few weeks after its maiden voyage, as Nadar's grand airship crossed into Germany.

It was evening. 'There is', according to one surviving onboard diary of the flight (and quoted at length by Fulgence Marion), 'talk about dinner, or rather supper, and night is now fast approaching. Everyone eats with the best possible appetite. Hams, fowls and dessert only appear to disappear with an equal promptitude, and we quench our thirst with bordeaux and champagne.'

As night fell, however, a heavy fog descended. 'The water

Nadar's Géant flew only once, in 1863. Jules Verne wrote a novel about it.

which had collected on the balloon during its ascent now began to take effect, and caused it to descend with such rapidity into the dark abyss that the ballast, which was immediately thrown overboard, was overtaken in its descent and fell on our heads again.' (You have to wonder how much they'd had to drink.)

The balloon stabilised, and the voyage continued: 'We still continue to pass over fires, forges, tall chimneys, and coal mines at frequent intervals. Not long after we distinguish a large town on our right hand, which, by its size and brilliant lighting by gas, we recognise as Brussels.'

At an altitude of about 3,000 feet, a storm struck the balloon. *Le Géant* fell like a stone and then, at the last second, was borne away on a 100 mph gale, knocking down chimneys, trees and whatever else stood in its way. According to the correspondent for *Harper's* magazine, 'sometimes it struck the ground, then, springing upward, it would rise into the clouds, with the apparent velocity of a rocket, dashing its occupants from side to side with fearful force'.

At last, near Newburg in Hanover, the balloon, much deflated, came to rest against trees long enough to allow the passengers to escape, 'and the wounded, almost crippled travellers, were at length enabled to go home – wiser and sorer people.'

Balloons have no means of propulsion. They go where the air takes them. Depending upon your mood, and what you're trying to do, this is either their great charm, or a source of great inconvenience. Here are two old faxes from my scrapbook, both from attempts to circumnavigate the world by balloon.

The first was received on board the *Virgin Global Challenger* as it neared Algerian airspace on 7 January 1997: 'YOU ARE NOT, REPEAT NOT, AUTHORISED TO ENTER THIS AREA.'

The second was sent on 23 December 1998 after we had received a dispatch from Chinese government. The dispatch said we had to land the *ICO Global* as we were entering Chinese airspace. We had no doubt that they would shoot us down if we did not comply. The trouble was that we couldn't:

WE KINDLY ADVISE THAT IT IS NOT POSSIBLE TO LAND NOW WITHOUT SEVERELY ENDANGERING THE LIVES OF THE CREW AND ANY PERSONS ON THE GROUND. WE CANNOT STEER THE BALLOON AS IT GOES WHERE THE WIND TAKES IT. WE HAVE FULL CLOUD COVER AND CANNOT SEE THE GROUND. WE CANNOT DESCEND THROUGH CLOUD AS IT WILL CREATE ICE ON THE BALLOON RESULTING IN US CRASHING. WE KINDLY BRING TO YOUR ATTENTION THAT WE ARE DOING EVERYTHING IN OUR POWER TO RESOLVE THE SITUATION AND APOLOGISE PROFUSELY FOR NOT BEING ABLE TO COMPLY WITH YOUR INSTRUCTIONS.

WE ARE NOT BEING DISRESPECTFUL TO THE CHINESE AUTHORITIES. WE ARE JUST IN AN IMPOSSIBLE SITUATION THAT WE CANNOT RESOLVE AT PRESENT WITHOUT ENDANGERING LIVES. WE KINDLY REQUEST THAT YOU GIVE OUR TEAM MORE TIME TO WORK ON THIS PROBLEM.

You can take it from me: sitting in a pressurised capsule halfway to space, exchanging ever more desperate and heated messages with foreign governments, is a frightening experience. I should count myself lucky that both exchanges ended well.

In September 1996, two American balloonists, Alan Fraenkel and John Stuart-Jervis, took part in the Gordon Bennett Cup. They had filed flight plans and had received permission to overfly military airspace in the former Soviet republic of Belarus. As they entered Belarus territory Alan, an airline pilot with TWA, contacted Minsk air-traffic control. The balloonists received a garbled reply, then nothing.

Later a military helicopter approached and tried to contact the ballooning team in Russian. It circled around the balloon for nearly half an hour, then opened fire. The envelope and the basket were hit by twenty bullets. The balloon crashed in a forest. Alan and John were killed.

Four months later, Steve Fossett was carried over Libya and received this gem: 'BECAUSE OUR COUNTRY HAS AN AIR EMBARGO YOU CANNOT COME THROUGH THE AIRSPACE OF LIBYA. YOU SHOULD CONTACT YOUR GOVERNMENT AND ASK THEM TO LIFT THE EMBARGO ON OUR REPUBLIC.' As Steve told it in his autobiography, *Chasing the Wind*, Colonel Gaddafi took his finger off the trigger only when his intelligence people learned that Steve was an Eagle Scout.

There was never any doubt that these 'incursions into sovereign airspace' were inadvertent and unavoidable overflights by civilians of good will, conducting themselves in a spirit of sportsmanship. Still, balloons seem to be to sovereign powers what red rags are to bulls. (The great and shining exception to this rule was, astonishingly, North Korea, one of the most closed, heavily militarised countries in the world. In 1998, and given no forewarning of *ICO Global*'s approach, the government faxed Per, Steve and me a message of welcome!)

Many a viable long-distance ballooning attempt has had to be scotched in mid-flight so as not to antagonise a prickly government. In January 1997, rather than encroach on China, Steve Fossett came down in a remote region of Uttar Pradesh, whereupon a local priest, with unnerving seriousness, greeted him as Hunaman the Monkey God. For years, the Soviet ban on balloon overflights ruled out a good sixth of the world's land mass and made round-the-world attempts a virtual impossibility.

From the start, ballooning pioneers were looking for a way to direct their balloons where they wanted to go, rather than where the wind wanted to take them. One of the more remarkable of these figures was Dr William Bland, who was born in London in 1789, the son of an obstetrician. In January 1809, he became a surgeon, boarded the sloop *Hesper* and travelled the world. In Bombay, India, he got into an argument with Robert Case, the ship's purser. A duel was set for 7 April 1813. Bland won, and Case died. Bland was convicted of murder and transported to Van Diemen's Land (Tasmania) for seven years. He was pardoned on 27 January 1815. (Australia needed doctors, and Bland was, by all accounts, a good one.)

For Australian readers, Bland hardly needs this introduction. A farmer, politician, founder and first president of the Australian

Medical Association, Bland is one of the country's founding fathers. He was also a visionary inventor, and one of the great pioneers of the aviation business. Bland designed an airship.

The steam-powered 'Atmotic Ship' had two propellors, a payload (passengers and cargo) of one and a half tons, and could be driven at fifty miles per hour, covering Sydney to London in less than a week. In March 1851 Bland sent his designs to the Great Exhibition at the Crystal Palace in London, where they caused a sensation.

The Atmotic Ship was never built. It was – to borrow today's term – a 'concept aircraft'. Bland designed it to get people talking – and he succeeded. It was hugely influential. Less than a year later, on 24 September 1852, the engineer Henri Giffard built and flew the world's first successful full-scale steam-powered

Henri Giffard's steam-powered airship, which flew across Paris in September 1852.

airship across Paris, from the Hippodrome to Trappes and back – a distance of seventeen miles.

The golden age of airships had to wait a while, however, until lighter, more efficient engines were developed. Count von Zeppelin began drawing up airship designs in the 1890s, and with the launch of the Luftschiff Zeppelin *LZ 1* in July 1900, the most successful airship line of all time took to the skies.

While biplanes were still hedge-hopping, falling apart and crashing into trees, airships were being constructed to be ever more flexible and weather-resistant. They could go further than planes, for longer, and – an often-overlooked point – they were *safer*. After all, a faulty motor on a Zeppelin can be fixed in the air. An early plane with a mechanical fault simply crashes (a point ably demonstrated by W E Johns, creator of Biggles, who in 1918 contrived to write off three planes in three days owing to engine failure, crashing into the sea, then the sand, and then through a fellow officer's back door).

The worst you could say of the great airships was that they were filled with explosive hydrogen. As the century turned, even that objection seemed surmountable. In 1903, oil workers in Dexter, Kansas, hit on an unusual find: a gas well that absolutely refused to burn. Samples of the gas turned out to contain a small amount of an element so rare, it had never before been gathered in any quantity.

The gas was helium. It was inert: it didn't burn, or react chemically in any way with anything. It had, according to the scientific report on the find, 'no practical application'. The most you could say about it was that it was lighter than air. But then, so was hydrogen, and that was much easier to produce.

Then came the First World War – and a change in the way wars were fought. As had been predicted throughout the nineteenth century, in books by visionary authors like H G Wells and Jules Verne, 'war from the air' was coming into its own. Germany was sending Zeppelins to bomb London. They weren't very accurate – the first casualty of the bombardment was the coastal town of Great Yarmouth, 117 miles from the capital. Nor were they very effective. More German aircrew were killed than British casualties on the ground. (An eerie highlight of Howard Hughes's film *Hell's Angels* has gallant German airmen jumping to their deaths in a desperate effort to keep their Zeppelin bomber airborne over London.) Still, the airships of the First World War were a worry: they could fly higher than any plane of the day could reach, and the only way to bring them down was to have pilots fire incendiary bullets at them, to ignite the hydrogen with which they were filled.

If Germany got hold of helium, then German airships would be effectively invincible. So Britain and the US hurried to corner the market in the stuff. Britain built the first helium-extraction plant in 1917, and by the end of the war, the Americans had established their own source of supply. Still, we're not talking great quantities. When the US Navy's experimental airship *Shenandoah* was torn apart by winds over Ohio in 1925, around 90 per cent of the world's captured helium reserves were lost to the air!

The Zeppelin company – for many years the world leader in airship design – had long been planning to swap hydrogen for helium in its aircraft, just as soon as supplies were sufficiently plentiful. Its new flagship commercial liner – the *LZ 129 Hindenburg*, the largest flying machine of any kind ever built – was designed specifically with helium in mind. However, by the terms of the Treaty of Versailles, the defeated Germans were to have no access to this new and expensive technology.

The Hindenburg over Manhattan: later aircraft couldn't match it for luxury.

The designers were hopeful that the Allies would change their minds; in the end, though, they were forced to re-engineer the *Hindenburg* to use hydrogen.

After five years of on-and-off construction, the *Hindenburg* was finally completed in early 1936. It offered passengers the most luxurious airborne experience yet: they drifted elegantly from lounge to dining room to study, before levering their way into (admittedly rather cramped) private cabins. In 1936 – its only full year of service – the Hindenburg made seventeen round trips across the Atlantic, with ten trips to the US and seven to Brazil. It was on its first return from South America in 1937 that tragedy struck. At around 7 p.m. local time on 6 May, it approached Naval Air Station Lakehurst in New Jersey. Twenty-five minutes later, the airship caught fire. Possibly an electrical spark ignited the ship's highly charged, aluminium-coated skin. The skin evaporated and, an instant later, the hydrogen exploded. The *Hindenburg* crashed, completely engulfed in flames.

Incredibly, the conflagration spared two-thirds of the passengers and crew. Still, the disaster, covered by a live radio broadcast and caught on film, etched itself on the public mind. The great age of airships was over.

Even when faster, hardier, more manoeuvrable aeroplanes succeeded them for most purposes, airships persisted, serving niche markets that exist to this day. In 1909 the suffragette Muriel Matters, aboard 'quite a little airship, 80 feet long', threw political leaflets over King Edward VII.

Our Virgin blimp, towing one cheeky marketing message or another, never achieved quite Muriel's level of political notoriety. But it was good for us. We used it to promote the brand. Flying an airship said something about our sense of fun. We teased British Airways when they ran into difficulties assembling the London Eye, flying a banner over the construction site. It read: 'BA can't get it up'.

The chief measure of our airship's success was its visibility. Ours were the only airships that lit up from the inside. Once, while one of our ships was filming above an American football stadium during the Superbowl, we decided to get ourselves some free publicity. The message 'CBS's cameramen are the best-looking cameramen in the world', scrolling across the envelope of our blimp, secured Virgin many seconds of free network advertising!

On 31 March 1989, Virgin invaded Planet Earth. The glowing flying saucer – in reality, a balloon equipped with an internal lighting system – brought motorways to a halt and brought thousands of early-morning London motorists out of their cars to stare as we floated over the city. Studying the prevailing winds, we had hoped to land in Hyde Park; in the end, we came to rest in a field near Gatwick, on the city's outskirts. The loneliness of the landing site, and its nearness to the airport, only doubled the concern of the authorities, spooked as they were by dozens of phone calls warning them of an alien invasion.

The police arrived on the scene with admirable speed: one brave constable crept towards us through the early-morning fog, truncheon at the ready, as the craft popped open and I stepped out in a bacofoil space suit and a fishbowl helmet. The whole affair was very foggy, very cold, and very, very odd, so it says nothing against the policeman that he ran away, very fast.

'Hang on!' I shouted, removing my helmet. He turned and visibly sagged with relief: 'Oh, am I glad to see you!'

We were in the aviation business because we loved flying. We weren't just another boring airline: we were looking for new things to do in the air. In 2001 we set a world speed record for airships, and Mike Kendrick, who ran our airship operating company, was always on the lookout for new ideas and opportunities. He dreamed up an airborne mine-clearing system, and deployed it in Bosnia, and when he left Virgin he set up the charity Mineseeker to develop the idea further.

World events overtook our plans and dreams for the Virgin airship. Following the terrorist attacks of 11 September 2001, blanket bans were put in place that prevented airships from overflying most major cities. It pretty much wrecked this tiny industry. (An airship's visibility is, and always has been, a key selling point.) So we sold the Virgin blimp – and, yes, I still miss it.

I wish I could think of a way to return airships to our skies. I think they're beautiful and dramatic and ingenious. I fancy our cityscapes would be immeasurably improved by the spectacle of fleets of airships. It's an Englishman's instinct to champion the underdog, I suppose, but I reckon airships tug at the heartstrings in a way that other aircraft don't. More than once, the airship has been hailed as a world-beating commercial idea – and each time, developments in heavier-than-air flight have elbowed it aside.

The airship was once safer and more reliable than the aeroplane. Those days are long past. Once, airships could fly much further than planes. Today, at least one plane – the *Virgin Atlantic GlobalFlyer* – can circumnavigate the Earth without even refuelling. Fans of the airship mostly praise it for being an environmentally friendly form of transport. Given the composite materials available to aircraft designers, and the number of exciting 'green' fuels being developed – not to mention the number of solar-powered microlight aircraft out there now – I can't imagine that even this perceived advantage will last much longer.

I still nurse one hope: that airships will find a niche in the tourist market. I cannot imagine a more enjoyable, more cost-effective way of viewing African game than from the gondola of a blimp. Anyway, I remind myself that, as new materials are developed, the aviation landscape changes dramatically. In a hundred years' time, who knows what strange craft will have succeeded our *GlobalFlyers* and *WhiteKnights*? Who knows which old ideas will merit another look?

The *Rozière*

After crossing the Pacific with Per Lindstrand, in 1991, all I wanted was a drink and a roaring fire, but I could see a gleam in Per's eyes. He said we'd broken all these records, and now it was time to try for the last one – a flight around the world. I thought he was mad at first. But when I thought about it some more, I realised that for all the horrendous moments – and there'd been plenty of them! – these flights had been the greatest adventures of my life. So I let Per persuade me.

On 18 December 1998, Per Lindstrand, Steve Fossett and I launched our final bid to circumnavigate the Earth in a balloon. We expected to be airborne for anything up to three weeks, flying at altitudes that would require us to travel in a heavy, pressurised capsule. For such a feat, there was only one kind of balloon we dared put our trust in. In 1987, when we started our adventures together, Per's genius had got us across the Atlantic in a hot-air balloon; but for a circumnavigation of the Earth, only a *rozière* would do.

Pilâtre de Rozier, who 'put flame to powder' and came to grief so spectacularly while trying to cross the Channel, believed that a combination gas-and-hot-air balloon was a natural choice for long-distance flying. He was right. Once its inflammable hydrogen could be replaced with helium – a safer, non-inflammable gas that was almost as light – the *rozière* became the balloon technology of choice. The modern *rozière* was designed and tested in the 1980s by Don Cameron, the Scottish hot-air balloon pioneer who now runs Cameron Balloons, the world's largest hot-air balloon company. (He's also, incidentally, one of very few balloonists ever to have been awarded the prestigious Harmon Trophy for 'the most outstanding international achievements in the arts and/or science of aeronautics'.) The rozière balloon is normally a sphere of helium gas with a hot-air cone underneath. In daylight, the helium warms and expands, squeezing hot air out of the envelope. By night, when the helium cools and shrinks, you light a burner, heating and expanding the air in the inner envelope. You don't need to vent any helium in the day, or replenish it at night; and you don't have to heat the entire envelope in order to stay airborne. The fuel consumed by your modest burner is relatively small, so the length of your voyage is pretty much up

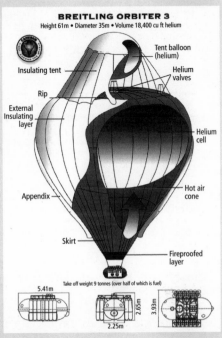

BREITLING ORBITER 3
Height 61m • Diameter 35m • Volume 18,400 cu ft helium

Insulating tent

Tent balloon (helium)

Helium valves

Rip

External Insulating layer

Helium cell

Hot air cone

Appendix

Skirt

Fireproofed layer

Take off weight 9 tonnes (over half of which is fuel)
5.41m
2.25m
2.65m
3.93m

to you and the weather. How comfortable do you want to be? How much food do you want to take? And – the big one – at what height do you want to fly? A pressurised cabin weighs around three tons, putting Nadar's *Géant* to shame; but a *rozière* can keep it in the air for weeks at a time.

Ours was one of the more terrifying flights I've ever experienced: a catalogue of near brushes with death. I remember us flying along a narrow land corridor between Russia, Iran and Iraq, expecting any moment to be blown into hostile airspace. I remember dashing off frantic communiqués to Libya and China as we strayed right into their air defence networks. I remember us hurtling towards Everest and K2, in a wind so fierce, the turbulence could have dashed us against the lee of either mountain (a phenomenon that goes by the none-too-comforting name 'deadly curl-over'!) and passing, with incredible ease, right between them. The balloon, *Virgin Global Challenger*, performed magnificently, right to the end, when, at last, our luck ran out and the record fell from our grasp.

Bob Rice, our meteorologist, informed us that the sub-tropical jet stream carrying us across the Pacific was about to fail abruptly. Our survival chances were bleak. The Pacific is big. It's relatively featureless: there are a handful of islands, but none to offer the castaway a realistic chance of being saved by a land-based rescue. In the Atlantic, you can ditch near a boat. Ditch in the Pacific, and you're as good as dead. But miracles do sometimes happen. The next we heard, Bob Rice had found us winds that would take us straight towards the only islands for thousands of miles: Hawaii! We ditched some sixty miles offshore, bouncing off wave tops as we summoned up the courage to abandon the capsule and jump into the sea. Helicopters rescued us.

The years 1998 and 1999 were great years for long-distance ballooning – perhaps the greatest. There can never be another 'world first' like that achieved by Swiss psychiatrist Bertrand Piccard and British pilot Brian Jones in March 1999. After a twenty-day flight – itself a staggering endurance record – they became the first to circumnavigate the Earth, in *Breitling Orbiter 3*: a *rozière*, of course, designed by Cameron Balloons.

three

'To Fly Is Everything'

'To invent an aeroplane is nothing. To build one is
something. But to fly is everything.'
Otto Lilienthal

Saturday, 5 July 2003.

'They keep telling me I should learn to fly, but I've
never bothered,' I told assembled journalists. 'Right
now, I wish I had.'

I was standing in a field at Brompton Dale, near Scarborough,
in the north-east of England. I was dressed as a coachman, and
was preparing to restage man's first ever controlled flight.

Sir George Cayley, a prolific engineer (and, for three years,
Scarborough's MP), was the first person in history to explain
aerodynamics using proper Newtonian physics. Born in 1773,
Cayley spent an active and happy life devoted to the study of
manned flight. By 1853 he had worked out how to build a 'flying
parachute': a confusing name for something that was, in fact,
very like a modern aeroplane.

Cayley was not on board when it flew. He was a baronet,
a man of means, eighty years old and no fool: he bunged his

coachman John Appleby a few coins for his trouble. The *Cayley Flyer* flew 200 yards, and by the time it came to rest, none too gently, on the other side of the dale, Cayley had lost a loyal servant. 'Please, Sir George,' said Appleby, 'I wish to give notice. I was hired to drive and not to fly.'

Standing in front of our replica, I knew how he must have felt. I was fifty-three, and I still hadn't got round to getting my pilot's licence. The glider ace Allan McWhirter had tried to give me the basics, but by the end I was still about as clueless as the *Flyer*'s original pilot.

Above our heads, the Red Arrows screeched past. A Virgin 747 was due overhead any second. Three generations of Cayleys were on hand to buttonhole the press, explaining excitedly how their ancestor was responsible not just for the aeroplane but for tank tracks, prosthetic limbs, the spoked bicycle wheel, the first polytechnic . . . I looked around for my coachman, cursed the fact that I didn't have one, and climbed aboard.

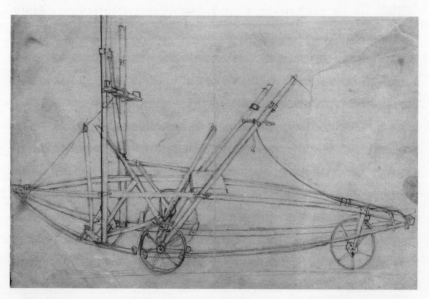

Not bad for a schoolboy doodle: young George Cayley's sketch for a flying machine.

'They keep telling me I should learn to fly,

but I've never bothered,'

I told assembled journalists.

'Right now, I wish I had.'

I'm not the only Cayley nut out there. So – at a remove of fifty years – were the Wright brothers. The Wrights studied Cayley's writings closely. In later years, deluged by legal actions, they found that Cayley was one of the few forerunners they could acknowledge without weakening their patents.

Cayley was the first true aeronautical engineer. Only a couple of years ago, his school notebooks turned up (they're held in the archive of the Royal Aeronautical Society Library in London). They reveal that even at school he was developing theories of flight.

Cayley studied the anatomy of birds. He spent hours watching them in flight. Seeing no easy way to simulate the flapping of a bird's wing, he developed fixed-wing gliders that relied on some other form of propulsion. Typically, they were models. Later, full-size gliders were hauled down hills by a rope until they attained enough speed to take off. The gliders were successful in carrying people over short distances. Arguably, Appleby's laurels for being the first aviator belong to others: a nameless ten-year-old boy, or maybe Cayley's grandson George John Cayley, both of whom covered a few feet in an earlier prototype.)

By happy coincidence, the centenary year of the Wright brothers' first flight was also the 150th anniversary of Cayley's achievement. We could leave it to others to look after the splendid Wrights, but Cayley, like his *Flyer*, needed a shove. We had talked with friends at BAE Systems, put some money together – about £50,000 – and oversaw the reconstruction of Cayley's invention. Together, BAE engineers and the local branch of the Royal Aeronautical Society had done a bang-up job. Now all I had to do was fly the thing without breaking it – or myself.

Perched on a wooden plank over a hollow canvas hull (no comfy cockpit here) and clinging, more for balance than anything else, to the primitive controls, I gave the signal, bumped down the hill, and – glory be – rose fifty feet into the air.

Even before there were planes, there were airlines. The logistics and economics of passenger flights were worked out before anyone even knew how to fly, and investors were ploughing their capital into airline companies a generation before Orville Wright left the ground.

Born in 1812, William Samuel Henson followed his father into the lacemaking business. In 1840, and inspired by the work of George Cayley, Henson and the lace-industry engineer John Stringfellow designed a lightweight, steam-driven aeroplane they called an 'aerial steam carriage'.

Henson and Stringfellow were far-sighted enough to realise that passenger services were the future of aviation: so they set up an international airline. The Aerial Transit Company launched a massive publicity campaign to raise investment capital. They released illustrations of their carriage in flight over London and exotic settings in Egypt, India and China. (In much the same spirit, you can find animations of *SpaceShipTwo*'s maiden flight

Henson's vision of international air travel. Sadly, his plane couldn't fly.

on YouTube.) They put a bill before Parliament, allowing them to raise funds and operate international air routes. The House of Commons resounded with laughter – a sure sign that they were on to something! The press responded with incredulity and enthusiasm. Caricatures of their aeroplanes flying over Egypt's pyramids promptly appeared in *Punch* and in the newspapers.

The Aerial Steam Carriage ('Ariel' for short) was to be made of bamboo and hollow wood, and braced with wires. It was to be powered by a stripped-down steam engine driving two six-bladed propellors. To call Henson's craft prophetic is to undersell it. There was virtually nothing about his design that wasn't later adopted in real aircraft. There was only one problem: it couldn't fly.

Henson built a scale model, which did manage to hop off its guide wire. A larger model, with a twenty-foot foot wingspan, never left the ground.

The besetting challenge of all heavier-than-air flying machines is how to fit enough power into a light enough vehicle. Ariel was never going to get off the ground, because the more power Henson added, the heavier his machine became. The only motors available to Henson were steam engines!

Surprising as it seems, as the years went by, steam-driven prototype aircraft did become almost feasible. In 1877, in a park in Milan, Enrico Forlanini's steam-driven helicopter rose to a height of thirteen metres and hovered there for twenty seconds – a surprisingly light and elegant machine with its fabric counter-rotating sails. Clément Ader's invention of 1890 was a sort of mechanical bat powered by a four-cylinder steam engine driving a four-blade tractor propellor. During its 150-foot trip it rose to an altitude of eight inches. Don't laugh: Ader – coincidentally, the inventor of broadcast stereo – went on, as I mentioned earlier, to achieve manned heavier-than-air flight a full thirteen years before the Wright brothers, in machines that look like conceptual sketches for a Batman movie (though, if his achievements have been sorely neglected, it may be because his every public demonstration ended in a crash).

By the time Orville and Wilbur Wright were paying close attention to aviation, it was clear that you couldn't use powerful

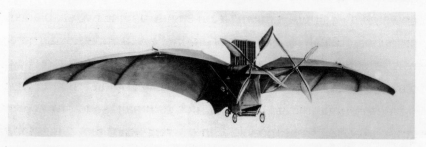

Clément Ader's 'Bat' was powered by a steam engine. It very nearly worked.

engines to simply thug your way into the air. What you needed was a better sort of wing.

Orville and Wilbur ran a chain of bicycle shops in Dayton, Ohio. They didn't gamble, smoke, or drink, and they had precious little to do with women. They didn't hanker for distractions, and they didn't need entertaining. They had each other. 'From the time we were little children,' Wilbur wrote in 1912, 'my brother Orville and myself lived together, played together, worked together, and in fact, thought together. We usually owned all of our toys in common, talked over our thoughts and aspirations so that nearly everything that was done in our lives has been the result of conversations, suggestions and discussions between us.'

The idea of flight obsessed the brothers from the moment their father brought them home a helicopter from one of his business trips. The toy, made of cork, bamboo and paper, was powered by rubber bands and could rise fifty feet into the air. This was a treat, as their mother usually constructed the boys' toys herself. The daughter of a carriage-maker, Susan thought nothing of knocking together simple household appliances. Her example was the solid foundation on which her boys' love of mechanics grew.

The Wright boys' obsession with flight was not unusual or eccentric. On the contrary, they were growing up in an age captivated by new engineering ideas, new materials and the possibilities for manned flight. Just as today's young engineers are drawn into climbing and kite-surfing, so the brothers' love of new technology led them into the cutting-edge technical sport of their day: cycling. Bicycles were transforming small-town life in America. Orville and Wilbur loved the work, and they were very successful: had they stayed in the business they would by now probably deserve more than a footnote in the history of the bicycle. Instead, they stumbled upon news of a death.

'My own active interest in aeronautical problems,' Wilbur Wright recalled in 1901,'dates back to the death of Lilienthal in 1896. He had run across a report of the death of glider pioneer Otto Lilienthal in a newspaper while reading to his brother Orville, who was laid up – indeed, dangerously ill – with typhoid fever.

Of all the men who attacked the flying problem in the nineteenth century, Lilienthal was easily the most important. Since childhood, the German engineer had been fascinated with the flight of birds, and that interest, as it matured, produced arguably the most influential book on aeronautics ever published: *Birdflight as the Basis for Aviation*. Lilienthal's book, published in 1889, contains reams of original data on the effectiveness of different sorts of wing. Though the book itself was not translated into English for many years, its tables and figures were exchanged in letters by flight pioneers all over the world.

Lilienthal was also a practical inventor. Over six years he made some 2,000 flights in sixteen glider types, launching himself from various sites, including an artificial hill he built himself near Berlin. Based on his study of birds – and particularly storks – the gliders were recognisable prototypes of modern hang-gliders, but with one vital (perhaps I should say lethal) difference: rather than hanging off them from his waist, Lilienthal wore his gliders on his shoulders. If his glider nosed up, he threw his feet forward. If his right wing rose, he shifted his weight to the right. It sounds precarious; and it was. On 9 August 1896, Lilienthal fell from a height of seventeen metres and broke his spine. He remained conscious just long enough to remark to his horrified rescuers that 'sacrifices must be made', and died the next day.

Not long after this sad news, the Wright brothers stumbled upon another obituary. This time the newspaper reported the

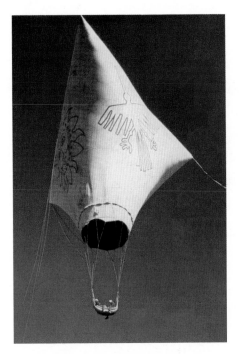

A 1,500-year-old idea: Julian Nott and Jim Woodman hover over Peru's Nazca Plains.

M.GARNERIN'S ASCENT and DESCENT with his Balloon and Parachute.

1797: André-Jacques Garnerin pendulums to earth, wearing the world's first fabric parachute.

A highly idealised view of Blanchard and Jeffries' chaotic first crossing of the English Channel. Note the oars!

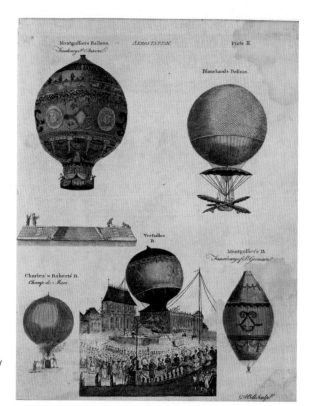

Pioneers of manned flight: balloon designs by Charles, Blanchard and the Montgolfieres.

The Gordon Bennett Cup is the world's oldest balloon race: begun in 1906, it still draws the crowds.

To celebrate 150 years of controlled flight, I take to the skies in a reproduction Cayley Flyer. (The inventor was smarter: in 1853 he got his coachman to fly the thing!)

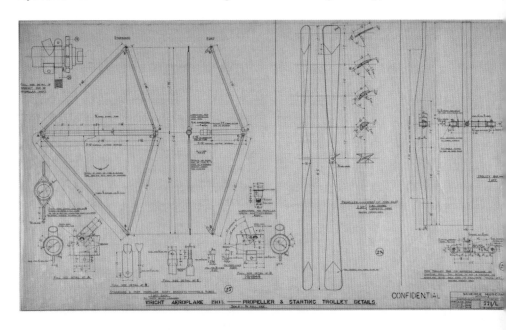

'It is so simple it annoys one': the Wright brothers' plans for the Kitty Hawk.

10:35 AM, 17 December 1903: Wilbur Wright watches anxiously as his brother takes the world's first aeroplane into the air.

From London to Paris, alone: Charles Lindbergh.

Intercontinental air travel began in 1913, with Roland Garros's celebrated flight across the Mediterranean.

Saluting an aviation great: a Tintin magazine from 1938 commemorates the life and achievements of Amelia Earhart.

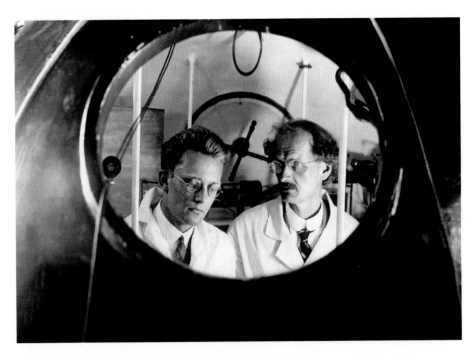

1931: Auguste Piccard (right) and Paul Kipfer take to the stratosphere in their prototype 'space capsule'.

My childhood hero (and he rather fancied my aunt): Group Captain Douglas Bader in 1950.

Hughes's H-4 Hercules was supposed to take the world's sea cargo into the air. The plane got off the ground; the project didn't.

Unsung achievement: Rostislav Alexeyev's mysterious and terrifying KM ekranoplan skims the Black Sea.

'Lord, take care of me now.' On 16 August 1960, Joe Kittinger jumped from 102,800 feet – and accomplished the world's longest free-fall.

The first man ever to visit space twice: USAF Captain Joe Walker beside his 1960s-vintage X-15 rocketplane.

Sitting comfortably: individually moulded chairs are prepared for NASA's astronauts.

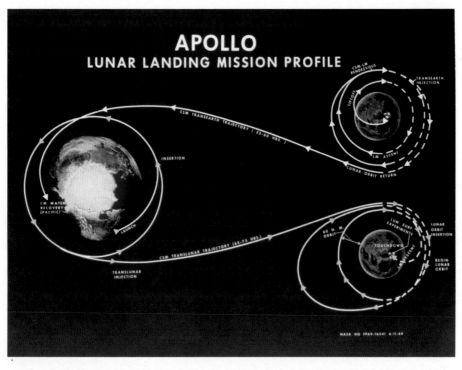

In 1962 NASA's Apollo project set out to realise Jules Verne's dream of landing a man on the Moon.

Otto Lilienthal's gliders were inspired by studies of birds in flight.

passing of Scotsman Percy Pilcher, Britain's most important glider pioneer. A follower of Otto Lilienthal, he held the world distance record for flying his 'hawk' glider over 800 feet in the grounds of Stanford Hall in Leicestershire, England. It was as he was flying an experimental triplane for potential sponsors that the plane's tail snapped; he plunged thirty feet to his death. The newspapers reported that the days of powered flight, surely just around the corner now, had suffered another small and tragic postponement.

The brothers, reading between the lines of these two reports, began to wonder. First Otto Lilienthal; now Percy Pilcher. Both had suffered virtually identical fatal accidents. Could these great men have missed something vital about the nature of flight? The Wrights had little formal education, but they had been brought up in a house that made up in books and magazines for what it lacked in creature comforts. The boys had enough self-confidence, if they didn't know a thing, to make them go out and ask. They were brilliant, indefatigable researchers.

In May 1899 Wilbur wrote to the Smithsonian Institution for a reading list of technical works on aviation, assuring the recipient that he was 'an enthusiast, but not a crank'. He received, by return, a whole caseful of journals and papers, generously thrown together by Richard Rathbun, the institution's assistant secretary. Among the papers were articles by the American engineer Octave Chanute, who later championed the brothers' work.

At the end of their reading the brothers felt they knew what had killed Lilienthal and Pilcher. Both men had attempted to create gliders that were inherently stable. As a consequence, neither had developed any real system of flight control.

The Wrights knew this was the wrong approach, because they knew about bicycles. They knew that the faster you rode a bicycle, the more stable it became. Stop, and you keeled over. Bicycles are not stable, but when they are in motion, they are exquisitely responsive to the movements and adjustments of their riders. The Wrights' breakthrough was to conceive an aeroplane that, like a bicycle, had no inherent stability, but responded sensitively to the movements of its operator.

Like Otto Lilienthal and so many pioneers before them, the brothers had spent many hours watching birds. Among their observations was one that proved to be the key to their success. They had noticed how a buzzard handles sudden gusts by twisting its wing tips, lowering one tip while raising the other to maintain its stability. The story goes that, some time in July 1899, Wilbur was goofing around with an empty inner-tube carton when it dawned on him: if you twist the ends of the box, the corner of one end goes up, while the opposite corner goes down. Imagining the box in flight, Wilbur realised that, by twisting, the box would alter the flow of air around it in a way that would cause it to tilt in the air, just like a buzzard. In his mind's eye, this box in his hands wasn't a box any more: it was a wing – and what he had in his hands was the first ever aeroplane control surface!

As Eureka moments go, this one takes some unpicking. First, I'd better explain how a wing works in level flight to hold a body – an aeroplane, or a bird – up in the air.

Blow up a balloon and tie it tight. Squeeze the walls of the balloon. The air inside resists you. The further you squash the balloon, the harder you have to squeeze. That's because you're increasing the pressure of the air inside the balloon. So far, so obvious – and you'd be forgiven for thinking that whenever you constrict a fluid in this way, the pressure will increase. But there is one big exception to the rule, described by the Dutch mathematician Daniel Bernoulli in 1738, and it's why birds – and planes – manage to stay in the air.

Bernoulli's exception has to do with how fluids flow, and it's most easily demonstrated not with air but with water. (Just to be clear: though water is much thicker than air, air and water are both fluids; they both obey the same physical rules.) Turn on your garden hose. Now pick a spot on the hose and squeeze. This time, the more constricted the hose becomes, the *easier* it is to squeeze!

This is what's happening. Something – in this case, the pump that maintains the mains water pressure in your tap – has given the water the energy it needs to run through your hose. Some of that energy pushes the water forward, and some of it pushes the water against the sides of the hose. (If you punctured your hose, the water would fountain out.) The flow of water is constant; the same amount of water is trying to pass through every part of the hose. If you pinch the hose, then the water has to pick up speed to get through the bottleneck. More of the water's energy is used to flow forward, which means less energy is available to push against the walls of the pipe. Squeeze the hose, and the water pressure against the walls of the pipe *decreases*.

Let's cut to the chase here and have a look at a cross-section of a wing. (This could be a bird's wing or the wing of a plane; it doesn't make any difference: they both work the same way.) Air passing from left to right in the diagram hits the wing. The wing squeezes the air passing over it. The air moves faster to compensate for the squeezing, and the pressure over the top surface of the wing drops. Planes and birds are sucked into the air.

So much for level flight on a calm day. What happens if it's blustery? What if the air over your left wing is blowing harder than the air over your right wing? How do you stay level in real, unpredictable, constantly moving air? This is where Wilbur's cardboard carton comes in.

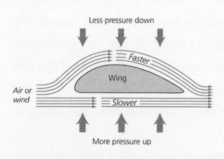

A wing in motion sucks its payload into the air – with a little help from Daniel Bernoulli and his principle first published in 1738.

If you progressively bend the front tip of your wing down, you will increasingly squeeze the air passing over it; the pressure over the wing will drop, and the wing will lift. If, at the same time, you progressively raise the front tip of the opposite wing, it will squeeze the air passing over it less, and the wing will drop. Orville and Wilbur proved this theory by attaching control lines to twist the sides of a box kite while in flight, in just the same way as Wilbur had twisted the cardboard carton. Sure enough, pulling the control lines made the kite roll over to one side or the other. Later, in combination with a moveable rudder, this technique of 'wing warping' would allow the Wrights' machines to turn in the air with grace and ease . . . but I'm getting ahead of myself.

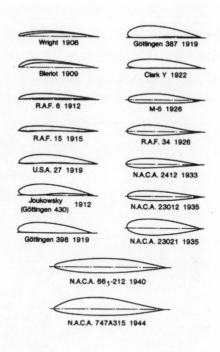

Evolution among the machines: a chart summarising four decades of wing design.

The brothers' kite experiments began in 1899, but they could never find enough wind. Wilbur wrote to the US Weather Bureau and was told that they couldn't do better than move their experiments to Kitty Hawk, a narrow beach off the coast of North Carolina.

Late in September 1900, Orville Wright wrote to his sister, 'We certainly can't complain of the place. We came down here for wind and sand, and we have got them.' Along with the wind and the sand came mosquitoes. Their arrival 'was the beginning of the most miserable existence I ever passed through,' Orville complained. 'They chewed us clear through our underwear and socks. Lumps began swelling up all over my body like hens' eggs.' To make matters worse, there were precious few buildings

The Wright brothers Orville (front) and Wilbur fly a kite at Kitty Hawk.

in Kitty Hawk, and none for rent, so the brothers were living in tents.

To begin with they flew their prototype wings from a derrick twelve feet high, but the winds proved so strong and blustery they soon abandoned the tower and controlled their wings from the ground, as they would with ordinary kites. By the end of October 1902, Orville and Wilbur had become skilled pilots of their prototype glider. Launched from a nearby hillock with a daunting name, 'Big Kill Devil Hill', the glider carried its pilots hundreds of feet in each flight. It was time to add an engine.

They decided to build their own, ultra-lightweight engine, and gave the job to Charles Taylor, a young mechanic who worked in their bicycle shop. Taylor rose to the challenge. He shaved every fraction he could off the machine. He later recalled: 'I cut the crankshaft from a solid block of steel weighing over a hundred pounds. When finished, it weighed about nineteen pounds.' Taylor's four-cylinder engine used bicycle chains to drive two counter-rotating propellors. The Wrights had calculated that two propellors turning slowly would be more effective than one propellor spinning fast; and they arranged the propellors to spin in opposite directions so that the spin of the motors didn't twist the frame of the plane.

While Taylor worked on the engine, the brothers worked on the propellors. These were much harder to make than anticipated. The Wrights assumed that there were figures and charts explaining the shape of ship's propellors, and that they could adapt these numbers to come up with a propellor ideally suited to the air. As it turned out, however, no one had ever done any serious work on the shape of ship's propellors; they had simply evolved over decades of use! The Wrights had no choice but to figure their propellors out for themselves.

A propellor is a sort of moving wing. It works by creating a vacuum in front of the blades and a zone of high pressure behind. What makes it complicated is that, as Orville complained, 'nothing about a propellor, or the medium in which it acts, stands still for a moment.'

Imagine trying to work out the speed of each point along a propellor blade without really knowing how fast the engine should be turning, or even how long the propellor blade should be! What the Wrights ended up with, after countless, long,

A propellor from the *Wright Flyer*: designed from first principles and carved by hand.

involved arguments and many sleepless nights, was propellors of astonishing beauty, each blade twisted in a way that looks, with hindsight, perfectly natural, like exquisitely polished driftwood.

Indeed, much the same was said of the brothers' whole invention. The sculptor Gutzon Borglum (the man who would later be given the job of sculpting US presidents' faces into Mount Rushmore) wrote: 'It is so simple it annoys one. It is inconceivable, yet having seen it, it now seems the most natural thing in the air. One is amazed that human kind has not built it before.'

The machine that emerged into the near-freezing 30 miles per hour wind blowing across Big Kill Devil Hill launch site on Thursday, 17 December 1903 would carry Orville into the air and into the history books: at a ground speed of about 6 mph, the *Wright Flyer* rose, dipped and climbed into the air, on a flight that lasted twelve seconds and covered 120 feet.

It was the first aeroplane. And it was only the start.

four

The Golden Years

My life and my work have given me fantastic opportunities to fly in every imaginable kind of plane, from gliders to flying boats to jumbo jets. I have walked the wings of a biplane, crossed from balloon to balloon on a plank, hurled myself off Brighton pier in a less-than-successful attempt to be a birdman and for the TV show *The Rebel Billionaire* I took one lucky contestant up a rope ladder, on to the top of the envelope of a balloon. We drank tea at 10,000 feet and gazed over the bowl of the earth. I have flown in warplanes and balloons and for a few scary months I was even the back-up pilot for Steve Fossett's transglobal flight in the *Virgin Atlantic GlobalFlyer*.

I find it impossible to choose an absolute favourite. Some planes tremble beneath you as though they were alive. Others fly so smoothly that if you felt the slightest tremor, you would have them grounded for safety checks. I have flown at multiples of the speed of sound in perfect comfort and felt sick with fear at twenty feet. How do you pick from such experiences?

Certainly I can rattle off any number of favourite moments. There was the time I flew in the lead plane of the Red Arrows aerobatic display team and had the surreal experience of flying so close beside other planes I felt I could reach out and touch them. There was the time I landed a newly restored Dornier flying boat on Lake Winnebago, and discovered that touching down on water feels, for those first few seconds of contact, just like touching down on concrete.

These experiences have taught me something important about the history of flying, and how we should preserve it. Planes are meant to be flown and to be seen flying. Maintaining old planes is expensive, and flying them can be risky. With the best will in the world, it's not possible to preserve all the skill and knowledge and understanding that went into making them. I believe, however, that if we want to preserve the planes of the past at all, we have to do what we can to preserve them in operational condition. Strange to admit it, but I look back with special fondness to the day I was taken up in a Spitfire – strange, because I spent most of that flight with my head in a bag.

In 2003 the Discovery Channel organised a series of TV programmes and a national poll to celebrate the centenary of powered flight. They got celebrities to act as advocates for their favourite machines, and it was my job to sing the praises of the Spitfire. I had some lines prepared to deliver to the cockpit camera and, in between gagging fits, I delivered them. On the ground again, white, trembling and thankful to be alive, I found a microphone under my nose: how had I enjoyed my flight? I think the Spitfire won the public poll in spite of my advocacy rather than because of it!

The most remarkable aspect of that flight was the pilot. Spitfires are very much planes in the Wright brothers mould: they are *inherently unstable*. Fling them around in the air, and you have some hope of controlling them. But if you lose your nerve, or drop your speed too far, you can't expect a Spitfire to stay airborne. It is as thrilling, and as unforgiving, as a sports car.

Planes are only as good as their pilots. This is true even aboard jetliners with onboard flight computers. Those computers carry inside themselves insights from a century of aviation. And that is why, important as the machines are, the history of aviation is really about people. There is nothing we can do to preserve the spirit of the early aviation pioneers: but we can foster it for a new generation. As I'll explain in a later chapter, I think we foster it rather well. The pioneering spirit of the first exhibition flyers is still with us.

The early 1900s *were* special time, of course, and unrepeatable, because no one at that time quite knew how this great new technology would develop. They were years when an aerobatic display thrilled a crowd, demonstrated the abilities of a plane, promoted an airmail service, won a prize, provided footage for a movie and trained a military pilot – all at the same time! Back then, the magic of flying was concentrated around two or three companies, a handful of people and a couple of dozen venues, and its achievements and terrors were splashed across every newspaper and newsreel. From the early 1900s to the beginning of the Second World War, the sky offered countless opportunities for everyone – or anyway, that was the promise. Celebrity, success, wealth, knowledge, the satisfaction of making something new, the chance to see things no one had ever seen before: with these goals before them, the flyers of the golden age came together to create exceptional communities – plane-makers and barnstorming troupes, airlines and experimental associations. People lived hard, and frequently died hard. The English motoring pioneer Charles Rolls – who went into partnership with Frederick Royce in 1904 to create one of the world's great aero-engineering companies – was killed in a flying accident when the tail of his *Wright Flyer* broke off during a flying display in 1910. Aged thirty-two, he was neither the first nor the youngest casualty.

Because the Wrights' machines allowed them to control their flights, they discovered something new each time they rose into the air. They weren't just testing machines; they were learning how to fly. They learned quickly, too, breaking their own records virtually every time they left the ground. On 3 September 1908, Orville tried out a new Wright plane at Fort Myer for the US Army. He managed one and a half circles of the parade ground and pranged the machine on landing. By 8 September he was flying for ten minutes at a time. The next day, he flew fifty-two laps in fifty-seven minutes and thirty seconds of unbroken flying time, shattering the record set by his brother in France just four days earlier. So it went on – until, on 17 September, as he was flying at 125 feet with the young army officer Tom Selfridge, himself a keen air pioneer, one of the plane's two propellors split, cutting a guy wire. The plane's rudder collapsed and the men fell to earth. Selfridge died a few days later of his injuries. Orville would live the rest of his life in pain.

The Wrights' later careers make for grim reading. Their patents covered virtually every aspect of winged flight, but their very generality made them difficult to defend. The brothers swapped airfields for lawyers' offices in a losing battle for proprietorship that alienated them from the young generation they inspired. Glenn Curtiss, an indefatigable engineer who would go on to set a world motorcycle speed record of over 136 mph on a motorcycle of his own invention (it didn't have any brakes), first met the Wright brothers in 1906. It was they who inspired his interest in aviation. Soon they would be suing him. It was a sour sort of birth for manned flight.

Glenn Curtiss in flight: some say he did more for aviation than the Wrights.

On 30 September 1907, Curtiss became a founder member of the Aerial Experiment Association. Other founders included Alexander Graham Bell, the inventor of the telephone, who described their venture as a 'co-operative scientific association, not for gain but for the love of the art and doing what we can to help one another'.

The Wrights took a dim view of that, and when Curtiss began building planes with steering flaps called 'ailerons', they cried foul. The Wrights claimed that in the 1906 patent for their wing-warping system they had described alternative systems for roll control, including ailerons.

This, while true enough, hardly spoke to the matter. The world wanted to fly, while the Wrights were interested only in defending their patents. They turned down invitations to races and prizes and competitions and lost themselves in endless legal wrangles, leading one federal official to accuse them of single-handedly causing 'the United States to fall from first place to last of all the great nations of the air'. The Wrights had the law on their side, but they may as well have joined King Canute and told the tide not to roll in. The Aerial Experiment Association, meanwhile, built plane after plane after plane, and Curtiss went on to become the most successful of all first-generation American aircraft-makers.

The first great sea crossing by plane was achieved on 25 July 1909 when, 124 years after Blanchard and his sponsor John

Understandably worried: Louis Blériot takes off in his self-made monoplane.

Jeffries narrowly avoided a dunking, Louis Blériot crossed the English Channel and won the £1,000 *Daily Mail* Prize.

Blériot was an aircraft-maker. He designed some real death traps in his time, but he was also the first person to make a working monoplane. 'It is not beautiful,' one reporter remarked, 'being dirty and weather-beaten, but it looks very businesslike.' It certainly was, dashing over the water at 250 feet, at just over 40 mph. Not until 1927, and Charles Lindbergh's solo flight across the Atlantic, would a single flight have such an impact. National borders – even ones marked by physical boundaries – lost some of their meaning that day.

Blériot won the *Daily Mail* Prize by the narrowest of margins: twelve days earlier his compatriot Hubert Latham had launched his own attempts, all three of which ended in a crash. With his cigarette holder, chequered cap and fashionable clothing, Latham epitomised the European daredevil aviator and was hugely popular. Born in Paris to a family of wealthy Anglophiles (he had British citizenship, though he never lived there), Latham used his phenomenal fortune to finance glamorous adventures. He may not have flown across the Channel, but he ballooned across it with his cousin Jacques Faure. He raced cars and motorboats and led safaris to Africa. And that, sad to say, is in the end how he died, aged twenty-nine: gored to death by a buffalo during a hunting expedition.

Blériot's triumph, and Latham's celebrity, reflect France's obsession with manned flight. In 1910, France had more than three times as many licensed pilots as America, and most of its pilots were inventors and designers. Blériot alone produced forty-five experimental machines, including airbuses capable of carrying eight passengers. By 1913 his aircraft construction business had thirty-three domestic competitors.

Belgian airwoman Hélène Dutrieu won prizes, records and a nickname: Girl Hawk.

France's golden year was 1913. France flew higher, further and faster than any other nation. By the end of the year the top speed of an aeroplane was 125 miles per hour, set by the Frenchman Marcel Prévost, while his compatriot Edmond Perreyon set a new altitude record of 19,281 feet. In 1913 the athlete Roland Garros flew across the Mediterranean in a French monoplane, and Hélène Dutrieu – a world-champion cyclist and racing driver – was awarded the Légion d'honeur for her services to aviation. Adolphe Pégoud became the world's first aerial acrobat, attracting thousands of spectators to displays of loops, rolls and other stunts.

Look at the figures, though, and you'll notice something important: by 1913, the Germans had already spent more than the French on aviation. At the outbreak of the First World War, Germany took to the skies.

With eighty confirmed victories in the air, Manfred von Richthofen – the German fighter pilot known to posterity as 'the Red Baron' – was the most successful German flying ace of the war. A wealthy aristocrat, he came to flying comparatively late. As a youth, he had been much more interested in horses and hunting, and liked nothing better than to ride out with brothers Lothar and Bolko to hunt wild boar, elk, birds and deer.

When war began, he served as a cavalry reconnaissance officer. 'I was entirely ignorant about the activities of our flying men,' he recalled later, 'and I got tremendously excited whenever I saw an aviator. Of course I had not the slightest idea whether it was a German airman or an enemy.' Machine guns and barbed wire made traditional cavalry operations impossible. Richthofen's men were drafted into the infantry, while their commanding officer looked around for some other kind of 'dashing' action. Within a few weeks, reconnaissance operations were being conducted from the air, so Richthofen signed up.

In the first few months of the war, the planes of both sides were unarmed, and flyers had only shelling from the ground to contend with. In 1915, however, Tony Fokker, a Dutch aeroplane builder working for the Germans, invented a gear system that shot machine-gun bullets between the blades of the aeroplane's propellor as it turned. For a time, Germany's Fokker Eindecker fighters gave the Germans an edge. But British pusher biplanes (whose propellors were mounted to the rear fuselage) and the French Nieuport 11 were effective opponents, and there were more of them, so, all in all, the sides were evenly matched. Victory in the air depended less on the equipment, more on the character and calibre of the pilots. This wasn't war as it was being fought on the ground. This was more like jousting.

It took Richthofen a while to adapt to the grime and discomfort of flying. 'The draught from the propeller was a beastly nuisance. I found it quite impossible to make myself understood by the pilot. Everything was carried away by the wind. If I took up a piece of paper it disappeared. My safety helmet slid off. My muffler dropped off. My jacket was not sufficiently buttoned. In short, I felt very uncomfortable.'

The planes used in the war were fast, topping out at around 100 mph. And when they caught fire (which was often) they went up like matchwood – which is, largely, what they were. Some were quite easy to fly. The British ace Cecil Lewis was told by his instructor to keep his plane above 5,000 feet and then throw her around as much as he liked: 'Whether you're on your back or on your ear, she'll always fall out of it.'

Lewis had joined the Royal Flying Corps in 1915, after lying about his age. He was already so tall (six foot, three inches) that the planes could scarcely hold him. When he began his training, the average life expectancy of a British pilot on the Western Front was three weeks. He loved flying for its own sake, and wrote a magnificent memoir, *Sagittarius Rising*, about his experiences. From the air, a rainbow was not an arc but a perfect circle. You could dive and turn to watch the shadow of your plane on the clouds. Below, yellow mustard gas crept 'panther-like over the scarred earth, curling down into dugouts, coiling and uncoiling at the wind's whim'.

After the First World War ended, Lewis was hired by the Vickers company to teach the Chinese how to fly, married the daughter of a Russian general and co-founded the BBC.

Richthofen was not so lucky. Acknowledged by the enemy as the most dangerous man in the air, Richthofen evolved rules for combat that turned his squadron, Jasta 11, into living legends. To help them identify each other in the melee of battle, Jasta 11 painted their aircraft bright red, and became known as 'the Flying Circus'.

On 6 July 1917, Richthofen received a serious head wound. While he was recuperating, a writer from the German propaganda unit turned up to ghost his autobiography. *The Red Battle Flyer* is a thrilling read but the arrogant tone can be hard to take: it thoroughly embarrassed Richthofen.

The Red Baron returned to combat in October 1917, but his head wound had left him a changed man. He suffered nausea and headaches and mood swings, and these may well have contributed to his death, shot down while pursuing a young Canadian pilot over Morlancourt Ridge near the Somme River.

Manfred von Richthofen with his father, and sporting a near-fatal head wound.

Within a few years of the Wright brothers' first exhibition flights, the public was hankering for more. They had witnessed numerous take-offs and landings. They wanted to see what these strange craft could actually *do*.

Exhibition pilots would scout out suitable open areas for their shows, then fly over neighbouring towns dropping advertising leaflets. America's early 'barnstormers' earned a fortune. An aerobatic display could net you $1,000 in a day – more than twice the country's average annual earnings. The trick was to live long enough to spend it. 'When it was blowing hard, nobody wanted to fly if they could help it,' remembered one barnstormer, Beckwith Havens. 'But the crowd would demand that you go up. The programme said you were going to fly at two-thirty. Well, maybe the wind was blowing pretty hard. You were always watching the wind, you know – watching smoke, watching flags, laundry on the line, and everything. I still do it.'

By 1911, more than a hundred people had died in aeroplane accidents. That people were prepared to accept such risks seems extraordinary today, but it's worth remembering that back then there were plenty of other things that could kill you. Charles 'Daredevil' Hamilton survived a staggering sixty-three aeroplane crashes and died at the tender age of twenty-eight – of tuberculosis.

After the First World War ordinary men and women got their hands on thousands of surplus and decommissioned planes. In the US, a $500 course of instruction often came with a free biplane, and second-hand engines could be had for as little as $75. Amateur pilots with a taste for adventure flew from town to town selling five-dollar rides at county fairs. Aerial mapping, skywriting and crop-dusting kept body and soul together out of season. (Continental Dusters began crop-dusting in 1924; they subsequently became part of Delta Air Lines.) As one pilot put

Bessie Coleman was the first African American airwoman.

it, the most dangerous thing about this kind of life was 'the risk of starving to death'.

Barnstorming was a tough life, and it forged a tough breed of pilot – though few were tougher than Bessie Coleman. Born 1892, Bessie Coleman escaped rural poverty and moved to Chicago, where she became a beautician. Inspired by stories of French women aviators like Thérèse Peltier and Elise Raymonde Deroche (the first woman to earn a pilot's licence), she moved to France to learn to fly. She returned to the US a different woman: Bess Coleman was now 'Queen Bess, the Daredevil Aviatrix'. She gave exhibition flights – sometimes with the Jamaica-born aviator and parachutist Sam Fauntleroy Julian ('the Black Eagle of Harlem') – and lectured on aviation. She died in a plane crash in 1926.

Florence Barnes came from the other side of the tracks. Born into privilege on 22 July 1901, Florence already had an aviation pedigree: her grandfather, Thaddeus Lowe, had pioneered American aviation by setting up the Union Army Balloon Corps during the American Civil War. A tomboy, and difficult to control, Florence was married off, aged eighteen, to the Reverend C Rankin Barnes of South Pasadena. She stuck with this dismal arrangement for nine years before she snapped. Abandoning her husband and daughter, she

Hellraiser: Florence 'Pancho' Barnes flew stunts for Howard Hughes.

disguised herself as a man and stowed away on a freighter bound for Mexico. She got work on a banana boat and acquired the nickname 'Pancho'.

Four months later, Pancho came home. If her family was relieved to see her, their relief was short-lived. A few weeks later, while driving her cousin to flying lessons, she got it into her head to learn to fly. After six hours of lessons she was flying solo.

Pancho took to 'buzzing' her ex-husband's congregation each Sunday morning. When that palled, she set up a barnstorming show and competed in air races, breaking Amelia Earhart's world women's speed record with a fly-by of just over 196 mph. She went to Hollywood, got work as a stunt woman, and can be seen, *going very fast indeed,* in Howard Hughes's Oscar-winning air adventure *Hell's Angels.*

She blew all her money just in time for the Great Depression, and with the last of her cash she bought a chunk of California's Mojave Desert, near the March Army Air Base. There she built the business she retired into: the Happy Bottom Riding Club – a dude ranch and restaurant that catered to airmen at the nearby Muroc Air Field. We'll meet some of those airmen in later chapters: the test pilot Chuck Yeager and the astronaut Buzz Aldrin were among their number.

Not every barnstormer was a pilot; in 1908, at a state fair in Raleigh, North Carolina, carnival crowds cheered Charles Broadwick as he descended from a balloon on a home-made parachute. Broadwick was one of the first parachutists to pack his chute into a wearable container – an innovation that would make skydiving possible.

In the audience that day was a fifteen-year-old single mother called Georgia Ann Thompson. Married at twelve, a mother at thirteen and abandoned by her husband, Georgia – a cotton-mill worker – had by then very little to lose. Even her mother agreed, and gave her blessing as Georgia hooked up with Charles Broadwick's World Famous Aeronauts.

At just over four feet tall, Georgia was billed as 'The Doll Girl', and quickly became the sweetheart of crowds all across the country. Charles Broadwick adopted her as his daughter. As Tiny Broadwick, Georgia used to jump from a swing attached to a balloon, she used to jump from biplanes, and she was the first person

Georgia 'Tiny' Broadwick made her first parachute jump at the age of fifteen.

ever to deliberately free-fall before pulling her cord. She quit while she was ahead, in 1922, after 1,100 jumps, but she stuck with the aviation business. When she died, on 25 August 1978, members of the US Army's elite parachute team, the Golden Knights, served as her pall-bearers.

Parachutists developed a number of daredevil stunts to wow the crowds at county fairs. One lethal escapade involved wearing two parachutes. After the first chute opened it was cut off, allowing the jumper to free-fall. The second chute would burst open just before the jumper hit the ground. The crowds loved it.

Art Starnes made his first parachute jump in the mid-twenties at the age of eighteen with a barnstorming troupe at an airfield outside Charleston, West Virginia. As parachutes go, Art's was, to say the least, basic: 'Instead of having a harness there was a large rope loop with a piece of garden hose covering it.' Starnes's show name, Aerial Maniac, was not calculated to inspire confidence. In truth he was a meticulous pilot, famous – among aviators – for his relentless preparations and rehearsals. It was Starnes who first developed the techniques of free-falling.

Regular parachutists viewed the prospect of free-fall with terror. Free-falling spelt uncontrolled tumbling and spinning and certain death. Military pilots were taught to pull the ripcord the moment they left their planes. In war, though, this left them exposed to enemy fire. No one yet knew what position they should adopt to stay stable as they fell in the air. Starnes thugged out the answer by trial and error, enduring any number of rolls, tumbles and flat spins before he hit upon the ideal skydiving posture: spread-eagled; chest out; knees bent. By the early 1930s, Starnes was jumping out of planes and falling for three and a half miles before pulling his cord.

Another great, iconic stunt of the era was to climb out of your cockpit and walk along the wing of your plane. We owe this piece of craziness to Ormer Locklear, a carpenter and mechanic in Fort Worth, Texas, who joined the US Army Air Service in October 1917, just a few days short of his twenty-sixth birthday.

As part of a pilot's test, Locklear needed to read and correctly interpret a signal flashed to him from the ground; but the plane's engine housing and wing kept blocking his view. Fed up, Locklear left the plane in the hands of his instructor and climbed along the wing to read the message. On landing, his instructor bawled him out – and passed him.

Locklear's wing-walking saved his bacon on other occasions,

Ormer Locklear, 'King of the Wing Walkers', pioneered countless aerial stunts.

too: he'd wander out to fix a loose radiator cap, or re-attach a spark-plug wire. He got his honourable discharge from the Army Air Service in May 1919 and immediately became a barnstormer, quickly establishing himself as 'King of the Wing Walkers'.

Locklear pioneered virtually all the stunts that other wing-walkers would copy. He did handstands, he hung from a trapeze by his teeth and he was the first person to switch from one plane to another while in mid-air and from a car to a plane by grabbing a rope ladder.

He claimed there was method in all this madness: 'I don't do these things because I want to run the risk of being killed,' he once protested. 'I do it to demonstrate what can be done. Somebody has got to show the way someday we will all be flying and the more things that are attempted and accomplished, the quicker we will get there.'

'Somebody has got to show the way someday we will all be flying **and the more things that are attempted and accomplished,** the quicker we will get there.'

Ormer Locklear

On New Year's Day 1914 the world's first scheduled commercial flight took off from the water near St Petersburg, Florida, and headed north-east over Tampa Bay. Twenty-three minutes and twenty-one miles later, the single-engined flying boat landed St Petersburg's mayor Abe Pheil, in the town of Tampa.

The Airboat Line was the brainchild of Tony Jannus. Born 1889 in Washington, DC, and nicknamed 'the Birdman', Jannus began life as a barnstormer. Popular, brave and charming, he dated movie stars, tested machine guns and parachutes and, with his brother Roger, started his own firm, Jannus Brothers Aviation, co-ordinating pilots, aeroplane designers and builders. Two years after starting the firm, delivering bombers to the Czar of Russia, Tony Jannus's Curtiss K flying boat developed engine trouble and ditched into the Black Sea. Jannus was lost at sea. He was twenty-seven.

Jannus's airline was short-lived, and it would be many years before civil aviation took hold in America. After all, the continent had working railroads: what did it need an airline for?

Civil aviation began sooner in Europe, kick-started by the First World War. The conflict had virtually destroyed the railways of France and Belgium, and for a while, flying the 200 miles between London and Paris was easier – and certainly quicker – than picking one's way overland from Paris to Brussels. In 1920, about 6,500 passengers flew between London and Paris. The airlines lost money on every ticket but the British and French governments picked up the tab. Both had colonies to govern, and saw air travel as a way of holding their empires together.

Pierre Latécoère pioneered France's empire of the air, establishing Lignes Aériennes Latécoère, often called simply 'the Line'. Just six weeks after the end of the First World War services began between the Line's base in Toulouse and the Spanish city of Barcelona. Month by month, year by year, the line grew

Henri Guillamet and Jean Mermoz pioneered countless international air routes.

Larry's chair

Larry Walters had always dreamed of flying; but his eyesight wasn't good enough for him to join the United States Air Force. He did not stop dreaming.

In 1982, while working as a truck driver in southern California, Larry visited his local Army & Navy surplus store and bought forty-two weather balloons and several tanks of helium. On 2 July, in his girlfriend's back yard in San Pedro, he anchored his favourite deckchair to the bumper of his jeep, inflated his weather balloons with helium, tied them to the chair and sat down, clutching an air gun, a pack of sandwiches and a six-pack of Miller Lite beer. His plan was to drift about at a height of about thirty feet for a few hours, use the gun to pop the balloons one by one, and float gently to the ground. But when his friends cut the cord, Larry's lawn chair rocketed up at a rate of 1,000 feet per minute.

Larry, whose spectacles had flown off during his ascent, reached an altitude of about 16,000 feet and drifted into the primary approach corridor of Los Angeles International Airport, where he endured fourteen hours of fright and freezing cold. A Pan Am pilot was the first to spot him. He told air-traffic control he had just passed a man in a lawn chair brandishing a gun.

One by one, Larry shot his weather balloons, but the freezing cold made him clumsy and he dropped the gun. An offshore breeze picked up and carried him out to sea. Finally a rescue helicopter approached, dropped him a line and tugged him back to earth. On his way down Larry's cables got caught in a power line, causing a twenty-minute blackout in Long Beach. On the ground, Larry was arrested. Safety Inspector Neal Savoy of the Federal Aviation Administration was not best pleased: 'We know he broke some part of the Federal Aviation Act,' he told reporters, 'and as soon as we decide which part it is, a charge will be filed.'

Larry was shaken, but not very repentant. When asked by a reporter why he had done it, he replied, 'A man can't just sit around.'

longer. By March 1919, the Line was flying to Rabat in Morocco. In September, it launched a regular service to Casablanca. In 1922 Latécoère began services within North Africa itself, flying from Casablanca to Oran. Three years later, he pushed down the western coast of Africa to reach Dakar, in what was then French West Africa.

Latécoère's most famous pilot was Jean Mermoz, whose adventures became the basis for best-selling novels by his fellow pilot, Antoine de Saint-Exupéry. On one occasion Mermoz's plane crashed in the Sahara and he was taken hostage by Tuareg tribesmen. He wasn't the only one. The risk of being kidnapped was so great, Latécoère ordered his pilots to fly in pairs, employed friendly Arabs to ride on the flights as interpreters, and put the word out that he was prepared to pay ransom for the safe return of downed pilots.

Once the Line conquered the Sahara, Latécoère turned his ambitions west – to the jungles of South America, and the virtually impassable highlands of the Andes. 'Here,' wrote Saint-Exupéry, 'the crust of the earth is as dented as an old boiler. The high-pressure regions over the Pacific send the winds . . . into a corridor fifty miles wide, through which they rush to the Atlantic in a strangled and accelerated buffeting that scrapes the surface of everything in their path.'

On one occasion Mermoz and his mechanic were forced down on to a plateau 12,000 feet up and with a sheer drop on every side. After two days of makeshift repairs, they rolled the machine off the plateau and over the edge. Luckily, the plane's controls responded!

If, in America, civil aviation remained a distant prospect, airmail was, thanks to the truly heroic efforts of the US Postal Service, fast becoming an essential and familiar part of life.

The modern US Air Mail service had an inauspicious beginning (the young lieutenant charged with the first delivery was fresh out of flying school and had an atrocious sense of direction), but it steadily wove that vast country together. The planes used by airmail pilots, mainly de Havillands, were fondly christened 'flaming coffins', because if you landed heavily (easy to do – these planes had the glide angle of a brick), the fuel tank would blow up in your face.

'Map-reading was not required,' one airmail pilot recalls. 'There were no maps. When visibility was at a minimum, I was in trouble and could even be upside down.' He got through by his ability 'to recognize every town, river, railroad, farm and, yes, outhouse along the route.' Thirty-two aviators died on US Postal Service duty, piloting routes that airlines would one day follow.

In 1925 Charles Lindbergh, the son of a US congressman and a talented barnstormer, was hired by the Robertson Aircraft Corporation in St Louis to plan and fly a new airmail route between St Louis and Chicago. Twice during the ten months that he flew the route, Lindbergh had to bail out of his mail plane owing to bad weather or equipment problems. After that sort of work experience, flying the Atlantic can have held few terrors for him.

The first prize announced for an air crossing of the Atlantic – a purse of £10,000 – was put up by newspaper magnate Lord Northcliffe. Appalled at the laggard state of the British aircraft industry, Northcliffe hoped the prize would inspire British aviators to close the distance between them and their American and French rivals. It was the kind of patriotic project the readership of his *Daily Mail* newspaper appreciated. But the first crossing was undertaken by Americans! Led by Lieutenant John Towers of the US Navy in 1918, the mission involved four aircraft, multiple stops and forty-one US destroyers.

The Navy declined to accept the prize. Aeroplane technology was moving so quickly, it was obvious to all that, whatever the rules said, the prize should be reserved for a more purely aeronautical achievement. On 14 June 1919, RAF Captain John Alcock and Lieutenant Arthur Whitten Brown, an American citizen born and living in Britain, set off from St John's, Newfoundland, and after sixteen hours and 1,890 miles of mechanical problems, disorientation, ice clouds and wind, they landed, nose-down but safe, in a Connemara bog. They had flown the Atlantic non-stop, and were worthy winners of the *Daily Mail* Prize.

A month before their historic flight, however, an even more prestigious prize was announced: New York hotel owner Raymond Orteig offered a $25,000 purse to the first allied aviator to fly non-stop between New York City and Paris. The prize, driven by Orteig's enthusiasm for Franco-American co-operation following the First World War, fostered nine separate attempts to cross the ocean. Altogether, $400,000 was spent in its pursuit. Six men lost their lives in three separate crashes. Another three were injured.

By this time, aircraft technology had taken another big step forward, with the development of bigger, heavier tri-motor aircraft. The Russian inventor Igor Sikorsky designed and flew the world's first multi-engined fixed-winged aircraft, the Russky Vityaz, in 1913, ten years before he emigrated to the US. That plane, so big many claimed it was a hoax, pointed the way forward for civil aviation. In the US, and in competition with the Dutch designer Tony Fokker, Sikorsky developed a generation of three-engined workhorses, powered by a propellor at the front and one propellor under each wing. These, everyone assumed, were the kind of planes that would one day conquer the Atlantic.

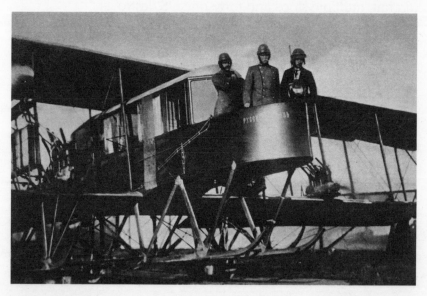

Early riser: Igor Sikorsky's trimotor aeroplane of 1913 could carry eight people.

The Orteig Prize threw up a surprise, however. Rejecting the big three-engined machines preferred by his competitors, Lindbergh got into discussions with companies producing light, single-engine planes for the US airmail. These were the sort of planes he knew like the back of his hand. These were a proven technology, and less likely to throw up unpleasant surprises when he was halfway across an ocean. The airframe he finally settled upon was loosely based on the 1926 Ryan M-2 mail plane. The fuselage was two feet longer than the production model; the wings were longer and stronger; the landing gear was strengthened. But there was really nothing radical about it.

The *Spirit of St Louis* wasn't nice to fly. Putting fuel tanks in front of the cockpit meant that there could be no front windshield, and a periscope had to be installed so that Lindbergh could see straight ahead. The *Spirit of St Louis* wasn't very stable, either, although Lindbergh later wrote that this instability helped keep him awake during his thirty-three-and-a-half-hour flight.

Charles Lindbergh with the mail plane that carried him across an ocean.

On the evening of 21 May 1927, Charles Lindbergh landed at Le Bourget Air Field in Paris, after a flight of 3,614 miles. Lindbergh and his team had succeeded because they didn't bite off more than they could chew. Their technology for the Atlantic crossing was about as off-the-shelf as it could be at that time. They extracted extraordinary performance from ordinary machines. They didn't wildly overspend, and they didn't empire-build. They stayed small, so that everyone involved knew what everyone else was doing and thinking. The Orteig Prize had inspired more than an achievement: it had inspired a way of working. And this, in the end, is how prizes push technology forward.

After his historic crossing, rather than return to service as a regular US Air Mail pilot, Lindbergh used his fame to help promote the use of the service, giving speeches and carrying souvenir mail on flights across the US and over routes in Latin America and the Caribbean. Lindbergh flew 22,350 miles in *Spirit of St Louis*, encouraging the construction of local airports. His Latin American tour took him to thirteen countries in two months.

People said his flight changed the world. It certainly changed America. In 1927 applications for pilot's licences in the US increased threefold, and the number of licensed aircraft quadrupled. In 1926, 5,782 passengers flew on US airlines. In 1929, 173,405 took to the air.

The story of the Orteig Prize shows that a well-timed, well-structured prize can change the mental landscape of an industry and a nation. Lindbergh, for his part, sowed a seed in people's minds – a revolutionary idea: that anyone could fly. The dream came true for some.

*

Wiley Post flew solo around the world in 1933 – and received a hero's welcome.

British aviator Amy Johnson, who flew her de Havilland Gypsy Moth biplane from England to Australia in 1930, scrimped together the money for flying lessons from secretarial work in London. She received the Harmon Trophy as well as a CBE for her trouble. In 1931, the American flyer Wiley Post, who'd spent time in a reformatory for armed robbery and whose aviation career began as a parachutist for a flying circus, flew around the globe with navigator Harold Gatty. Two years later he circled the globe alone. On 5 September 1934, wearing an innovative pressure suit of his own design, Post reached an altitude of 40,000 feet above Chicago. And he kept on going, reaching altitudes of up to 50,000 feet on later flights.

In 1904, seven-year-old Amelia Earhart persuaded her uncle to help her cobble together a home-made ramp, fashioned after a roller coaster she had seen on a trip to St Louis. Amelia's first flight ended dramatically. She emerged from the broken wooden box that had served as a sled with a bruised lip and a torn dress: 'It's just like flying!' she cried.

Amelia Earhart and navigator Fred Noonan vanished while circumnavigating the globe.

Amelia spent her childhood climbing trees, hunting rats with a rifle and filling a scrapbook with newspaper clippings about successful women. In Long Beach, on 28 December 1920, she and her father visited an airfield where Frank Hawks, later a famous air racer, gave her a ride that would change her life. 'By the time I had got two or three hundred feet off the ground,' she said, 'I knew I had to fly.' By 1927, she had accumulated nearly 500 hours of solo flying, and had set her first women's record, reaching an altitude of 14,000 feet.

One afternoon in April 1928, Earhart, now a Boston social worker, received a phone call: 'How would you like to be the first woman to fly the Atlantic?' The caller, publisher and publicist George Putnam, was perfectly serious, and on 17 June, Earhart, with pilot Wilmer Stultz and mechanic Louis Gordon, became the first woman to fly across the ocean. She shrugged off the achievement: 'I was just baggage, like a sack of potatoes,' she said, adding, 'Maybe someday I'll try it alone.'

Family investments, such as they were, had long since disappeared down a failed gypsum mine, and celebrity endorsements were essential if Earhart was to keep flying. Offered a position as associate editor at *Cosmopolitan* magazine, she handled her publicity well, campaigning for women in aviation. In 1929, she organised the first Women's Air Derby (which featured Pancho Barnes) and was among the first flyers to promote commercial air travel. Together with Charles Lindbergh, she lobbied for Transcontinental Air Transport (TAT), which later became TWA. She was also vice president of National Airways. By 1940, it had become Northeast Airlines.

In August 1928, Earhart became the first woman to fly solo across the North American continent and back. On 20 May 1932, she soloed the Atlantic in fifteen hours. The list of Earhart's 'firsts' would make a book. Following an unpublicised flight from Oakland to Miami, Florida, she publicly announced her most daring adventure yet: with ace navigator Fred Noonan (the man who had established Pan Am's China Clipper routes across the Pacific) she was off to circumnavigate the globe. They departed Miami on 1 June 1937, hopped through South America, Africa, India and South East Asia, and arrived in New Guinea on 29 June 1937. They were two-thirds of the way through their journey. On 2 July, they took off from Lae, in New Guinea, on the first leg of their Pacific crossing. The ocean swallowed them.

Filmed at a cost of nearly $4 million, *Hell's Angels* was, in 1930, the most expensive movie ever made. An epic tale of loyalty (it's set in the First World War), courage (it's about officers in the

The most beautiful racing plane ever built? Howard Hughes beside his H-1.

Royal Flying Corps) and sin (it stars Jean Harlow), *Hell's Angels*
features aerial stunts by actual First World War aces. None of
them – this, anyway, is the story – was crazy enough to perform
the film's final aerial stunt, a piece of acrobatics they all said
couldn't be done. The film's director, Howard Hughes, proved
otherwise – or tried. He flew the scene, got the shot – and
crashed the plane.

His injuries, this time, were minor, and a dashing reputation
was established – a reputation that would dominate US aviation
and US politics well into the post-war era.

Howard 'Sonny' Hughes was born into privilege: his family
owed their huge fortune to a patent on a drilling bit used by
the oil industry. Hughes learned to fly when he was a teenager,
and devoted his personal fortune and his life to aviation. He
was more than a stunt flyer, more than a tinkerer: he studied
every aspect of the business. To understand the demands of

commercial flying, in 1932 he adopted an assumed name and signed on for a while as a co-pilot with TWA. He learned aviation design by buying entire aeroplanes and setting to work on them with a spanner. This hands-on approach bore spectacular fruit in 1935, when Hughes collaborated with the engineer Glenn Odekirk and the designer Richard Palmer to realise the Hughes H-1 racer, arguably the most beautiful monoplane ever built. Because of its radically streamlined design (it had retractable landing gear, and its every rivet was countersunk flush to the aluminium skin of the plane) it was also the fastest: Hughes used it to set a world speed record of 352 mph in September 1935; two years later Hughes and the H-1 (sporting longer wings) set a new transcontinental record and Hughes won the Harman Trophy as outstanding airman of the year.

But the strangest, and in many ways the most impressive part of Hughes's design legacy has to be the 'Spruce Goose'. The Hughes H-4 Hercules was a military transport plane, and the largest flying boat ever built. It was the brainchild of Henry J. Kaiser, a shipbuilder who directed the construction of hardy merchant-marine 'Liberty ships' in the US during the war. Though the programme was turning out one cargo vessel every forty-five days, German submarine attacks on the Atlantic trade were sinking the ships as fast as they were being built. The human and commercial losses were horrendous, so Kaiser conceived a plan to take merchant shipping out of the water altogether and into the air! Only a giant like Hughes could have swallowed such a gigantic undertaking. And it might have worked: boasting the largest wingspan and height of any aircraft in history, the H-4 cargo transport was as big and unlikely as Hughes himself. It was built, not of spruce, but of laminated birch, because aluminium had become so scarce during the war. Events intervened to scotch its promise: it missed the conflicts it was supposed to serve by two years and flew only once, on 2 November 1947, before delays and cost overruns led to its cancellation.

Howard Hughes was no less of a legend as a businessman. Three years after he set a new transatlantic record in the H-1, Hughes set a very different kind of aviation milestone: one that would promote the cause of civil aviation in a civilian aeroplane. In 1939, Hughes flew around the world in a twin-engine Lockheed Super Electra airliner. He refuelled only six times and covered 14,672 miles in just over ninety-one hours of flying time. As well as demonstrating the potential of civil aviation, Hughes led its commercial development. He bought himself a company, TWA, and worked with the aircraft-maker Lockheed to create a revolutionary airliner, the Lockheed Constellation, exceptional at the time both for its speed and its endurance. Eisenhower picked it for his presidential plane. Orville Wright climbed aboard, too: forty years after his historic first flight, it was the last aeroplane Orville ever flew in. Hughes lived to expand TWA, broke Pan Am's monopoly of US international air travel, and along the way persuaded Walt Disney to build the TWA Moonliner at his theme park Tomorrowland, depicting what travel would be like in 1986. The former Nazi rocket scientist Wernher von Braun helped design the rocket, which looked remarkably like a wartime V-2!

Sadly Hughes, like Orville Wright, lived out his later years in constant pain, after being involved in a near-fatal air accident. On 7 July 1946, his XF-11 – an experimental US Army Air Force reconnaissance aircraft – suffered engine failure during a test flight. Hughes crashed through three houses in Beverly Hills before his plane buried itself in a fourth and burst into flame. Burnt and immobilised, Hughes required large amounts of highly addictive pain medication. His notorious 'eccentricity' in later years – subsisting on chocolate bars and milk, walled in by Kleenex boxes – was almost certainly exacerbated by his lifetime reliance on painkillers.

Even during his decline, Hughes wielded huge influence. He was the largest private employer in Nevada and spent about $300 million on his many properties in Las Vegas. Throughout the sixties and up until his death from kidney failure on 5 April 1976, Hughes's executives acted as

Howard Hughes at the controls of the world's largest cargo plane, the H-4 'Spruce Goose'.

though he was still lucid and still pulling the strings of his many business interests, from airlines to gambling to hotels and real estate. The truth was, he spent half his days watching thrillers, the other half in the bathroom. It is hard to imagine a crueller fate for such a major figure – and such a courageous individual.

Douglas Bader, my greatest childhood inspiration, also lived his entire adult life in constant pain. He had a wide and generous definition of what a fool was, and he didn't suffer them gladly.

This irascible old man was also one of the funniest and most generous a child could know. His example gave me my confidence. He also gave me and my generation one of the best pieces of business advice ever formulated.

Rules, he once said, were for the guidance of wise men – and for the obedience of fools.

His life story proves his point. Born in 1910, Douglas was twenty when he visited Reading Aero Club, performed acrobatic tricks in a Bulldog to fellow RAF pilots – and drove his left wing into a ploughed field. His logbook for that day reads: 'Crashed slow-rolling near ground. Bad show'. He wasn't kidding: he had lost both legs.

Though the RAF retired him in 1933, Douglas kept on flying. By 1940 he was back in uniform, operating Hurricanes and Spitfires. He shot down several enemy aircraft over Dunkirk, argued strategy with his elders and betters, and dropped eleven enemy aircraft during the Battle of Britain. In August 1941, during a fighter sweep over Europe, he was forced to bail out over Le Touquet, in German-occupied France.

He went one way, and one of his tin legs, still jammed in the cockpit, went the other. Stranded in almost the very spot where his father, a sapper in the Royal Engineers, had been fatally wounded in 1917, he was quickly picked up and imprisoned. The German authorities asked the British to air-drop their captive a spare leg. A British plane dropped him a leg all right – and then rejoined its fellows on the way to bomb Gosnay power station near Béthune; only bad weather saved their target from being destroyed.

That discourtesy soon paled into insignificance compared to the trouble Douglas caused his captors. Treated well, visited and entertained by just about every experienced Luftwaffe officer who happened by, Douglas devoted himself to mischief and escape. He succeeded, too – not once, but many times, until an exasperated prison official threatened to take away his legs. The threat had no effect and eventually Douglas was packed off to Colditz. Released by the 1st US Army in April 1945, he travelled to Paris and immediately requested a Spitfire. He was refused.

five

'A Great River of Air'

Practically the moment their first manned balloon left the ground in 1793, Joseph and Étienne Montgolfier were proposing to drop fourteen tons of explosives on the occupied city of Toulon.

Depressing as it is to report, by the time manned flight became a reality, the theory of war from the air had already been worked out. Detailed speculative accounts of aerial bombing date from the early seventeenth century. The advent of real balloons merely added detail and local colour to the picture. In 1842, in the poem 'Locksley Hall', Alfred, Lord Tennyson wrote of the 'ghastly dew / From the nations' airy navies grappling in the central blue', and he didn't have long to see his vision realised. Seven years later, during the siege of Venice, an Austrian artillery lieutenant called Franz von Uchatius bombarded the city with *mongolfières* made of paper.

This, the world's first air raid, was not a success. According to an eyewitness, 'the balloons . . . exploded in mid-air or fell into the water . . . Venetians, abandoning their homes, crowded into the streets and squares to enjoy the strange spectacle . . . Applause was greatest when the balloons blew over the Austrian forces and exploded.'

War is hell: air battles dominate Albert Robida's 1908 adventure serial.

By the end of the nineteenth century, it was generally accepted that future wars would be air wars. There's a reason Jules Verne was a best-seller: titles like *Robur the Conqueror* (1886) and its sequel *Master of the World* (1904) captured the fears of a generation. By the turn of the century, it was increasingly clear that in the aeroplane, the world possessed a weapon capable of destroying civilisation.

A few minutes after midday on 30 August, 1914, on the eve of the Battle of the Marne, a German Taube warplane appeared in the skies above the Gare de l'Est in Paris and dropped a handful of explosives on to the railway station, killing one woman. Another five hundred Parisians fell victim to the 'five o'clock Taube' before the war was over.

The practice of targeting civilians was not new. The fact that the attack came from the air, however, was extremely worrying. In the air, all bets were off. There were no rules of engagement; there were no precedents. As the war progressed and the technology improved, one German general observed that 'the distinction between combatant and noncombatant began to blur.'

If the First World War ushered in the era of the warplane, no one had any doubt that Europe's next war would usher in the purpose-built bomber – and European governments were under no illusions about what *that* would be like. One of the most influential pundits of the period was General Giulio Douhet, an

Italian military theorist whose book *Air Power* was translated into many European languages and became a best-seller. The really frightening thing about reading Douhet now is that he was mostly right. He wrote, 'The brutal but inescapable conclusion we must draw is this, the strongest army we can deploy in the Alps and the strongest navy we can dispose on our seas will prove no effective defence against determined efforts of the enemy to bomb our cities.'

In 1933 H G Wells, Douhet's English contemporary, published *The Shape of Things to Come* – a political speculation couched as a history written at a date far in the future. Wells, along with everybody else, believed that the next war would be primarily an air war, and that it would destroy civilisation. He had already written as much twenty-six years earlier. His potboiler *War in the Air* (serialised in 1907) ends with humanity reduced to a brute, feudal existence.

The Shape of Things to Come predicts the Second World War with uncanny accuracy. Though by the 1930s Wells the writer was past his prime, he still has the ability to raise the hairs on the back of the reader's neck, with his talk of Polish aeroplanes dropping gas bombs on Berlin, Italians 'administering the same treatment to Belgrade' and his description of 'a line of Permanent Death Gas across East Brandenburg'.

The British government's estimate of how people would cope under aerial bombardment was no less bleak. Medical analysts reporting to Whitehall believed the experience would send the survivors mad. In the early days of the war hospitals surrounding the capital sent home their non-urgent cases and made up beds ready for tens of thousands of 'nervous cases'. Following an air attack, it was assumed that survivors who made it into the city's tunnels would simply refuse to come out again. At the beginning of the war, London's Underground stations were locked at night to keep people out.

America, entering the war following the Japanese attack on Pearl Harbor in December 1941, believed itself immune from such terrors. Japan, its nearest enemy, simply didn't have the means to attack the US mainland from the air. That, anyway, was the assumption.

On 5 May 1945, a minister and his wife took some children on a fishing trip in southern Oregon, east of the Cascades. They came upon a curious device, tangled up in some trees. When thirteen-year-old Joan Patzke attempted to pull the balloon free, it blew up in her face, killing her, four other children and the pastor's wife.

The firebombs – reports were coming in thick and fast now – mystified the US authorities. They couldn't see how the balloons could have travelled all the way from Japan. The alternative explanations were even sillier: were they being launched from US beaches by Japanese landing parties? Were they being secretly manufactured by interned Japanese-Americans?

Finally an Army fighter managed to nudge one of the balloons to the ground intact, and the unbelievable truth emerged: these were extremely sophisticated weapons, and – yes – they bore all the hallmarks of Japanese manufacture.

It was one of the stranger episodes of the air war: from November 1944, Japanese schoolchildren from eighty schools laboured to construct 10,000 balloons, each carrying a bomb meant for the US mainland. Sumo halls, sound stages and theatres were commandeered for the work. The rubberised silk of conventional balloons leaked too much to sustain the ten-metre-wide balloons on their voyage over the Pacific, so an alternative material was found: *washi*, a paper made from mulberry bushes, impermeable and very tough. Manufacturers of *washi* paper could only produce the stuff in small batches, and squares, each no bigger than a road map, had to be glued together using vegetable paste. The workers – most of them schoolgirls just into their teens – were told to wear gloves, keep their fingernails short and not use hairpins. They volunteered for this, but they were not very well treated. Living conditions were worsening as the war in the Pacific turned against Japan. Hungry workers used to steal the paste to eat it.

Once stuck together, each envelope segment was drawn across a light-box. Inch by inch, the papers were checked and tears or weak spots reinforced with paper. Once the envelope was assembled, it was filled with air and lacquered, then deflated, boxed and sent to the project's launch site. Japan released the first of its bomb-bearing balloons on 3 November 1944.

The project – effectively, the building of the world's very first intercontinental ballistic missiles – was the brainchild of Major General Sueyoshi Kusaba, who assembled the best scientists from all over Japan to develop his secret weapon. The balloons were meant to start forest fires and cause explosions. They may have had a darker purpose, too. Chemical weapons including mustard gas and lewisite had been manufactured on the island of Okhuno under the direct control of the Army since 1929, and Okhuno also happens to be one of the places where the balloons were being made.

So much for the payloads. The balloons are worth mentioning not because of what they carried but because of how they travelled. Japan's fire balloons were built to cross the Pacific Ocean in just three days, borne by fierce, barely understood high-altitude winds. That no one but the Japanese authorities knew about these winds is one of aviation history's great ironies.

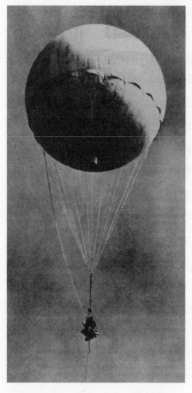

The jet stream carried Japan's fire balloons over mainland America.

They were first studied by Wasaburo Ooishi, a committed internationalist and pacifist whose European studies (at Berlin's Lindenberg Aerological Observatory) had convinced him of the importance of international collaboration. Returning to Japan, Ooishi set up his own upper-air observatory at Tateno: a barren, flat expanse, 100 miles to the north-west of Mount Fuji. It was from this unprepossessing spot that Ooishi released balloons and tracked them with a theodolite (a surveying instrument with a rotating telescope for measuring angles) as they shot suddenly away, snatched by the mysterious high-level winds.

Convinced that scientific work should be held in common for the world's advancement, Ooishi ensured that his findings would be read by the greatest number of people in the greatest possible number of countries. He wrote them up in Esperanto. Ooishi's optimism and idealism – his belief that world understanding was just around the corner, borne on the world's fastest-growing 'auxiliary' language – were, to say the least, misplaced. Nobody read him. Nobody *could* read him. In his desire to communicate with the world, Ooishi had effectively made his work a state secret!

The Japanese military assumed control of Ooishi's observatory in the early 1930s, and towards the end of the Second World

War, it was his data that made the balloon-bombing of America a reality. About 9,300 balloon bombs were released from Japan in the direction of the United States. They were ingenious. They were automated, laden with weights, altimeters and timers, strung together so that they would drop sand bags at night to compensate for the shrinking of the hydrogen inside their envelopes. If the balloon rose too high, an altimeter opened a valve to vent hydrogen. As the project leaders expected, only one in ten made it across the ocean. Of those, 285 caused damage; but it was never very significant. One bomb fell on a power line in Harford, Washington, and shut down the reactor making plutonium for the Nagasaki A-bomb; but power was restored a few seconds later.

The bombs were more effective as terror weapons. They could appear anywhere. One even got as far as Michigan. The randomness of the threat was its strength. The US War Department, concerned about what news of this and other balloon incidents would do to civilian morale, forbade all mention of the balloons in the press. On several occasions, officials claimed that bombs had accidentally fallen off planes belonging to the Royal Canadian Air Force!

Once the scale of the threat was appreciated, the race was on to disable the Japanese project before balloons arrived on US soil carrying something far more deadly than a few incendiaries. The Military Geology Unit of the US Geological Survey hit upon a plan. They set about studying the sand in the ballast bags. They thought it unlikely that the Japanese would go to all the trouble of shipping sand long distances, merely to use as ballast. More than likely, the bags were being filled from a beach near to the balloon factories. Studying the microscopic creatures contained in the sand, they traced the ballast to specific Japanese beaches

– and America's B-29s took to the air. Two of the three hydrogen plants supplying gas to the Japanese balloon project were destroyed, and Major General Kusaba's project was cancelled.

Still, the mystery remained: how on earth had the balloons travelled so far, so fast?

The Second World War had taught the Allied powers something about these high-level winds, but in a disorganised, piecemeal way, from the reports of mystified pilots. American B-29 aircrews returned from bombing raids on Japan full of wild and wonderful stories: of tail winds of 150 mph and westerlies topping 200 mph. In Europe, bomber squadrons, flying at between 30,000 and 35,000 feet were the most likely to be affected. In some regions, they found a high wind propelling them to their targets. In others, the jet stream really ruined their day. In 1943 an English bomber squadron met headwinds of nearly 240 mph as it returned from a raid over Gironde, on the west coast of France. The crews had no choice but to parachute from their stalled aircraft, and were picked up and interned by the German Army.

These winds were so fast, so narrow and so seemingly fixed in their courses, the Swedish-American meteorologist Carl-Gustaf Rossby coined the name 'jet stream' to describe them. What makes a jet stream? To answer this question, I'll have to explain about the weather – all in a couple of pages!

The earth is constantly heating the air, like an electric ring under a pan of water; and when warm air rises, it sucks cold air in after it. This is where winds come from. If the Earth did not spin like a top, winds would blow smoothly and regularly. On a planet that did not spin, warm air would rise at the equator, cool as it moved towards the poles, sink to near ground level, and roll back towards the equator. The Earth, however, spins really fast, from west to east. This means that the warm, high winds moving away from the equator move a little bit east as they go; and cool, wetter winds moving towards the equator move a little bit west.

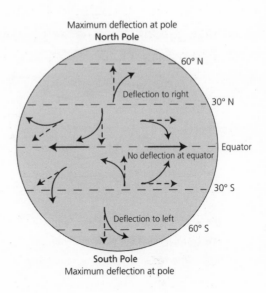

This cross-section through the earth's atmosphere shows the way the winds blow.

This isn't the end of the story. Because the Earth is a ball, the further you move away from the equator, the slower your movement from west to east. Stand on the equator, and you'll be zipping along at around 1,038 mph. At the poles, it's possible to spin on the spot. London spins at 656 mph. So winds leaving and approaching the equator don't just veer off in straight lines. They curl in on themselves, so that the nice, single circulation I just described is broken up into three independent circulations. This curling is important to our story, and it has a handy name: the Coriolis effect.

In the tropics, and in the far north and far south, bands of roiling air circulate with a certain regularity. Sandwiched in between these circulations, however, are what we optimistically call the 'temperate' zones. Here the air tends to blow from west to east and from east to west doing absolutely nothing to even out the temperature difference between the equator and the poles. Where these large bodies of warm air and cold air meet, naturally the cold air wants to rush in and fill the vacuum created by the warm air. But it can't: the Coriolis effect means that the

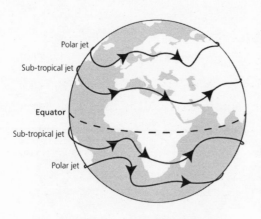

Polar jet
Sub-tropical jet
Equator
Sub-tropical jet
Polar jet

The world's jet streams offer speedy one-way travel around the world – if you can find them.

cold air, instead of rushing *in*, ends up curling *around* the warm air. This is where cyclones come from.

High up in the stratosphere, where the heat emitted and reflected off the earth can't jiggle them about so much, these winds are very strong and very stable; they move much more quickly than the winds below them, and they curl much more slowly. These are the jet streams.

In 1991, Per and I were planning to cross the Pacific in a hot-air balloon, and had come to Miyakonojo, a small town in the south of Japan. The same jet stream that had carried Japan's balloon bombs to the US mainland would soon, we hoped, be carrying us across the Pacific. We wanted to be first to make the crossing. We had not come to race. When we arrived, however, we found a charming Japanese balloonist, Fumio Niwa, challenging us to be the first over the Pacific. Both of us were grounded by the weather for a while; all we could do was kick our heels, waiting for the jet stream to pick up strength enough to bear us across the world's biggest ocean – waiting, too, with mounting tension, for war to break out in the Gulf.

The previous October I had flown with a Virgin crew to Baghdad to bring back British hostages. I wanted to be on the ground if war broke out, not gallivanting around in a balloon. But it would be a massive waste of many people's time and effort if we did have to abort.

Christmas came. I went with the family to Ishigaki, an island off the south Japanese coast. Then my wife Joan took the children back to London to start school. As my parents and I walked through the airport to catch an internal flight back to Miyakonojo, I saw a television screen. A helicopter was hovering over the sea and winching a body on board. It was Fumio. He had taken off the day before we were due back, hoping to steal a march on us. The strong winds had torn the envelope of his balloon, forcing him to ditch. By the time the rescue helicopter arrived, Fumio was dead from exposure. His body was recovered only ten miles off the Japanese coast.

On Tuesday, 15 January, Per and I walked through crowds of thousands towards our balloon. Japanese children held up candles and waved Union Jacks at us. They sang 'God Save the Queen'. I couldn't get Fumio's death out of my head. Our balloon towered over everyone, large enough to swallow the dome of St Paul's Cathedral. We released some white doves as a rather futile peace gesture and turned to enter the capsule.

We ignited the burners, then Per fired the bolts that released the steel hawsers and we rocketed upward. On the radio Will Whitehorn shouted: 'The crowd down here are cheering like crazy. It looks amazing. You're heading up fast.' (Will was in charge of the recovery crew. He was watching our backs, chartering rescue boats to the limits of their range to cover our progress.)

Within five minutes we were out of sight of Miyakonojo and within half an hour we were well over the Pacific Ocean. At 23,000 feet, we hit the bottom of the jet stream.

It was as if we had struck a ceiling. However much we heated it, the envelope refused to go in. It simply squished itself flat against the wall of wind. We put on our parachutes and clipped ourselves to the life rafts in case the balloon should rip.

At last, the balloon edged into the jet stream. I watched aghast as the silvery envelope went screaming off ahead of us. Dully, I wondered: if the ballon was hurtling all the way over *there*, what's keeping us in the air *here*? Before puzzlement could turn to panic, the balloon dipped *below* the level of the capsule – and tugged the capsule after it, into the stream.

The shock was vicious. We were knocked flying. From travelling at 20 knots we were suddenly flying at 100 knots. For a moment I thought we were going to be torn apart, but then the balloon rose above us again and we were safely tucked into the jet.

'Nobody's done that before,' Per announced, cheerfully. 'We're in uncharted territory.'

The real trouble began about seven hours into our flight. The capsule my friend Alex Ritchie had designed for our 1991 Pacific balloon crossing carried six propane tanks in a necklace around it, and we had just emptied our first. Per pressed the button to jettison the tank – and the entire gondola suddenly lurched to one side and hung at an angle. The empty fuel tank had fallen away all right – and had taken two full tanks with it.

The implications were horrific. We had flown only around 1,000 miles. Now we had just half the fuel we had started out with, and we were crossing the most dangerous and remote part of the Pacific Ocean.

'Watch out!' Per said. 'We're rising.'

Without the weight of the two full tanks, the balloon was soaring.

Thirty-one thousand feet.

Thirty-four thousand feet.

'I'm letting air out,' Per said. 'We've got to come down.'

We had no idea how strong the capsule was. We knew that the glass dome was able to withstand pressure of only around

42,000 feet, and even that was something of a guess. If we reached 43,000 feet the dome would explode. Per had opened the vent at the top of the balloon, but we were still rising.

'It's slowing,' I said. 'I'm sure it's slowing.'

The altimeter ticked up: at 41,000 feet we were in the realm of the unknown. None of our equipment had been tested at this kind of height. Anything could go wrong.

At 42,500 feet, the balloon levelled off; and, now we had avoided a quick and spectacular death, it was time for us to face the slow and miserable one: with so little fuel we seemed doomed to ditch into the Pacific. To reach land before the fuel ran out, we would have to fly at an average speed of 170 miles an hour – twice as fast as any hot-air balloon before us. It was round about then that our radio link gave out: the storm raging below us had wiped out the signal. We were alone.

We descended into the jet stream and for the next six hours we sailed high above the storm-tossed ocean. No polar explorer had ever seen such an expanse of white. The clouds beneath us were wrinkled, like cauliflowers or brains. As night fell, lightning lit them up from within. I paid the sight little notice. I was too busy staring, barely daring to blink, at the altimeter, tweaking the burners to keep the balloon where the winds were fastest.

Per and I had no idea what fate had in store for us over the Pacific...

'Nobody's done that before,'
Per announced, cheerfully. 'We're in uncharted territory.'

And – this was nothing short of a miracle – it seemed to be working. Per and I were hurtling eastwards towards America at well over 200 mph! No balloon had travelled so fast. The jet stream, which had threatened to destroy us when we first encountered it, was saving our lives.

While Per, exhausted, grabbed some sleep, I stayed glued to the altimeter, every nerve singing as I strained to detect the slightest wobble or buffet in our flight. The jet stream had an inner core only about 4,000 feet in diameter. If we stayed in the core, we might cross the ocean and live. If I let us slip out of the core, we would slow down and surely die. The slightest roughness would suggest that the balloon and the capsule were in different airstreams.

A very beautiful white-and-orange flickering lit up the capsule. I looked up – and saw lumps of burning propane falling from the burners on to the capsule! I imagined one of those lumps falling on to the freezing cold glass of the canopy: it would surely shatter.

Per, waking to my shout, quickly lifted us to where the oxygen gives out and the fire would be extinguished – at around 43,000 feet – and again we found ourselves staring, silently and prayerfully, at the glass dome.

It held.

We sank back into the jet stream.

After eight hours of communications blackout, our radio came on again.

'Thank God we've got hold of you,' said Bob Rice, our chief meteorologist. 'I've worked out your route. You've got to change course. Right now.'

'Yes?'

'Come down immediately,' he said. 'Your jet stream is turning.'

Our relief at hearing Bob's voice was cut through with shock at his news. Our jet stream was turning, all right – a few minutes later, and we'd have been on our way back to Japan!

One of the odd aspects of the record-breaking fraternity is the close bond you form with people you might never see again. I run into Per very seldom now; outside the capsule of a high-altitude balloon, we live and work in different worlds. I haven't spoken to Bob Rice in years. Yet there was a time – there were many times – when I would be hanging on Bob's every word. At times, he has been my only hope, the one man who could save my life and the lives of my crewmates.

Bob Rice is a weatherman – one of the very best. Among the adventure community in particular, he's a legend. He first trained in the US Air Force during the Korean War, and by the time he retired in 1999, he'd amassed over fifty years' meteorological experience, half of it focused on special projects and adventure support. He took a key 'mission control' role on twenty-six long-distance manned balloon flights, as well as countless sailing races and record attempts.

When Bob worked with *Earthwinds* (an ill-fated round-the-world ballooning project that Virgin Atlantic sponsored back in the mid-1990s), balloonist and PR man William Armstrong was watching: 'Beginning his workday ritual at 3.30 each morning, Rice would stuff his pipe with Black-and-Tan (his exclusive private brand), ignite the tobacco and proceed to incense the room like the high priest of forecasting before celebrating the weather mass.'

'What captured me was the idea of weather as a living, breathing thing,' Bob says. 'You don't just type in a bunch of numbers and data. You visualise it. You see waves, you see storm clouds, you see the system.' Bob's speciality was to apply to ballooning something called the Trajectory Model – a nifty piece of mathematics developed to track the path of volcanic dust and radioactive particles from nuclear explosions. Bob used it to say where a balloon would travel at given altitudes.

Using the Trajectory Model Bob had worked out that if we dropped down to 18,000 feet, the prevailing winds would carry us north. We were then pretty much guaranteed to complete our journey – although we would have to kiss Washington State goodbye, and settle for a very chilly landfall in the Arctic! The prospect of taking the largest balloon ever built out of the stratosphere and down into bad weather wasn't an appetising one. The waves beneath us were topping fifty feet, so if we ran into trouble, even if we ditched near a ship (hardly likely on an ocean that covers virtually half the planet) it would not be able to reach us. Turning in seas that high would snap a boat in half. After so long out of radio contact, however, and after such a close shave, we were only too glad to follow Bob Rice's advice.

Meanwhile, on board their United Airlines flight to America, Will Whitehorn and the ten-man retrieve team were having kittens. They were getting messages passed to them from the flight deck and knew only that the balloon had lost almost half its fuel. By the time their flight landed at LAX, Per and I were already heading north. There was a flight already arranged to take the team up to Seattle. After that, they would have to make things up as they went along.

There had always been a slim risk that Per and I would find ourselves whisked into the Arctic, and the team were carrying gear for us. But they had no survival gear for themselves, and conditions were worsening by the minute. In Seattle, the retrieve team became a pure raiding party, gathering cold-weather gear wherever they could find it. Ground crews at the airport handed over boots and gloves. Within minutes of their landing, a Learjet was powering up on the tarmac, cleared for Yellowknife.

On board the capsule, we listened to Mike Kendrick over the radio: 'You're heading way north,' he told us. 'The rescue team is chasing you to try to get to where you're going to land.' After thirty-six hours of flying, we finally crossed the coast of northern Canada. It was too dark to see, but we felt safer. Even though we were now heading for the Rockies, one of the most inhospitable mountain ranges you could find, at least it was land. We hugged each other and shared a chocolate bar. It was an incredible feeling. As we started flying over the Rockies, we made radio contact with the local ground control, Watson Lake Flight Service.

'Put your rescue beacon on,' they told us. 'You're heading into a blizzard. There's zero visibility and a wind of 35 knots.'

We weren't the only ones risking our lives now. Our retrieve team had boarded two helicopters and were trying to scissor their way to our likely landing place. It was hopeless. It was snowing, and the winds were topping 35 knots. At one point Will lost all visibility and had to put his helicopter down on a road.

Per and I knew we had to land soon after dawn. If the morning sun heated the envelope, we would end up in Greenland, maybe even further – and well beyond the reach of any rescue team. When we were at 750 feet, I opened the hatch and climbed out on to the top of the capsule. I crouched there for a minute and watched the snow whirl around me. It was very quiet.

I shouted down to Per: 'Don't get too low. It's all forest. We'll never get out of there.' Then: 'There's a space ahead. Can you see it?'

Per shut off the burner, I climbed back into the capsule and we headed down. We landed heavily and went skidding across the ground. Per fired the bolts and the capsule came to a halt. The envelope flew off without us. We wrenched open the hatch and clambered outside. It was minus 40 degrees Celsius out there. I made radio contact with Watson Lake Flight Service. 'We've done it!' I cried. 'We've arrived! We're all in one piece!' We were the first people to cross the Pacific in a hot-air balloon. We had travelled 6,700 miles, from Japan to Canada, in forty-seven hours. We had broken the world distance record and travelled at speeds of up to 245 mph. It had been, by the world's reckoning, a triumph.

'Where are you?'

I looked around me.

'Richard?'

'Ah, we've landed on a lake,' I said. In the distance, the envelope draped itself across the pine trees. The wind shredded it. 'Ah, we're surrounded by trees.'

It took a Canadian Hercules eight hours to find us and scramble a helicopter to pick us up. Not bad going, when you consider that our lake was one of about 800,000 other, virtually identical lakes. Per had frostbite in one of his feet, and I had frostbite in a finger. We huddled together, eating our supplies, desperate for warmth as the snow and wind howled around us.

'Per?' I said.

'What?'

'Why aren't we in California?'

The American ballooning pioneer John Wise, born in 1808, amassed over 400 ascents during his long career and, by the by, became the first airmail carrier in the US. It's perhaps not so surprising, then, to learn that he knew all about the jet stream – or, at least, he understood that there was, at a certain height, a 'great river of air which always blows from west to east'. He even hoped to use that stream to cross the Atlantic – a project doomed to failure given the materials of his day, but which nonetheless carried him to a new world distance record of about a thousand miles. (He left St Louis at 4 p.m. on 15 August 1859 and was wrecked in a treetop on the shore of Lake Ontario in Jefferson County, NY, at 3 p.m. the following day.)

Wise's dream of exploiting the jet stream for air travel would only be realised a century and two world wars later, in Pan Am's pioneering passenger flights from Tokyo to Honolulu. Flying in the jet stream cut the time of that flight by over one-third, from eighteen to eleven and a half hours. Before those flights, the jet stream was a dangerous and often unpredictable mystery. I should know: the jet stream could have killed my mother.

Before I was ever thought of, my mum Eve was a pioneer several times over. Her adventures began, inauspiciously enough, at

Heston airfield. She turned up there one day at the start of the Second World War to ask what her chances of flying were. She was given the brush-off. Still, one instructor had seemed more sympathetic than the rest, so Eve – a beauty, and a professional dancer – turned on the charm. Disguised as a man, she learned to fly gliders, and soon she was instructing new pilots – men who a few years later were fighting the Battle of Britain.

Civilian life posed new challenges for her: after the war she became one of the first – maybe the very first – British stewardess on an international airline. Hers were pioneering years for air travel: glamorous certainly, also uncomfortable and – by modern standards – dangerous. Seriously: looking after the passengers on the planes of British South American Airways must have made glider-flying look like sailing paper planes. Today's cabin crews provide a prompt and courteous supply of drinks and nibbles. When BSAA's planes reached 25,000 feet, Eve was dishing out oxygen masks. My dad proposed marriage to her as soon as he dared in a desperate bid to stop her flying. She flew Comets, while Comets were falling out of the sky (we'll come to that story later), and Avro Lancastrians, one of which vanished over the Andes just a couple of days before she was due to fly in it, on 2 August 1947.

BSAA's *Star Dust* was less than two years old when it took off from Argentina's capital Buenos Aires for Santiago in Chile. The flight crew were RAF veterans with hundreds of hours of flying experience. The captain was an experienced navigator. The passenger list reads like the cast of a period thriller: a King's Messenger carrying diplomatic documents, a German émigré suspected of Nazi sympathies and a rich Palestinian with a large diamond sewn into the lining of his jacket. This was a pioneering period, when only the very rich and the very well connected flew.

Shortly before the airliner disappeared, it radioed ahead to report that it expected to enter airspace over Santiago in four minutes. Just over fifty years later, an Argentinian mountain guide came across the wreckage of a Rolls-Royce engine at the foot of a remote glacier in the Andes, about fifty miles east of the city.

Swords into ploughshares: the Avro Lancastrian was a modified RAF bomber.

It was the jet stream that killed them. The Lancastrian was one of the very few airliners flying high enough to nudge the bottom of the jet stream, which in this area normally blows from the west and south-west. According to their reckoning – calculating the aircraft's position from its direction and speed and time – they should have been heading in to Santiago. Heavy cloud hid the terrain from view and the crew had no idea that a powerful wind was pushing them over fifty miles off course.

The moment they entered the cloud layer, they were finished. The crew and passengers of flight CS 59 flew into a nearly vertical snowfield near the top of the Tupungato glacier. An avalanche buried them.

Today, as I mentioned, commercial airlines make as much use of jet streams as possible, to shorten journey times and save fuel. There are four major jet streams, two in each hemisphere, circling the globe at middle and polar latitudes. If you've flown across the Atlantic, and wondered why it's quicker to get to Europe than it is to fly from Europe to America, it's because your eastbound flight hitched a lift on the jet stream.

In future, the jet stream may have other uses, too. Ken Caldeira, an atmospheric scientist at Stanford University, certainly thinks: 'My calculations show that if we could just tap into one per cent of the energy in high-altitude winds, it would be enough to power all civilisation,' he told the *San Francisco Chronicle* in May 2007. Plenty of people agree with him. Designs for high-altitude wind turbines come in a dizzying array of shapes and sizes. Some resemble Zeppelins, others futuristic helicopters. There's much buzz at the moment around a wind-power company called Makani. They are developing kite-assisted high-altitude turbines. They're keeping the details a close secret and may be years away from setting the world alight with their technology, but you have to love their background: a president who made self-replicating machines at MIT and writes comic books in his spare time showing children how to make gadgets; a professional wind-surfer; and a world frisbee champion. As we've already seen, it's exactly Makani's sort of people who (if they're lucky) take technology forward. Larry Page, the co-founder of Google, reckons the thirty-strong gang of kite-surfers at Makani are the Wright brothers of their age. He has put $30 million of Google's money where his mouth is. Who knows? He may be right.

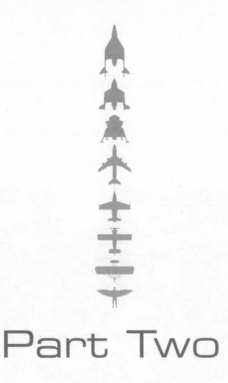

Part Two

Up and Away

A first-class cabin, *c.* 1960. Just looking at this picture makes my back ache!

six

Shrinking the World

I seem to have spent my life – in the aviation business and elsewhere – separating the Things Not Done Because They Don't Work from the Things Not Done Because We Don't Do Them.

Here's something not done because it doesn't work. Not long ago I suggested we tow our planes from their berths to the start of the runway. In theory, this ought to have saved us an extraordinary amount of aviation fuel. It turned out after tests, however, that tugging a jetliner around by its nose isn't very kind to the airframe. We're now looking at installing electric motors in the front wheels of our aircraft instead.

Next, by way of contrast, is something that's Just Not Done.

If you want to arrange seats on a plane so people can lie down and have a decent kip, your best bet is to arrange the seats in a herringbone pattern. That way you can fit more people into the cabin and give everybody greater comfort. Everybody in the industry told us this couldn't be done. Everybody explained that it was because, in the event of an accident, the seatbelts would cause an injury. Nobody, it seemed, had heard of airbags.

Today, our herringbone seating, complete with airbag-equipped seatbelts, is the glory of Virgin Atlantic's upper-class cabin.

Over the years we've pioneered comfortable reclining seats, flat beds, lounges with hairstylists and masseuses, and a motorcycle and limo home pick-up service. Virgin Atlantic was the first to provide personal video screens in every seat-back, so our travellers could choose the films and television shows they wanted to watch. These are some of the ideas that worked. There were plenty that didn't. Does anyone remember our live in-flight entertainment?

One of the most difficult and exciting challenges of running an airline – and it amazes me how few airlines take it seriously – is how to maintain the glamour of air travel. Many of our passengers have only ever flown economy class on commercial jets. Given how thrilling and magical flying can be, I think it's up to us to make their experience different and exciting or, at the very least, comfortable.

11 September 2001 changed air travel for ever. Nineteen hijackers flew two passenger jets into the twin towers of New York's World Trade Center, one into the Pentagon, and a fourth into a field: the plane's passengers had somehow, and at the expense of their own lives, stood up to the hijackers.

Needled by silly measures, inconsistent rules and careless government scaremongering, we too easily forget that security is an important issue, and that airport security has been greatly improved since the attacks. No. Really. It's easy to forget how lousy it used to be, especially on US domestic flights. In 1997, the US Federal Aviation Administration tried to smuggle 173 imitation firearms past airport security. They were caught only fifty-six times – that's a detection rate of less than one in three.

After the 11 September attacks, something had to be done. I have no complaint with extra security: I just don't understand why it has to be done so shoddily. You want to take my mother's knitting needles away? OK, but why can I still buy a glass bottle full of inflammable liquid once I get past the gate? Why can I buy *razors*? You want me to queue for half an hour? If you must – but how about a bottle of water while I'm waiting? You want to X-ray my shoes? Fine. How about giving me a chair so that I can put them back on?

What with the rigmarole of customs beforehand and the dread prospect of immigration afterwards, making flights fun for people is, to say the least, challenging. So we start with the little things. We try, against all the odds, to make you smile. 'Please ensure that your seat is in the upright position,' says V Australia's new safety animation; 'check that your tray-table is folded away, and that your hair is just right.' V Australia's CEO Brett Godfrey had epic arguments with the Civil Aviation Authority over that one: they thought it was demeaning. Brett took a few weeks out and came back with data to prove that passengers were paying far more attention to his 'demeaning' presentations.

I can't quite believe we're still having these arguments. Virgin Blue's cabin crew have been turning safety briefings into vaudeville performances for years, for good reason, and to good effect. When the cabin crew tell you the whistle on your life jacket is just about perfect for attracting sharks, you'll laugh, you'll shudder, and you'll surely remember that there's a whistle tied to your life jacket.

It's always been my philosophy that airline staff are in the entertainment business. They have to be. Every day, the industry ties one and a half million people down in narrow metal tubes for hours at a time, and insists that they do *exactly what they're told*. For the sake of everyone's safety, we must never forget that we're asking a hell of a lot from human nature.

I spend much of my life in the air. I've grown used to sleeping on aeroplanes and, at the risk of sounding like an advert, that herringbone seating of ours really does guarantee me a comfortable night. Comfortable – but short. I get up well before we land to walk the aisles and say hello to our passengers. Showing my face is good for the brand; even more useful, I get to see for myself where we can improve and strengthen our service. For the cabin staff especially, there is no getting away from me.

Hence the lookalike competition.

Madame Tussaud's waxwork museum in London is an eerie place at the best of times, but for Virgin Atlantic's twenty-fifth birthday, our marketing people went one better. They filled a room with people who had the misfortune to look an awful lot like me. It had sounded great on paper. I entered the room. I grinned and greeted myself, again and again and again. I tried not to hyperventilate.

After the party, I went off to circumnavigate the world. This time, Joan would not have to fear for my safety. I wasn't attempting to break any records. I was simply circling the world in comfort, on board passenger jets. From Heathrow to Hong Kong, to Sydney, to Los Angeles and back to Heathrow was going to take me about eight days. What made my journey a first was the tickets in my pocket: each one bore the Virgin brand.

The last thing I ever expected when I entered the field – a Freddie Laker fanatic wielding a single second-hand 747 – was that one day I'd be able to fly around the world on Virgin-branded airlines. Boarding Virgin Atlantic's Heathrow service to Hong Kong that night, I was struck by how much these companies had achieved. The airlines I've invested in and helped create over the years are now, indisputably, playing their part in making the world a smaller place.

What does that mean for the world? Back in the 1940s, and after the terrors and losses of two world wars, shrinking the globe seemed a good idea to pretty much everybody. Passenger aviation would make all places local. It would bring the world together. I firmly believe that it has done just that – as surely as I know, beyond a doubt, that a price has been paid.

During the 1950s, aeroplanes carried Western culture – and American brands – around the globe. By 1961, there were Hilton hotels in every continent except Antarctica – and already, people were starting to complain that international travel was beginning to feel less vivid. Charles Lindbergh remarked: 'I never feel more keenly the separation of tourist from native life than when I stay in an "American hotel" abroad.'

The smaller we make the world, the more we have to cherish its richness and diversity. The global airline industry, with its expensive, identikit machinery, its great manufacturing monopolies and its pan-national regulatory framework, doesn't look much like a champion of diversity.

There is no pressing logical reason why the air industry should look this way. Much of its shape and character was set in 1944 by the Convention on International Civil Aviation, which became known as the Chicago Convention. The idea was to regularise and control the planes crossing our skies, for the world's greater good. The convention was shaped by ideas that seem strange to us now, but which made good sense considering the firestorms of Dresden and Hamburg and the atomic annihilation of Hiroshima and Nagasaki.

The convention's primary assumption is that *all planes are military assets*. At the time of signing, there was no distinction to be made between commercial aircraft and military aircraft. Planes simply fulfilled the requirements of the time. The fighters and bombers of the First World War were old mail planes. The early commercial airliners, like the Boeing 377 and the Avro York, were all converted Second World War bombers.

The Convention assumed that civilian planes had military capability. Therefore (ran the logic) whoever owned the most planes posed the most serious global war risk: private aviation companies were effectively private armies!

The spectre haunting the Chicago Convention was of an international criminal mastermind launching terrorist raids in the hope of destabilising world order. The idea goes back further than Wells, to Jules Verne's *The Master of the World* (1904), and by the 1940s it was cropping up in virtually every comic, radio show and cinema serial. (*Sky Captain and the World of Tomorrow* (2004) is a deliriously accurate big-screen pastiche of that kind of story.) Many of us must at one time or another have smiled at the quaintness of the idea – until the smiles were

Boeing's 377 Stratocruiser: a world-beating civilian version of the B29 bomber.

wiped off our faces by the attacks of 11 September 2001 and the videotaped posturings of Osama bin Laden.

The last thing the signatories of the Chicago Convention wanted to create was a free market in passenger air travel. From their point of view, that would be tantamount to creating a free market in mercenary air power! Far from setting civilian air travel free, they did their level best to leash and muzzle it. The Convention took aviation under the wing of government. The US, with its large internal market, went down the road of heavy regulation and protectionism. The Europeans, who were much better placed geographically to fly the world, from India to Africa to the Americas, preferred uniform regulation and state control – hence the creation of flag carriers like Air France (founded 1933) and the British Overseas Airways Corporation (BOAC, founded 1946).

The Chicago Convention was a compromise; it ensured that no one nation state would dominate world air travel, while in the same breath enshrining Britain and the US as the world's most powerful commercial air operators (an unsurprising bias, given that they had just won the war). Among the 'freedoms of the air' guaranteed by the Convention were the right to overfly a country without landing; the right to refuel without disembarking passengers (the most famous example being Ireland's Shannon Airport, which was used as a stopping point for most North Atlantic flights until the 1960s); and the right to operate connecting flights from another country. To win those rights, each airline needed to obtain government approval.

Government set the schedules. Government controlled the number of flights per day, the number of destinations covered and the number of aeroplanes. It controlled the prices. Airlines did not serve the customer; they served the government. If an airline could not meet its obligations, the government ensured that it did not fly at all.

Pan American Airways – the airline immortalised in Stanley Kubrick's *2001* as an operator of orbital space shuttles! – typifies the kind of airline that did best out of the Convention. Pan Am, as it became known, was the brainchild of Juan Terry Trippe, one of the most celebrated of the early airline moguls, and the undisputed pioneer of international aviation in the US.

Trippe saw his first plane in 1909 when his father took him to see Wilbur Wright fly. Inspired, he and his friends became Navy pilots when America entered the First World War; but they saw no action. This youthful non-adventure behind him, Trippe – a Yale graduate with a privileged New York background – was all set for a steady and lucrative Wall Street career, but boredom got the better of him. After receiving an inheritance he went to work with New York Airways, an air-taxi service for the city's smart set. He invested in a company called Colonial Air Transport, scared the life out of his colleagues with ambitious plans to fly all over the Caribbean, and eventually created the Aviation Company of the Americas – the company that would eventually become Pan Am.

Trippe secured US airmail contracts, flew the ninety-mile airmail route from Key West to Havana, and lobbied successfully to become a 'chosen instrument' of American policy in South America, where the US had many strategic and economic interests. With State Department backing, Trippe's company secured landing rights, built terminals and won customs privileges all along the seaboards of South America, and by 1929, the year its celebrity advisor Charles Lindbergh opened the company's route to Panama, Pan America Airways' routes covered 11,000 miles. Ten years later Pan Am straddled the Atlantic: all this before transatlantic airliners were invented!

For its ocean crossings, Pan Am needed a plane that could fly 3,000 miles (long enough to reach Europe or Hawaii) while carrying a payload equal to its own weight. The successful design was the work of Glenn Martin, described by *Time* magazine in 1939 as 'exhibit A1 of what a human being can do by channeling all his time

Juan Trippe founded Pan Am, for years America's flagship airline.

and talent in one direction'. This backhanded compliment presumably refers to Martin's being possibly the least colourful figure in aviation history. Martin lived with his mother Minta until she passed away and inherited his fascination with planes from her. She used to read him to sleep at night with newspaper articles about the latest experiments of aviation pioneers, from the American engineer Octave Chanute to the German inventor Otto Lilienthal. Martin's first aviation experiments were box kites; he turned them out at a rate of three a day and sold them out of Minta's kitchen for 25 cents each. He also experimented with sails, and found novel ways to harness the wind, propelling himself along on ice skates and even his bicycle.

He founded the Glenn L Martin Company in 1912. (It survives to this day, as part of the aerospace giant Lockheed Martin.) Martin, who mostly made planes for the American military, turned out three huge, four-engined flying boats for Pan Am – aircraft that came to symbolise the glamour and luxury of flying.

Though designed for transatlantic service, Martin's M-130s

were to spend their working life flying in the opposite direction – over the Pacific. Much as Trippe wanted to establish lucrative air routes to Europe, he was at first stymied by politics. Britain wanted to protect its own 'Empire' flying boats, manufactured by Short Brothers and operated by Imperial Airways, so the British were not likely to give Trippe landing rights on their territory. Given that their territory included both Newfoundland and Bermuda, this made an Atlantic crossing impossible.

So Trippe bided his time, christened his first M-130 *China Clipper*, and turned towards the Pacific. Again, Trippe lobbied the US government. Pan Am's ambitions to open air routes across the Pacific as far as China chimed perfectly with the US government's own desire to spread the American sphere of influence into areas that would otherwise fall to Japan. Trippe got government assistance to build facilities across the Pacific, in Hawaii, Midway, Wake and Guam – and Pan Am became what, according to the Chicago Convention, a civil airline was supposed to be: an instrument of foreign policy. A flag carrier.

China Clipper made its most famous flight on 22 November 1935, before a crowd of 25,000. Carrying fifty-eight mailbags bound for Manila, it lifted off from the waters of San Francisco Bay. It was supposed to fly over the San Francisco–Oakland Bay Bridge, which was then still half-built, but it proved too heavy and flew under it instead. At last it lumbered into the air, and headed west to Honolulu: the first stop on its five-leg trip across the Pacific.

Pan American's three Martin M-130 seaplanes made it the dominant international airline of the Americas and the Pacific region. The clipper service was dependable and elegant, and it seemed to its passengers to magically shrink the world beneath its wings. Imagine it: travelling all the way from San Francisco

Early air travel was bumpy and expensive – but at least you got a real cup!

to Hawaii *overnight*! Hollywood bestowed on Pan American its supreme accolade – a movie called *China Clipper*, starring Humphrey Bogart.

Clipper passengers dressed in private dressing rooms, took in the view of the Pacific from large windows while eating gourmet meals in the dining room, and drank sizable cocktails – not least to deaden the persistent drone of the M-130's rackety engines. Failing the cocktails, there was always the bridal suite. The Clipper's seventy-four seats converted into forty bunks for overnight travellers (no, I can't make the maths work, either). The flight to Manila took sixty hours of flight time, over five days.

At least, that was the theory. Unfortunately, the fuel load required to reach Hawaii from California – an eighteen-to-twenty-hour flight – meant that Pan Am could carry only eight passengers on that leg, which was the lynchpin of the whole service. As huge an improvement as the M-130 was on every airliner that had gone before, Trippe would need a new machine if he was truly to conquer the world's oceans.

Early in 1936, Pan American offered a $50,000 prize to the manufacturer who could build it an airliner for its long-awaited Atlantic service.

On 20 May 1939 – twelve years to the day after Charles Lindbergh crossed the Atlantic in *Spirit of St Louis* – Pan American's first Boeing B-314 flying boat, *Yankee Clipper*, left New York on a transatlantic mail run. Passenger services began a few days later, on 28 June, when *Dixie Clipper* left New York with twenty-two passengers on Pan Am's southern route, via Horta and Lisbon to Marseilles.

The Boeing Clipper could carry seventy-four passengers and ten crew by day, and by night accommodated forty passengers in seven luxurious compartments, including a fourteen-seat dining room and a private honeymoon suite at the tail end of the plane. It was large, luxurious, and reliable – and it could fly an astonishing 3,500 miles in one go. It operated the first non-stop service across the Atlantic, between Southampton and New York. After the outbreak of war, Winston Churchill himself commandeered a Clipper and made it his personal transport. The B-314 made intercontinental air travel possible, and it did so much sooner than anyone in government could have predicted.

As far as the signatories of the Chicago Convention were concerned, civil aviation was a genie that had to remain firmly bottled, for the safety and security of the world. Scheduled airlines were never meant to operate in a free market, but were really part of the air arm of each nation state. Commerce didn't come into it.

Juan Trippe's vision for Pan Am was much more political than commercial: he dreamed of creating a vast global airline system, servicing virtually every airport everywhere without strong worrying too much about volume or profit. During the Second World War, his vision was very nearly realised. Pan Am became a major contract carrier for the US government, ferrying planes from Brazil across Africa to the Middle East. It flew Franklin D Roosevelt to and from the Casablanca conference in early 1943. (On the way home, the President celebrated his birthday in the flying boat's dining room.) Pan Am was, effectively, a civilian arm of the Air Force's global Air Transport Command.

Eventually, though, Trippe's vision for Pan Am proved false. Pan Am was by far the most successful expression of Chicago Convention thinking. But by the time the convention was signed, realities on the ground and in the air had changed out of all recognition.

For a start, commercial planes could no longer be considered military assets. Planes were no longer mere variations on one

Pan Am made intercontinental air travel a reality. Next stop, the Pacific!

theme. They had diversified. Modern military aircraft were flying ever faster and higher, and giving way here and there to other, quite different technologies: to rockets, and guided missiles, and satellites. The new military planes had no commercial application at all.

Commercial airliners, meanwhile, were getting bigger, and safer, and more capable: and people were waking up to the possibility of mass transit. Commercial aviation became a lot bigger, and a lot more international, much faster than expected. The result was a commercial disaster so profound its effects reverberate through the industry to this day.

When you operate a scheduled airline, you are effectively told what to do by the government: take these slots, and fly to these destinations, at this frequency. There is no room for manoeuvre. Every change of destination, every change to the schedule, is a matter of international negotiation.

When you sell tickets to the public, those tickets entitle them to a seat on the plane. If the aeroplane isn't full, you still have to take off and fly the people who did buy tickets. Now this is fair enough: of course ticket holders should be guaranteed a flight. The problem is when the same flight runs empty, over and over again, week after week.

In most other customer-service industries, if business goes bad, you can retrench. You can mothball a wing of your hotel; you can cancel those poorly attended matinees at your cinema. As a scheduled airline, you can't do that. You have to stick to your schedule. If you don't, the government will take you out of the air. An airline seat is not a hotel room, or a cinema seat. If a cinema seat goes empty for a night, or a hotel room goes empty for a week, you won't earn any money, but you won't incur much of a loss, either. An airline seat, on the other hand, costs you money every time you haul it up into the air.

Because scheduled flights are given fixed departure times, airlines can't expect to fill every plane all the year round. Hurling empty seats about the sky is expensive, and the costs have to be recouped somehow. The only solution is to put up the fares. That is why, from the end of the war to the late 1970s, international flights were largely the preserve of the rich. The Chicago Convention made it possible – even *necessary* – for state airlines to offer identical services at high prices, all with the sanction of the International Air Transport Association (IATA).

But there were exceptions.

From its opening in May 1928 to its closure in August 1939, Croydon Airport – the first purpose-built international air terminal in the world – was arguably the most visited tourist spot in Britain. Crowds gathered to watch the arrival of aviators and film stars. What they could not do was fly. For ordinary people,

London's airport between the wars was in Croydon: a place of glamour and romance.

tickets were astronomically expensive. (In today's money, a trip in the Boeing Clipper across the Atlantic would have set you back over £50,000, or $85,000!)

Holiday travel underwent a true revolution only after the Second World War. Shortly before Easter 1950, and after a series of fights with the Ministry of Transport, charter flying began in Britain, operated by Vladimir Raitz – later the inventor of that iconic sun-sea-and-sex charter outfit, Club 18–30.

I should explain quickly how charter airlines work. They supply equipment and staff to whoever wants to operate a plane. Usually it's a tour operator, but they'll take calls from anyone. Once when American Airlines stranded Joan and me in the Virgin Islands on our way to Puerto Rico, I called a local charter company and paid $2,000 to fly to Puerto Rico. I borrowed a blackboard, divided the charter cost by the number of people stranded and wrote down the number. We got everyone to Puerto Rico for $39 a head.

Charter is a different way to run an airline. It's simple, it's fair, it doesn't cost much and it's commercially stable.

The airline establishment hated it. Everything was done that could be done to limit the growth of charter air travel and preserve the monopoly of state flag carriers. One bizarre IATA rule stated that charter passengers needed six months' membership of an 'affinity group' whose main purpose was not travel. It was a petty inconvenience; spurious organisations sprang up at every airport and you could pick up backdated memberships when you arrived for your flight. 'People would make up names like the Left-Wing Club or the Right-Wheel Club, or the Birmingham Rose Growers' Association,' remembered Freddie Laker, whose company Laker Airways was repeatedly fined for carrying bogus rose growers to America!

By 1971 it was a circus – and Freddie Laker had become the ringmaster.

Freddie Laker's fascination for air travel goes back to the 1930s. He was standing with his mates outside a fish-and-chip shop in Canterbury, in Kent, looking down the road to the cathedral,

Freddie Laker's affordable air fares made him some powerful enemies.

'and we were having our fish and chips out of the old newspaper. Standing on the corner. And damn me if the *Hindenburg* was coming from Germany, of course going to America, and the Handley Page 42 with a four-engine biplane was coming from Croydon to go to Paris. I mean, you couldn't think of two more dissimilar aerial objects than these two, and they crossed right over the top of Canterbury Cathedral. And I said to my mates: "That's for me. I'm going into aeroplanes."' Freddie would grow up to be rich, and famous, and loved: the man who tilted his lance at the Chicago Convention – and almost won.

Freddie Laker's early mentor in the airline business was Arnold Watson, the publicity manager for Castrol, later chief test pilot at the Air Transport Auxiliary. The ATA flew planes from the factory to the RAF stations, from one station to another, and from the field back to the factories for repair and servicing. ATA pilots weren't trained for combat, but during the war they put in more hours than anyone else in the air. Of all the thousands of auxiliaries employed in the war effort, ATA pilots had real kudos.

With Arnold Watson, Freddie made all sorts of ideas and plans about what would happen to civil aviation after the war. They were good plans, and on April Fool's Day 1946 Laker became one of the first eight employees of Britain's original flag carrier, British European Airways. 'But I only stayed three months. It was rather boring and, you know, sort of *nationalised.*'

Freddie went instead into the war-surplus business, the scrap business, even the fruit business. It took the Soviet blockade of Berlin to drive Freddie back to his first love, aviation.

At the end of the Second World War, the remains of the Third Reich had been divided among the Allies. Portions of Germany were assigned to Britain, France, the US and the Soviet Union. The capital, Berlin, lay to the east, well inside the Soviet sector;

and since it *was* the capital, it was treated separately. As a signatory to the Yalta Agreement you received, along with your portion of Germany, a side helping of Berlin.

In 1948, as the Cold War grew ever chillier, Soviet forces blocked the Allies' land routes to the city. The stand-off was bloodless and, short of shooting planes out of the sky, there was no way the Soviets could stop planes flying in and out of the capital.

The government offered to pay air carriers to break the Soviet blockade; Freddie just treated it as another job – at first. 'The way we looked at it, it was: "Oh well, let's go and do this and get on with the job and we'll earn a few pounds." But after a bit, you know, two or three months down the road, it became a crusade.'

A remembrance stamp recalls the Berlin Airlift.

Allied supply planes were buzzed and harried, but no shots were fired. The Soviets assumed that the hastily organised airlift to relieve besieged Berlin – an effort that would have to feed, clothe and heat two and a half million Berliners – could not be sustained. They assumed it would dribble away after a few weeks, and then the Allies would concede the capital. They were proved wrong.

It was Dunkirk all over again. The British government minister Ernest Bevin told the Secretary of State for Air, Arthur Henderson, to 'fill the sky with our planes'. In just over a year, from August 1948, 2.3 million tons of aid was flown into the beleaguered city.

British, Commonwealth and US planes brought Berlin 13,000 tons of food each day.

Only a fraction of the total cargo airlifted to Berlin was carried by civilian aircraft, but this takes nothing away from the pilots and companies that took part in the operation, flying battered old warplanes that were by then, most of them, little better than a few thousand rivets flying in close formation. Freddie's company – a near-bankrupt business vehicle called Bond Air Services, which he'd revived with six war-surplus Halifax bombers and hangars full of spares – was a typical airlift outfit. Freddie's Halifaxes were, in his own estimation, 'absolutely useless. But having said that, it was the only thing that we had.'

In their biography *Fly Me, I'm Freddie!* Roger Eglin and Barry Ritchie capture the spirit of the time: 'In March 1949, Bond pilot Joseph Viatkin was taking off from Berlin's Gatow airport after delivering a load of dehydrated potatoes. When an engine failed at 10,000 feet, he shrugged, flew on three and the engineers promptly slotted in another engine.' Six weeks later the same plane ran into a construction trench, and was promptly bulldozed out of the way to make way for the aeroplanes already taxiing up behind it. 'Laker's men cut the Halifax up for scrap at the side of the runway.'

The cargo Bond's Halifaxes could carry was extremely limited.

> We carried oil drums, coal, vegetables, potatoes and things like that. I think we did something like 4,700 flights. And after the airlift I thought, well, what are we going to do now? We've made some money, what's going to happen? And I came to the conclusion that most people would stay in flying aeroplanes, and that they'd all get very competitive, and that nine out of ten of them would go out of business. So I thought well, this is the time for me to stop. And I actually stopped flying for over a year.

Freddie went into the scrap business full-time, turning old warplanes into aluminium ingots. He claimed he was more than happy servicing and recycling planes, and that his flying days were over. But by then the business had got into his blood.

First, in 1949, he flew joyrides and charters for Billy Butlin's new post-war holiday camps. Then, once the 'nine out of ten' little air companies set up after the war were dead and gone, and seeing that the government, too, was a large and growing customer for charter air services, Freddie bit the bullet and set up an airline.

It didn't take him long to run up against the petty regulations restricting the development of charter air. The stupidity of the thing drove him to breaking point: why couldn't passengers who wanted a cheap flight simply queue for a ticket at the bloody airport, the way they already queued at railway stations and bus terminals?

Freddie turned up at Gatwick with his lawyer and a Bible and got his passengers to swear allegiance to their make-believe clubs. The authorities were unimpressed; some thirty people were removed from a flight. 'I shouted and got headline treatment and vowed to fight it,' Freddie recalled. Seven years of legal battles followed.

Throughout the 1970s, Freddie fought through every imaginable obstruction to realise his dream. On 15 June 1971 Laker Airways submitted an application to launch Skytrain, the world's first low-fare scheduled service between London and New York. The 'walk on, walk off' operation would sell tickets to whoever turned up first. The fares were incredibly low: £32.50 in winter, £37.50 in summer – a third of what it would cost you to fly with a flag carrier. His opponents tried to force Skytrain to use Stansted rather than Gatwick, and even tried to limit the number of seats he could sell each day to 189, though his DC-10s had room for 345!

'I fought, kicked, shouted at them day after day,' Freddie recalled. When he won through the British courts the right to fly across the Atlantic, he had to fight the same battles all over again in the courts of the US, where Pan Am and TWA did everything possible to keep him out. Nevertheless, in June 1977, President Jimmy Carter finally gave Skytrain the green light.

'I fought, kicked, shouted at them day after day.'

Freddie Laker

Skytrain was a huge financial success from the start – but, as Freddie once said, to become a millionaire in the airline business, it helps to start out as a billionaire. On 4 February 1982, the operation went suddenly and spectacularly bankrupt, owing over a quarter of a billion pounds. I think it was in 1988 that Freddie Laker first explained to me exactly how it happened.

The scheduled airline industry favours big airlines over small ones. Suppose a big airline slashes its fares and operates at a loss, taking custom away from the little guy. By cutting its fares, the big airline fills its seats, so it's getting at least some return per seat. And it can always recoup money from its other routes and from the profits it will make once it has killed its competition. The little airline, meanwhile, has to lug empty seats into the air. (That's the deal you have to sign, if you want to fly a *scheduled* service.) In doing so it incurs spiralling costs.

Big airlines have been putting small competitors out of business this way for decades. When BA created the budget carrier Go, it essentially copied easyJet's business plan. Stelios Haji-Ioannou, easyJet's founder, protested: 'Go', he said, 'has been given permission by BA to lose £29 million and then close in three years having put its rivals out of business.' (Luckily for Stelios, it didn't work, and Go was eventually sold to easyJet!)

Squeezing a competitor is ugly. When a big airline cuts prices on all the routes a small competitor flies and makes up its losses by increasing fares on its other routes, it is, in my opinion, behaving unethically. Often enough, the game gets dirtier still, and flag carriers of several nations gang together to share the burden of squeezing a competitor out of business. This is what happened to Freddie.

Flying empty seats is expensive. An airline that suddenly finds itself having to fly empty seats will bleed to death, not over years or even months, but in a few *weeks*. An airline that's healthy in March can be bankrupt by the middle of May. As a consequence, airlines are notorious for collapsing like houses of cards the moment they run into trouble – and rumours that a competitor is collapsing are self-fulfilling. By the time you've denied the rumours, you're toast.

To put a competing airline out of business, you don't even need to lower your prices. All you have to do is *suggest* that the competitor has sustained a loss. Rumours of this sort are more credible if they're aimed at low-cost airlines, because low-cost airlines work to narrower margins. Sometimes they're less well capitalised. In addition, they are more reliant on leisure travel and the package-holiday industry.

Why is this a factor? Well, imagine you're a tour operator, and you've just heard an unlikely and probably scurrilous rumour that your regular low-cost airline is running out of money. What do you do? Do you ignore the rumour? Certainly not! Putting your customers on an airline that might just go bankrupt is the *last* thing you'll ever do. If the airline does file for bankruptcy, that's it: your clients have lost their money – and you can expect a world of grief from your entire customer base.

BA's campaign of dirty tricks against Virgin Atlantic was the worst example of this kind of rumour-mongering. BA sank, finally, to outright industrial vandalism, when a team accessed our booking system and messed with our passengers. But BA's lamentable campaign was also, I suspect, one of the last of its kind. It is very unlikely indeed that a whispering campaign of the sort that killed Freddie's business – and very nearly killed ours – would work today. The reason is simple: low-cost airlines like Stelios's easyJet adopted the Internet and put many traditional travel agents out of business. 'I knew nothing about the travel business,' Stelios told Simon Calder for *No Frills*, his book on budget air travel. 'I had no allegiances, I had no friends in that industry, I just said this doesn't make sense, we will not do it.'

The Internet has saved the airline business a shedload of money over the years. We were paying 7 to 10 per cent commission on every ticket to the travel agents. Cutting the agents out of the business was liberating. Stelios reckons it's changed our industry more than the jet engine. 'The jet engine was an improvement on the propellor and previous technology, but what really made it a mass market for everybody was the ability to fly someone for a pound. The ability to say, "I will rationally and economically speaking let that seat go for £1," is quite a revolution. You can only do that with the Internet.'

Not every airline turned its back on the travel agents. Virgin Atlantic didn't: as a business-class carrier, we needed them.

And while the rise of the Internet spelled the death of many traditional agencies, others embraced the new technology and were transformed. Much more than mere bookers of tickets, today's upmarket and specialist agencies, like Virtuoso in the US and Elegant Resorts in Europe, thrive by organising spectacular and thoughtful travels for their clients.

There is no denying that competition from the Internet has stabilised our industry. This is because a scurrilous rumour racing from travel agency to travel agency doesn't have the clout it once had. Today, the sort of rumours you'd have to sow to put a competitor out of business would have to address not just a handful of big, nervous agencies but the travelling population at large. Your claims would have to be so extreme, so outrageous, your bluff would be called long before you could do any real damage. Plenty of airlines have folded in recent years, but most were the victim of their business plans and wider economic difficulties.

There was a time, not very long ago, when air travel was for other people: the rich; the privileged; the powerful. The rest of us had to wait until 1952 before TWA launched the world's first economy class!

This is nothing: in the more remote parts of the world whole generations have lived, breathed and died in ignorance, mystified by the strange metal contraptions arcing over their heads. During the Second World War, for example, huge amounts of military equipment and supplies were airdropped on to New Guinea and the islands of the south-western Pacific as part of the Allied campaign against the Empire of Japan. Clothing, medicine, canned food, tents, weapons, radios . . . an unlooked-for bounty piled up around the bemused islanders right up to the end of the war, by which time most of their religious practices and institutions had collapsed in confusion.

The war ended and, overnight, the visitors left. Their airbases, deserted, reverted to jungle; and the flow of cargo ceased.

The islanders, bereft and abandoned, attempted to revive the flow of strange gifts that had transformed their lives and culture. To bring the planes to their islands again, they set about imitating the rituals they had seen performed by visiting soldiers, sailors and airmen. They carved headphones from wood and wore them while sitting in fabricated control towers. They lit signal fires and torches. They semaphored wildly, stamping up and down their newly cleared 'runways'. Many built life-size replicas of aeroplanes out of straw, hoping to attract more aeroplanes by a kind of sympathetic magic.

Today, it is almost impossible for our imaginations to conjure up that lost world. Aerospace technologies – aircraft and satellites, bombers and weather balloons – have made the world smaller. They have spread wealth and knowledge, disease and terror. If they have not yet spread universal happiness, they have at least done this: they have made just about everyone on the planet aware that we are one people, sharing one world.

At its simplest, aviation overcomes almost all the boundaries set by geography. The Soviets understood this. To bind their huge Eurasian empire together, they created Aeroflot: an unlovely way to fly, but – as the journalist Simon Calder reminds us – 'the biggest no-frills airline of them all'. Even in 1991, as the Soviet Union collapsed, you could travel from Minsk to Kiev, a distance of 275 miles, for just under £1.

America's domestic air market has shrunk the continent so effectively, visitors rarely grasp the nation's true size. The UK is the size of California. The state of Texas is bigger than France, Belgium, the Netherlands and Switzerland combined. Crossing the state by car will take you most of a working day; by plane, about an hour.

More than any other continent, Australasia has been shaped by the aeroplane, and it's no surprise to discover that the story of aviation there stretches back to the pioneering days of manned and powered flight. The Australian Flying Corps's involvement in the First World War gifted Australia hundreds of highly trained pilots, and a healthy supply of aircraft and hangars. Until the Second World War, Australians flew more miles, and boasted more pilots, than any other nation. The modern Australian state strung itself together with air services. Some of these were familiar, involving the carriage of cargo, mail and passengers. (The success of the Australian domestic carrier Virgin Blue came as no surprise: without good domestic air services, Australia simply can't function as a modern nation state.) Others were unique to Australia, and addressed the particular challenges of that vast country and its tiny, scattered population. The most famous of these, the Royal Flying Doctor Service, was the brainchild of John Flynn, a Presbyterian minister and aviator born on 25 November 1880, the same year as Australia's most celebrated outlaw, Ned Kelly, was executed.

In 1911, when Flynn began his missionary work, only two doctors were serving an area of nearly 2 million square kilometres! Flynn began establishing bush hospitals and hostels in remote outback areas, but these only scratched at the surface of the problem. As he campaigned for better medical care in the outback, Flynn told many true and harrowing stories. Perhaps the most distressing of these is the tale of Jimmy Darcy, a stockman who ruptured his bladder in a fall near Halls Creek, Western Australia, in August 1917. When the details of his harrowing and drawn-out death became known – a death that could have been avoided, had the

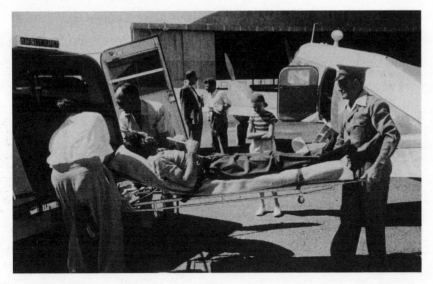

Since 1928 the Royal Flying Doctor Service has sustained life in Australia's Outback.

nearest doctor not been ten full days' travel away – it pushed news of the war off the front pages of Australia's leading newspapers. More than any other single event, it provided the impetus for the organisation that was to follow.

Lieutenant Clifford Peel, a young Victorian medical student with an interest in aviation, wrote to John Flynn, commending the aeroplane as the only credible means of 'ministering to the needs of the men and women scattered between Wyndham and Cloncurry, Darwin and Maree'. Peel had done his homework, too: his letter outlined costs, speeds, distances, and even a breakdown of the support facilities the service would require.

Peel was killed flying over German battle lines shortly before the end of the war. But Flynn had his letter, and adopted his vision. On 15 May 1928, the Aerial Medical Service was established as a one-year experiment at Cloncurry in Queensland. It serves the nation to this day.

The practicalities of life in Australia have been shaped from the air. So has its culture. Australia's white settlers have for years relied upon air travel to keep them in contact with their European inheritance. Today, cheap flights between Australia and Asia are shaping a new generation whose more self-confident, independent view of the world looks as much to Asia as to Europe. Native Australian and Maori cultures, meanwhile, are finally flourishing as their artists, musicians and writers travel the globe, performing, writing and filming their stories for audiences in every imaginable cultural setting.

Cultures have their pioneers, just as industries do. How many pioneers of all sorts has Virgin Atlantic carried over the years? How many adventures has it made possible? Business people, off to open up new markets; holidaymakers, steeling themselves for a couple of weeks surrounded by strangers, strange customs and strange ideas; writers, journalists and film-makers in pursuit of stories, literally to the far ends of the earth – these people have changed the world.

It's not that air travellers are particularly high-minded. It's simply that all our little acts of international trust and friendship add up. Barbara Cassani, who ran BA's short-lived budget airline Go, understood this: 'We change the way people live their lives,' she once said. 'I joke that I'm waiting for my Nobel Peace Prize for services to humanity.'

When people buy second homes over the border and commute by air, or use low-cost carriers to make regular visits to their girlfriends or boyfriends abroad, we all come to understand each other better. In France, dying rural communities have been revived by blow-ins from Britain. This was once a cause for anxiety – until the houses got rebuilt, the roads were repaired and the schools reopened. Ryanair and easyJet have bound war-weary Europe together more effectively than any number of post-war treaties, and their expansion into Eastern Europe can only improve the continent's political fortunes.

Today, every major city in the world needs an airport if it wants to develop and expand. Many nation states depend upon the traveller's dollar. Today, international tourist receipts are about $944 billion a year – or over $1 trillion if you add in the cost of the air tickets.

For even the wealthiest and most developed nation, operating a safe, efficient civil airline is a gigantic undertaking. From the planes, airports and maintenance crews to the ground transport links and air-traffic-control systems, the list of necessary investments and expenses is unending. The consequences for poor nations aren't good.

For a start, they'll be having to operate old planes. They'll be cheap to buy and inherently reliable, with all the kinks ironed out of them. But they'll cost money to maintain and they'll consume a lot of fuel. Straight away this puts the airline of a poor country at a commercial disadvantage. There's also a human cost: skimping on expensive maintenance will bring tried and trusted older aircraft toppling out of the sky. The air-safety record across parts of Africa is frankly atrocious. Planes crash quite regularly, particularly in Sudan and Nigeria.

More serious still, suppose you want to improve your air services. For that, you will need outside investment. The levels of investment required are so great they can trigger all manner of political crises, as we discovered when we created Virgin Nigeria. How to 'Africanise' African air services, and make them truly serve and support their local economies, is a problem no one yet knows how to solve. The creation of a truly global air industry, operated by all and for all, is still a long way off.

What of Juan Terry Trippe's vision of a vast airline monopoly, operating everywhere for the good of the whole world? Well, the world thought otherwise. Other airlines learned the knack of flying across oceans. Unimpressed by Trippe's offer to turn his company into a 49 per cent state-owned monopoly, in 1950 the US Congress refused Pan Am permission to run domestic flights.

From being the chosen instrument of US foreign policy, with a monopoly on US traffic abroad, Pan Am became just another airline. It fought its corner. It did some work for NASA. It made some mistakes. It let its accountants rub away at its glamour and allowed its quality to drop. Then, in 1989, it suffered a terrible tragedy, not of its own making, over Lockerbie in Scotland. It filed for bankruptcy early in 1991.

seven

Fanning the Flames

Born in Bucharest in 1886, Henri Coandă grew up to be one of the more revolutionary engineers of his day. In 1905 he built a missile-aeroplane for the Romanian Army. Five years later, he designed, built and piloted the first jet-powered aircraft, and used it to wow the crowds at the second International Aeronautic Salon in Paris.

Thirty-six years later, a Gloster E-28 airframe took to the skies, driven by an engine designed by a British Royal Air Force Officer called Frank Whittle. It, too, was the world's first jet-powered aeroplane.

Frank Whittle invented the jet engine as we know it today. What makes the story slightly confusing is that there are many kinds of jet engine, and many engineers worked, quite independently, on the same ideas. Henri Coandă's *motorjet* engine deserves its place in aviation history, as does Hans von Ohain's *turbojet* engine, begun in 1934. Five years later, installed in a small, metal-fuselaged monoplane, it became the world's first practical jet.

Ohain combined original work with insights gleaned from reading papers by Whittle himself (which is why we celebrate Whittle, rather than Ohain). But Ohain was a talent in his

Henri Coandă's missile-aeroplane for the Romanian Army: was this the first jet?

own right, and it's a lasting mystery why Germany's Nazi administration sidelined his work, preferring to deal with big manufacturers. (Ohain was recruited by the Americans after the war and got to meet Frank Whittle. They became good friends.)

So what's a jet engine? It's simply anything that emits a jet of fluid out of one end, generating an equal and opposite force going in the other direction. An early Disney animation on space travel charmingly demonstrates this principle by means of a sneezing dog. As the dog sneezes in one direction, his bum skids (across very scientific-looking graph paper) in the other.

Rockets work by igniting fuel and jetting it out through a nozzle. The problem with rockets is that they have to carry all their fuel with them, *and* all the oxygen in which to burn it. Have a look at some Apollo footage: shortly before it blasts off, you can see dribbles of liquid oxygen evaporating in puffs of white cloud from the frame of the colossal 3,000-ton Saturn 5 rocket that carried men to the moon.

A jet engine compresses the air around it and uses this compressed air to burn its fuel. Coandă's motorjet used a regular combustion engine to drive its propellor; but some of the energy from the motor also worked to compress the air flowing into the engine. This compressed air was then mixed with fuel in a combustion chamber and ignited, producing an exhaust jet that helped drive the plane forward. Even as early as 1905, engineers understood the importance of Coandă's new kind of propulsion system. Propellors and the piston engines that drove them were getting better and better – but the higher planes went, the thinner the air, the less efficient propellors became. There was a second, bigger problem: once the tip of a propellor travels fast enough to break the sound barrier, it starts to lose efficiency. So even if they flew at low altitudes, propellor engines would be able to propel an aeroplane only so fast. Aviation designers knew that they were going to hit a speed barrier: Coandă showed them the way past it.

The turbojets created by Whittle and Ohain took Coandă's idea a step further. Rather than use an engine to compress the air in the combustion chamber, they use a spinning fan – basically a glorified propellor. The fan compresses the air entering the engine. Fuel is mixed with the compressed air and ignited. The exhaust jets out the back, and some of the energy released is used to drive the fan. The faster the fan spins, the more energy the engine produces, the faster the fan spins. Were friction, noise and heat not sucking energy out of the system, once a turbojet got going it would simply operate faster and faster until it exploded!

The turbojet has spawned a dizzying number of variations. A turboprop engine uses as much of the engine's energy as possible to drive a propellor. It's tremendously efficient at low speeds, which is why really big military transports still boast propellors, giving them a rather old-fashioned look. A turbofan is a turboprop engine with a cowling around the propellor. The propellor ducts air around the engine, compressing it. This compressed air then gets mixed with the engine exhaust, which improves the flow of the exhaust, reducing turbulence and improving the efficiency of the engine. It also makes the engine quieter: the engines in commercial jet planes are usually turbofans.

It all sounds rather complicated and difficult to do. And it is. There's a reason Frank Whittle had two nervous breakdowns while working on the thing.

Frank Whittle with his turbojet: it earned him almost nothing.

Born in 1907, Whittle was a lousy student at school, but used his own time well, reading every science book he could lay his hands on. He first applied to become an apprentice in the RAF in 1922 but, being only five feet tall, he was turned down by the doctors. A friendly PT instructor drew him aside and suggested exercises he could do to pass the medical board; six months later, and three inches taller, he entered the RAF College at Cranwell.

Whittle was a fearless aerobatic flyer and was selected to perform the 'crazy flying' routine in the 1930 Royal Air Force air display at RAF Hendon. During rehearsal, he wrote off two planes. Flight Lieutenant Harold Raeburn was not impressed. Whittle recalled, 'As I came up to him he stood there with his face flushed with rage and said furiously "Why don't you take all my bloody aeroplanes, make a heap of them in the middle of the aerodrome and set fire to them – it's quicker!"

That year, Whittle took out his first patent. By April 1937, he had his first jet engine running: a liquid-fuelled monster that kept on accelerating even after he'd switched the fuel tap off! One visiting RAF officer described the contraption as 'pure, unadulterated Heath Robinson'.

The Air Ministry decided not to develop Whittle's jet engine. You can understand their point of view: back then, operating Whittle's engine at full throttle would have melted it into a heap of steaming slag. It needed to be built of materials that wouldn't be available for years. In the meantime, the RAF put Whittle through Cambridge and funded his postgraduate studies, in the hope that, once materials *were* available, they could put him to work.

The trouble for Whittle really began in 1942, when the Ministry of Aircraft Production began to take a serious interest in his invention. Desperate to develop jet-powered warplanes in the shortest possible time, MAP gave Whittle's company Power Jets no time to work on proper prototypes. Drawing-board designs went straight from Power Jets to Rolls-Royce, who quickly discovered – to no one's very great surprise – that these untested engines worked very badly. Presented with a dud and with a contract of their own to fulfil, Rolls-Royce engineers went ahead and re-engineered Whittle's design. Their work was brilliant – but it flew in the face of Frank Whittle's proprietary rights to his own engine.

MAP's complete disregard for the way business is properly conducted left both Rolls-Royce and Power Jets fighting wasteful and unwinnable arguments about who owned what and who had done what to which part of whose engine. Those arguments soon became so inextricably knotted, MAP decided there was only one thing it could do: it cut Power Jets out of the equation. In 1944, Stafford Cripps nationalised Whittle's company. It was a decision as easy to accomplish as it was cruel to contemplate.

For all its work, Power Jets had very little it could call its own. It had been using government facilities for years. Now it was forced into becoming a research-and-development vehicle for the government's National Gas Turbine Establishment.

Was taking Whittle's company away from him a rotten thing to do? I think so. Cripps was an enemy of free enterprise and a great believer in central planning – over the coming years, his policies would virtually destroy British manufacturing. Whittle's long-time supporter and fellow director Rolf Dudley-Williams had no time for Cripps at all: 'I wanted to wipe the floor with him,' he wrote. 'Unfortunately he died and had himself cremated, so I couldn't even piss on his grave.'

In 1941, American research programmes were very close to developing the jet. They lagged behind the British, and in peacetime, that advantage might have had commercial meaning. But there was a war on: Whittle himself flew to the US to accelerate the American jet effort and, in the same year, Britain gave its jet technology to General Electric for free.

Much is made of how this gift lost Britain its lead over America in the jet business. But this is gloominess for gloominess's sake. Today Rolls-Royce is the second-largest aircraft-engine-maker in the world, behind GE Aviation. Its annual revenue in 2008 was over £9 billion. Britain's biggest aircraft manufacturer, the once-nationalised British Aerospace, now BAE systems, is the world's second-largest defence contractor and the largest in Europe, not to mention becoming, in 2009, the biggest ever target of a British Serious Fraud Office investigation – a distinction it could probably have done without!

Britain doesn't do at all badly in the world aviation business; but ever since the end of the war, it's been haunted with visions of what might have been. It's been haunted, in other words, by the Comet.

The de Havilland Comet was Britain's groundbreaking passenger aircraft. It was the world's first ever passenger jet with a pressurised cabin, and this enabled it to fly higher, further, faster and more smoothly than any other passenger plane. It was quiet, and reasonably spacious (there was a bar). Best of all, flying at 35,000 feet, the Comet was above the weather – weather its propellor-driven competitors had to slug through. On board the Comet, air travel became, for the first time, a relaxing experience. Television reporters covering the maiden flights invariably took shots of a pencil balancing on the end of a dining tray.

The Comet could carry only seventy passengers and could never have hoped to compete with the later big American airliners like the Boeing 707. But what did that matter? It was half as fast again as its rival, the Douglas DC-6, and was well on its way to becoming a staple small liner for the world's rapidly expanding civilian airlines. The Comet was a hugely popular machine, loved by flight and cabin crew, trusted by passengers.

BOAC Flight 781 was the first to break up; minutes after it took off from Rome's Ciampino airport, its scattered wreckage plummeted into the Mediterranean. This was 10 January 1954. Three months later, a South African Airways Comet crashed into the sea near Naples. All Comets were grounded while a public inquiry looked for the cause of the accidents.

Many accounts will tell you that there was a fatal flaw in the Comet's design; actually, there wasn't. We're told that the square windows were the wrong shape to cope with the pressure differential at 35,000 feet. In truth, there was nothing wrong with them. What happened was this: the window frames were supposed to be glued and heat-sealed to the airframe using a

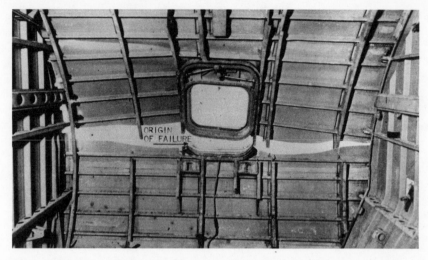

Painstaking reconstruction of a crashed aircraft revealed the Comet's fatal weakness.

patented British process called Redux. One of the supervising engineers, worried that Redux would not be enough to seal such a complex shape, ordered the frames to be riveted as well, just to make sure. Even the tiniest fatigue crack around an uneven rivet was enough to fracture the cabin's skin: explosive decompression and a catastrophic failure of the airframe followed in seconds.

Had the error shown up early enough, it could have been corrected. Had it shown up early, it wouldn't even have been considered an error: just a routine wrong turning on the road to researching and developing a new aeroplane. But no test, however meticulous, can predict the future. De Havilland's testing regime had been the most rigorous ever for a civilian aeroplane – and there had been no hint of trouble.

De Havilland didn't give up without a fight. They redesigned the Comet's windows, and produced the Comet 2. And in 1958, they came out with the Comet 4, a magnificent passenger jet, and the first to enter British transatlantic service. But while de Havilland's planes languished on the ground, US companies Boeing and Douglas had been learning valuable lessons from the company's misfortune.

Independently, and driven by a furious rivalry, they together evolved a new generation of airliner. Douglas's DC-8 was both faster than the Comet 4 and cheaper to operate. The Comet's demise left Britain lagging behind in air construction. There was one ray of hope. Engineers at the Royal Aircraft Establishment (RAE) working on the Avro Vulcan strategic bomber had studied German research into high-speed aircraft and now knew more about supersonic wing design than anyone on earth. With that knowledge, they might yet leapfrog Boeing and Douglas, and produce the world's first supersonic passenger plane!

Sound travels at around 750 mph. You might think flying at such a speed is a complex and difficult achievement, but it isn't that hard: all you have to do is aim for the ground.

The Second World War saw the development of some truly aerobatic fighting aircraft. One of them was the Mitsubishi Zero. It was a stunningly manoeuvrable fighter, and very fast. That was the problem: duck out of trouble in a Zero, and you had the devil's own job pulling out of your dive. The faster you went, the denser the air in front of you became. (Think of the rain piling up on your windscreen; slow down, and the rain seems magically to ease; speed up, and your wipers struggle to clear the glass.) Zeros could quite happily approach or even exceed the speed of sound with the force of gravity behind them; but their control surfaces weren't strong enough to contend with the thickness of the approaching air. Eventually, Zeros began to get a reputation, not so much for falling to earth, more for giving it a whacking great punch.

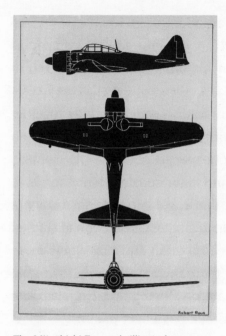

The Mitsubishi Zero: a brilliant plane –
until it broke the speed barrier.

Sound is a movement of the air. The air can carry information at around 750 mph – no faster. Hit the air at a higher speed, and it doesn't have time to get out of your way. It explodes. Many objects exceed the speed of sound: the leading edges of flags, the tips of bullwhips (the 'crack' of a whip is a tiny sonic boom), the tails of maliciously flicked bath towels – and, sometimes, the tips of propellors. If your blades are long enough, and spin fast enough, the tips exceed the speed of sound. When this happens, the air which would normally be fanned behind the blade, producing forward motion, simply explodes, constantly, producing a standing wave – a shock wave – that generates turbulence just forward of the blade. It's not as serious as it sounds: you'll stay aloft well enough. But you won't go any faster, and your fuel consumption will deteriorate.

It was these various, unconnected technical troubles met by aircraft (both jet- and propellor-driven) that weren't designed for supersonic flight, that led to the idea of a 'sound barrier'. It was real enough, but it was a technical barrier, not a physical one, and has long been superseded. These days most supersonic craft reach multiples of the speed of sound with no abrupt transitions at all.

Supersonic flight *is* different from subsonic flight, in some curious and fascinating ways. At supersonic speeds, aircraft get hot: Parts of the US Air Force's experimental X-15 spaceplane reached a highly significant-sounding *666* degrees centigrade! This is because the air doesn't have time to get out of the way of the aircraft. It piles up. Flying through this stuff is like flying through jelly. Neil Armstrong found this out the hard way on 20 April 1962, flying an X-15 spaceplane out of Edwards Air Force Base in California. Armstrong flew to a height of thirty-nine miles (the highest he flew before Gemini 8, and nearly two-thirds the distance covered by Burt Rutan's SpaceShipOne). During his descent, though, he held the aircraft nose up a fraction too high, and ricocheted off the atmosphere. Thirty kilometres too high,

(continued on page 202)

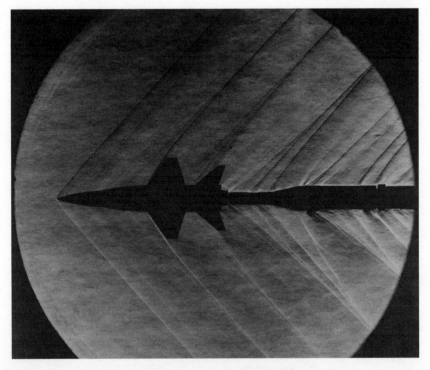

An X-15 generates cone-shaped shockwaves in this supersonic flight test.

The 'Sea Monster'

Look out over any decent-sized body of water and you are bound, eventually, to see a bird skimming its surface. The bird will be moving very quickly, because it is exploiting an aviation possibility that we humans have barely begun to explore.

The wing tips of both birds and aeroplanes generate considerable turbulence. Fly close to the ground, however, and air displaced by the wings cannot freely wheel and spread: the ground is in the way. Instead, this wind forms a high-pressure cushion upon which the bird or plane can surf. The result is an incredibly quick and energy-efficient flight – provided you don't mind flying just a few feet off the ground.

During the Cold War, US satellite pictures of the Caspian Sea revealed a disturbing object: it was huge, it was fast, and it made no sense. It looked like a derelict aeroplane: a gigantic fuselage fused to stubby, chopped-off wings. It wasn't a boat and it wasn't a plane: what the devil was it? At a loss, the Western intelligence community dubbed it the 'Sea Monster'.

The ekranoplan was conceived by revolutionary Soviet engineer Rostislav Alexeev. And, contrary to the impression created by decades of Western propaganda, it was one of the Russian military's great technological success stories. Ekranoplans were plying the Caspian Sea for years, in full view of a baffled NATO, carrying military materiel from one side of the sea to the other, far faster and more cheaply than any plane. The sea monster that so intrigued and worried the Western intelligence community was the KM – the grandest product of Soviet ekranoplan development. It was over 328 feet long, weighed 531 tons fully loaded and could travel at just a shade under 250 mph, mere metres above the surface of the water.

A baroque curiosity of the Cold War? Certainly: development of the ekranoplan idea was abandoned for years following the break-up of the Soviet Union. But good ideas linger, and the grandest ekranoplans of all are even now taking shape on the drawing boards of American and Russian companies.

Boeing has been developing the Pelican, a turboprop-driven military transport with a 500-foot wingspan. They are designing it to carry 1,300 tons of cargo up to 10,000 nautical miles – at an altitude of twenty feet. Meanwhile, at the Beriev Aircraft Company of Russia, plans are afoot to build the largest aircraft in the world. The Be-2500 Neptun is a super-heavy amphibian cargo-aircraft concept. Its maximum take-off weight will be 2,750 tons. It will function as both a conventional high-altitude jet and as an ekranoplan, and it will fly transcontinental routes, taking off from conventional seaports and requiring no special infrastructure.

Will it ever fly? If it does, remember to duck!

travelling at three times the speed of sound, Armstrong overshot the runway at Edwards by *forty-two miles.*

Because of all this air piling up in front of them, planes travelling at supersonic speeds run into problems similar to those faced by seagoing vessels. Waves of thick air, called shock waves, cling to a supersonic craft, the way a bow wave sticks to the front of a boat. (Bow waves *are* shock waves: waves in water move so slowly, it's relatively easy for a boat to throw up a shock wave in front of itself.) As early as 1933, wind-tunnel tests had shown German researchers that as air gathers in front of a plane travelling at supersonic speed, its shock wave spreads behind it as a cone. A plane's wings have to stay inside the cone, or the shock wave will put such pressure on the control surfaces, they can't be operated.

This is a problem for designers. If the plane's wings are too long, they'll cease to work at supersonic speeds and the plane will crash. If they're too short, however, the plane might not be able to get off the ground at all! Designing a wing that will function at subsonic and supersonic speeds is no easy task; but work on the problem had begun long before supersonic planes were ever built.

It was by a quite unpleasant mischance that Dietrich Küchemann, a Göttingen native, found himself developing ideas of supersonic flight. He had been planning to study pure physics at the university under the celebrated mathematician Max Born – a family friend, and one of the founders of quantum mechanics. When Born, a Jew, was expelled from the university under pressure from the Nazi regime, Küchemann was left casting around for other things to study.

Göttingen was home to Germany's largest institute of aerodynamics. There, Küchemann – somewhat to his own surprise – stumbled upon his life's work: aerodynamics. During the war, Küchemann designed the intakes for Germany's earliest jet fighters. It was important work, but it still left him time to develop ideas of his own, about wave drag, wingless planes and supersonic flight. Following the German defeat, Küchemann was picked up by Operation Surgeon, a no-nonsense British programme that removed German scientists and technicians out from under the noses of the occupying Russians 'whether they liked it or not'.

Küchemann, far from putting up any resistance, thrived in England. He had little cause for homesickness. At the RAE at Farnborough he found himself among men like Karl Doetsch and Adolf Busemann – both, like Küchemann, pioneers of supersonic flight. By the late 1940s the aerodynamics department of the RAE read like a Who's Who of German aeronautical design!

The primary purpose of the RAE was to research and develop new types of aircraft for the British government. What kind of aircraft would the post-war future demand? British aeroplane manufacturers and the RAE responded with three truly terrifying warplanes: the Handley Page Victor, the Vickers Valiant and the Avro Vulcan. Collectively known as the 'V-bombers', these planes were Britain's core Cold War deterrent until submarines equipped with the Polaris missiles came into service in 1969.

Even as V-bomber blueprints were being pored over at the RAE, it was becoming clear that unmanned missiles would one day do the job of manned bombers. The Minister of Defence, Duncan Sandys, went so far as to predict the end of manned military aircraft in his lifetime.

Engineers at the British Aircraft Corporation (BAC) disagreed, and responded with the TSR-2, a strike aircraft featuring an extremely fancy ground-following terrain radar, infra-red

The Concorde's engines and wing-shape owed much to the Avro Vulcan nuclear bomber.

cameras, side-looking radar and a sophisticated autopilot – features that had yet to be realised on any other military aircraft. When the TSR-2 was cancelled, it robbed Britain of the most advanced military plane of its day.

The RAE, meanwhile, had moved on to a string of rocket projects, every one of which – Black Arrow, Black Knight, Jaguar, Skylark – bit the dust. The RAE even tackled space-satellite design, with some success, but couldn't secure government backing to see their projects through to commercial launch. For Küchemann and his colleagues, fresh from the V-bomber projects, this was a time to regroup and rethink.

Freed from deadlines, Küchemann's team picked up their old work on the theory of high-speed flight and built a series of test aircraft to study the problem of wing design. They were by now expert at swept-back triangular wing layouts, called delta wings. (From below, the Avro Vulcans were virtually perfect triangles.) Delta wings had a surface area that could keep them in the air at normal speeds; pushed beyond the speed of sound, their swept-back shape kept them within the cone of the shock wave. The main problems were take-off and landing. The take-off and landing angles with wings like these were incredibly sharp . . .

At the same time, veterans of the TSR-2 project saw a way to save some of their hard work, by adapting their warplane designs to create a viable civilian aircraft. The stage was set for a remarkable meeting of minds – and a remarkable new aircraft. In 1961 Peter Thorneycroft, then Minister of Aviation, spoke to Cabinet. His excitement was palpable. He was proposing that the government develop a supersonic passenger jet. With it, Thorneycroft believed, 'Britain has an opportunity . . . of gaining the leadership we so narrowly missed with the Comet.'

At BAC, Archibald Russell – a notorious perfectionist – led the effort to create a British supersonic passenger plane. What he came up with would carry about 100 passengers across the Atlantic at around twice the speed of sound (or 'Mach 2' – a term that remembers the German physicist Ernst Mach, who did so much important early work on shock waves). The Bristol 223 boasted four Olympus engines, based on those originally developed for the Vulcan, a curiously scooped delta wing shape, courtesy of Dietrich Küchemann, and a droopy nose to cope with those sharp take-offs and landings – it helps if the pilot can see the runway!

The 223 was an extraordinary technical advance – and it would cost an absolute fortune. In November 1962 a treaty between Britain and France split the bill by merging Russell's project with a smaller supersonic project developed by Sud Aviation (later amalgamated into Aérospatiale).

When I say that the Concorde was a remarkable plane, I am not for a second forgetting its limitations. It lacked range, which lost it lucrative routes to the west coast of the US and Johannesburg. It carried only a hundred people. And it wasn't very comfortable: whoever dreamed up its plank-narrow seating certainly never predicted today's ever-expanding waistlines. The legroom on offer wasn't much better than you'd have got in economy class; and God help a tall person who tried to stand upright in the thing. BA made an effort, bless them, with their doll's-house Wedgwood crockery and stunted silverware, but Concorde was never going to be a comfort option.

At its maximum cruising height of 60,000 feet, the air is so thin that a sudden loss of pressure might well have knocked everyone out before they could get to their oxygen masks. Concorde's windows were made annoyingly small in an attempt to keep the air in for longer, giving passengers those vital extra seconds. The plane flew so high, there was a dial in the cockpit recording the amount of ionising radiation hitting it from space.

Concorde flew faster than the Earth spun; flying from east to west across the Atlantic, you could beat the clock and land before you arrived. It flew so fast, a commercial jet flying in the same direction would look to Concorde's passengers as though it was flying backwards. Air compressed by the plane's passage heated the windows in the cockpit so much, they became too hot to touch. The whole aircraft swelled in the heat of its supersonic passage, and a gap opened up on the flight deck between the flight engineer's console and the bulkhead. Retiring flight engineers used to place their hats in the gap before it cooled; the caps are there to this day.

Still the world's most futuristic-looking plane: a prototype Concorde draws the crowds.

Concorde was a plane to capture the imagination of an entire industry – always assuming, of course, that the industry had any imagination. It turned out to be a big assumption.

The Anglo-French consortium that built the plane secured a hundred non-binding orders, but a series of near-fatal coincidences knocked them for six. Bad enough that Concorde should go on sale at the height of the 1973 oil crisis; what really did for those initial orders (from the likes of Pan Am, United, Lufthansa – all the major global players of the day) was the dreadful and spectacular crash of somebody else's plane.

Some people say that the Soviet Tupolev Tu-144 – the world's first supersonic passenger jet, beating Concorde to the grid by two months – was the product of industrial sabotage: a mere Concorde rip-off. That's unfair. Yes, the Soviet designers had probably caught wind of the Concorde project. But the main reason the Tu-144 looked like Concorde – even down to its droopable nose – was that the technology of the day would only allow you to build one sort of supersonic passenger jet. Like its rival, the Tu-144 was a well-configured plane, much less fuel-efficient than its Anglo-French relation, but bigger and significantly faster.

The Tu-144 – instantly christened the Concordski in the West – was unveiled at the Paris Le Bourget air show on 3 June 1973. While in the air, it dipped violently, broke up and crashed, destroying fifteen houses and killing all six people on board and eight more on the ground.

The accident has never been fully explained. Tu-144s flew without trouble within the Soviet Union for years afterwards. Rumours still circulate: of a near-collision with a French chase plane; of a fatal souping-up of the Tupolev's automatic systems by a ground crew determined that it should outperform Concorde; of a deliberate flaw introduced into Concorde blueprints known to be studied by Soviet spies . . .

The much-maligned TU-144LL: the world's first supersonic passenger plane.

In any event, the Tu-144 was done for commercially; and Concorde, because it bore an obvious resemblance to the Tu-144, suffered by association. In the end, only Air France and British Airways took up their orders. Not that they paid for their planes: in the case of BA, the cost of buying the aircraft was eventually covered by a state loan, to be paid off by signing 80 per cent of the plane's operating profit back to the government.

The environmental movement was just getting going around this time, and one of its first targets was the noise pollution from aircraft. Concorde was particularly vulnerable because whenever it exceeded the speed of sound, a little of the air it displaced would explode. Over the years, aircraft designers have worked out ways to minimise this sonic boom, but at the time, it was popularly supposed that the sound barrier was some sort of real physical barrier that these newfangled supersonic aircraft simply had to punch through. No wonder some feared the future Concorde was ushering in – a cacophonous new world, its skies a-tremble with booms and bangs and the ever more raucous drones of ever more powerful engines! Noise abatement was a serious issue whose time had come, but it's a pity that Concorde should have been made a target. It was far from being the loudest plane in the sky – a point well made in the US Supreme Court in 1977, when the ban on Concorde imposed by New York's Port Authority was finally thrown out. (It was noted that the long list of planes noisier than Concorde included the US President's own Air Force One!)

The biggest brakes on the Concorde's future turned out to be the operators themselves. Concorde – the aeroplane that wanted to be a rocket plane – was a proposition so futuristic, so controversial, so *odd*, neither company quite knew what to do with it. They both made the same mistake. They treated Concorde like a regular passenger jet, only they stuck it on a pedestal: flying Concorde across the Atlantic was business as usual, they said, except that it was *exclusive*, it was *expensive*, it was . . . well, unaffordable.

In the last six months of Concorde's life, BA woke up. Someone there finally realised why people flew Concorde. And it wasn't for the silver service, which in such cramped conditions didn't mean anything anyway. People flew Concorde *for the experience.* It wasn't the workhorse the designers had imagined and the airlines had wanted. It was something quite different: a pleasure craft.

BA finally started thinking creatively. If you simply loved the plane, you could take a pleasure trip, taking off and landing at Heathrow. Or you could fly out on Concorde and catch a regular economy flight back again. For lovers of speed, BA offered discounted fares. Lo and behold, they were no longer hurling empty seats over the Atlantic at twice the speed of sound. And according to a report in the *Sunday Times*, they were earning a whacking profit, too: £50 million in six months!

But the axe had already fallen. Demand for air travel slumped following the attacks of 11 September 2001, damaging an industry already injured by rocketing fuel costs. The first-class cabins of flag-carrier airlines were even emptier than usual. BA and Air France committed themselves to withdrawing the Concorde from service so they could fill up their empty first-class seats.

On 25 July 2000, during take-off from Gonesse, France, Air France Flight 4590 rolled over a strip of titanium – part of a thrust reverser that had, only minutes before, fallen from a Continental Airlines DC-10. This fragment punctured a tyre on the Concorde's left wheel assembly. The tyre exploded, hitting the fuel tank and snapping an electrical cable. The tank fractured and fuel spilled out over the sparking wire. A fire broke out, and the landing gear refused to retract. Unable to gain height or speed, the plane pitched up violently, then rocketed into the Hotelissimo Hotel in Gonesse, killing all 100 passengers and nine crew, and four people on the ground.

It was the Concorde's only fatal incident, and it did not stop Concorde flying; but it did make abandoning the aircraft easier.

It was while Concorde was grounded following the Gonesse crash that BA and Air France noticed something interesting: regular users of their supersonic service were buying first-class seats on their regular jets and they seemed to be staying loyal to the companies that operated them. The penny dropped: if BA and Air France killed Concorde, they would not just save money on maintenance; they would make their other long-haul flights more profitable. They wouldn't even lose any passengers, because there were more than enough empty seats in their first- and business-class cabins to accommodate the demand from former Concorde flyers. It made a brutal sort of sense, and times for the airline industry were hard in 2003.

I offered to buy British Airways' Concorde fleet for the same amount BA had paid for it. By my calculations, that was about £1 a plane. When new, the Concordes had been valued at around £26 million each, but the government's loan had meant that BA had never had to hand over any real money. Later, a newly privatised BA bought two aircraft for a book value of £1 as part of their £16.5 million buy-out in 1983.

For some reason BA was unmoved by this logic! So I made the company another offer: five planes at a £1,000,000 a plane. Again BA would not budge. It was only by killing Concorde that they could hope to fill their first-class cabins. Flights by a Virgin Atlantic Concorde would only empty them again. I didn't like

BA's attitude, but I could understand it. What baffled me far more was why the British government had never had the wit to insist that they could give the plane to somebody else if BA decided not to operate it. After all, it was the taxpayers' plane, not BA's!

By this time all sorts of special interest groups – including members of BA's own staff – were lobbying to keep at least one Concorde in service for special occasions. Come a royal birthday, we can still muster a Vulcan, a Lancaster, a handful of Spitfires – so why not Britain's most instantly recognisable civilian plane?

So I pledged £1,000,000 to the idea of a heritage trust, to maintain a couple of Concordes for the nation. The Farnborough-based company Qinetiq were willing to maintain the aircraft, and the former Bristol Aeroplane Company – now the UK aerospace giant BAE Systems – said that their factory at Filton in Bristol could house the planes. What a magnificent homecoming that would have been, since Filton was the very place the Concordes were designed and built! It might have happened – if I'd only had British Airways to deal with. I was coming up with all sorts of ideas; at one point I suggested we paint one side of the plane BA colours, the other side in Virgin's livery! BA's responses were guarded, but we had hopes of bringing them around.

The trouble was France. Concorde's one fatal crash had occurred on French soil. Many had died and a nation had mourned. When the time came for Air France to wrap up its Concorde service, the French people were quite prepared to accept that Concorde was unreliable, outdated and done for. Now, here were a bunch of English aviation enthusiasts, convinced that Concorde was still a brilliant plane and prepared to maintain a Concorde in operational condition on English soil! If this went ahead, then Air France and the French government would be perceived

I offered to buy

British Airways' Concorde fleet

for the same amount BA had paid for it.

By my calculations, that was about

£1 a plane.

as having unfairly abandoned one of France's great technical achievements. Neither the company nor the government relished such a major embarrassment. Even as I was receiving positive messages from the European aeroplane manufacturer Airbus, who had the contract to maintain the planes, another set of Airbus top brass declared that they absolutely would not, under any circumstances, maintain the plane. Airbus, I should mention, is based in Toulouse, France.

So that was that. To help transport their fleet to museums, where today they languish on 'static display', BA and Air France sawed off their Concordes' wings. Britain's best-loved plane will never fly again.

Critics claim that Concorde was a white elephant: expensive to develop (which it certainly was), expensive to maintain (true, but exaggerated) and expensive to operate (absolute nonsense).

Concorde was a sports car. You don't buy a sports car for its fuel economy. So what if a 747 is four and a half times more fuel-efficient than Concorde? A fully booked 747 is more fuel-efficient than a family saloon! Playing with numbers is easy. The point is to ask what these vehicles are *for*, and to operate them responsibly.

Concorde wasn't what either its designers or its operators expected. In thrilling crews and passengers and lookers-on, it served to introduce us to a new model of the air industry: a way of doing things that took the 'long' out of long-haul flying.

Entertainment leads us into the future. Novelty and fun, more than anything else – more even than the ambitions and fears of nations – are the engines that carry us there. Concorde was never going to usher in a world of Concordes, any more than the Delahayes and Bugattis of the 1930s were going to usher in a world crawling with racing cars. The challenge today, for those of us inspired by Concorde's example, is to create supersonic passenger planes that are faster, cheaper and kinder to the environment.

Concorde was made out of the most advanced materials of its day. They were, most of them, metals; its children will be woven out of resins. Concorde burned fossil fuel by the barrel-load; its children will burn engineered fuels that have a minimal effect on the environment. Concorde climbed as high as it could, then slugged its way through the air; its children will escape the Earth's atmosphere entirely, increasing their speed and saving the atmosphere from harm. Concorde cut the journey times of its competitors by more than half; its children will carry passengers from New York to Sydney in under two hours. Concorde promised a future in which all parts of the Earth were accessible, convenient, and local. I believe that the technology being developed by Virgin Galactic will make good on Concorde's promise. I don't know whether this will happen in my lifetime, but successors to Concorde are already being developed.

Ordinary jets can't go faster than Mach 3 without their turbine blades melting. Rocket ships can reach Mach 25, travelling fast enough to reach Earth orbit; but they have to carry tremendous amounts of liquid oxygen to burn their fuel. Perched somewhere between the conventional jet and the conventional rocket is an idea of an engine so simple, so unconventional and so damnably hard to do, only a handful of such engines have ever been made.

Aside from the pump that injects the fuel into the engine, the ramjet has no moving parts: no turbines, no fans and no axles. Its shape alone compresses the air entering it as the plane moves forward. Its only glitch is that it only works at high speed.

The ramjet was invented in 1913 by French inventor René Lorin. Though his design made sense – and was granted a patent – Lorin couldn't find materials adequate to build a prototype. Another paper ramjet, this time by Hungarian inventor Albert Fonó, went even further: in 1932 a patent was granted to a design meant to power a high-altitude supersonic plane!

The world's first ramjet-powered aeroplane was Soviet, and followed only seven years later, but since then the ramjet has found few applications in anything other than the most exotic military craft. This is largely because a plane that requires two kinds of propulsion – one to bring it up to the speed at which the other can begin to work – makes for an expensive project!

Ramjets, which only become efficient above Mach 1, have an upper speed limit, too. This is because the air in the engine has to be slowed to subsonic speeds before the fuel in the engine will ignite. Slowing down the air makes the engine unbelievably hot. It doesn't matter what you do to cool it: above Mach 5, a ramjet will disintegrate.

Enter the scramjet: a *supersonic combustion ramjet*. By accelerating the fuel being injected into the engine to supersonic speeds, the scramjet doesn't need to slow down the air coming into the engine. The good news is that the scramjet can fly above

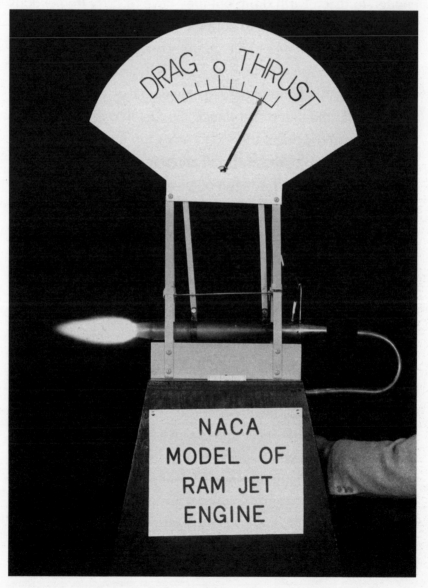

The US National Advisory Committee for Aeronautics lights some blue touchpaper...

Mach 5 and operate comfortably forty-six miles above the earth, where it can't do any damage to the Earth's atmosphere. The bad news is that if the speed of the air in the engine falls below Mach 1, the engine chokes and the whole thing blows up.

NASA's X-plane projects – we'll come on to them in the next chapter – already include experimental scramjets and, if Alan Bond has his way, Europe will not be far behind.

Bond is a former British aircraft engineer who began his career with Rolls-Royce's Rocket Division, and led a team of scientists to draw up an interstellar spacecraft design called Daedalus; he is currently receiving European Space Agency funding to develop an engine to propel aircraft at five times the speed of sound and punch spacecraft into orbit, and to do both at no appreciable cost to the environment.

Bond's company, Reaction Engines, based in Oxfordshire, is designing an airliner called the A2. A typical A2 flight will have it leaving Brussels international airport and flying quietly and subsonically out into the North Atlantic at Mach 0.9 before it reaches Mach 5 across the North Pole and heads over the Pacific to Australia. The total journey time will be around forty minutes. The same flight today takes about twenty-two hours.

The A2's secret is its engine: a ramjet with a fancy heat exchanger that transfers the heat from the incoming air to the hydrogen it uses as fuel. This means that the engine can run comfortably even when air is moving very fast through it. The faster the speed of the air through the engine, the cooler the engine. Reaction Engines believe that their ramjet, far from requiring exotic materials, could be made of light alloys.

Then there's Skylon. Skylon is Alan Bond's rocket ship – a hydrogen-powered aircraft that takes off from a conventional runway, accelerates to five and a half times the speed of sound and then – thanks again to that fancy heat exchanger – supercools the oxygen entering its engine intake for use later when the atmosphere gives out. At this point, Skylon mixes the liquid oxygen it's collected on its way through the atmosphere with an on-board reserve of liquid hydrogen, and becomes a pure rocket engine.

'It's a pretty unique concept,' says Mark Hempsell, Reaction Engines' director of future programmes. He can say that again!

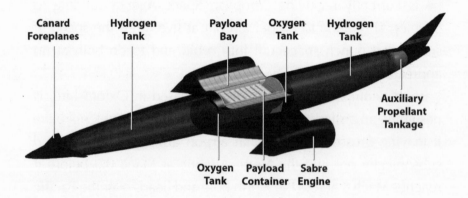

Alan Bond's Skylon concept: a plane that thinks it's a ramjet that thinks it's a rocket!

eight

Above the Sky

In Italy in 1670 a Jesuit priest, Father Francesco de Lana, published a scheme to create hollow spheres out of copper. The walls of the spheres were to be made thin, but strong enough not to crumple if you sucked all the air out of them. Once evacuated, de Lana reckoned, the spheres would become lighter than the air. They would float.

Over two hundred years later, in 1898, a sixteen-year-old boy from Worcester, Massachusetts, dreamed up much the same idea. He made his balloon out of aluminium and filled it with hydrogen. It didn't work. But the boy, Robert Hutchings Goddard, was by then hooked on the mysteries of flight. In 1919 he wrote a brilliant and meticulous book about the future of rocketry called *A Method of Reaching Extreme Altitudes*. In it, he mentioned the possibility of space travel. The idea was met with near-universal derision: he never lived it down.

He carried on working: on 16 March 1926 the tubercular, publicity-shy physics professor launched the world's first liquid-fuelled rocket from his aunt Effie's farm in Auburn, Massachusetts. The rocket, christened Nell, rose forty-one feet and landed in a cabbage field. The neighbours complained.

Goddard ploughed his own furrow his whole life, but he wasn't quite the lone voice in the wilderness that people sometimes make out. He was well liked and respected by his academic colleagues, even if they did smile at his crazy ideas. And a handful of influential people understood that his 'crazy' ideas weren't so very crazy after all. Chief among these was Charles Lindbergh, who put him in touch with the financier Daniel Guggenheim. In 1930, Guggenheim agreed to fund Goddard's research for four years for a total of $100,000. After years struggling for funds, Goddard must have thought he'd died and gone to heaven.

Heaven, for Goddard, was Roswell, New Mexico. He worked here with his team of technicians in near isolation and secrecy for a dozen years, launching solid-fuel rockets, liquid-fuel rockets,

Robert Goddard's idea of heaven: well-funded rocketry experiments in New Mexico.

even multistage rockets, and some of them attained speeds of 550 mph. (Theo Kamecke's marvellous 1970 documentary *Moonwalk One* has thrilling footage of their experiments.) American academia and the American public weren't ready for Goddard's futuristic advances. But the Germans were.

Rocket fever seized the German public imagination back in the 1920s, fuelling all manner of avant-garde films, novels and artworks. The idea of space travel was so popular that moon rockets became a regular item in carnival parades and rocket pioneers like Maximilian Valier, Fritz von Opel and Rudolf Nebel all achieved celebrity status from staging spectacular public experiments.

During the 1920s physicists like Hermann Oberth served as godfathers to the most important rocketry club of the day, the Verein fur Raumschiffarht (Rocket Society) or VfR. They personally encouraged and developed the country's most exciting young rocket talents: men like Willy Ley and Wernher von Braun.

Fritz Lang captured the feverish mood of the time with *The Woman in the Moon* (*Frau im Mond*, 1928). The screenplay was written by his wife, Thea von Harbou, who would go on to write Lang's masterpieces *Metropolis* and Herr Lang knew he would be addressing a well-informed audience and did everything he could to get the science right. He approached the VfR, who directed him to their most valued scientific advisor: the Austro-Hungarian physicist Hermann Oberth, and a remarkable collaboration began.

Oberth's interest in rocketry had been sparked at the age of eleven when his mother gave him a copy of Jules Verne's *From the Earth to the Moon*, a book that he read 'at least five or six times and, finally, knew by heart'. When Oberth discovered that

Verne's calculations were not simply fiction, the course of his career was set.

At the University of Heidelberg, Oberth caught wind of Goddard's *A Method of Reaching Extreme Altitudes*. When he couldn't get hold of a copy, he wrote to the author. Goddard sent him a treatise and a friendly letter explaining his experiments in liquid-fuelled rocketry. Oberth, staggered at Goddard's advanced knowledge, became his prophet in Germany. In 1923 he wrote *Die Rakete zu den Planetenraeumen* (*The Rocket into Interplanetary Space*) which set out the basic principles of space flight. While technically accurate, Oberth's writings went much further than Goddard's. His proposals included space stations, immense orbiting mirrors, explorations to the dark side of the Moon, and using detachable fuel capsules in orbit to power flights to the nearer planets!

The university rejected the treatise for being 'too speculative'. Still, Oberth's work never generated the kind of incredulity that Goddard's did. The rejected treatise, rewritten by German space-flight enthusiast Max Valier became *Ways to Spaceflight* (1929) and inspired new rocket clubs to spring up all over Germany.

Oberth not only advised Fritz Lang on *Frau im Mond*; he persuaded the director to bankroll a rocket! The liquid-fuelled rocket, 1.8 metres tall, was to have been launched from the movie-house roof during the film's première. Oberth expected it to reach an altitude of sixty-four kilometres over the Baltic Sea. Sadly, technical difficulties overcame the project, and the German studio Ufa took ownership of the equipment.

Among the fans of *Frau im Mond* were a circle of young rocket enthusiasts at the VfR headed by Willy Ley and a young aristocrat called Wernher von Braun, best known in those days for a boyhood prank. When he was twelve he'd attempted to power his toy go-kart with fireworks: it blew up, scaring the life out of the Berlin police.

When, years later, in October 1942, von Braun's ghastly wartime masterpiece, the V-2 rocket, first rose into the skies above Peenemünde on the Baltic coast, it had the *Frau im Mond* logo painted on its base.

Von Braun's ghastly V-2 missile was the first man-made object to reach space.

Long before I knew of his wartime work, his Nazi Party membership, his Waffen SS rank, or his likely knowledge of conditions in the Mittelbau-Dora concentration camp where his V-2 rockets were constructed – and where 20,000 died from illness, beatings, hangings and exhaustion – I thought of Wernher von Braun as a pal of Walt Disney.

Each Saturday for three weeks, von Braun – accompanied by various cartoon characters – showed me and my school friends how rockets would one day fly us all into space. The shows were a British cinema favourite during the 1950s; American kids got to watch the shows on television. After a lifetime closeted away in the service of military power, they were von Braun's chance to relive the enthusiasms of his boyhood, and to remember, in public, why he had fallen in love with rocketry in the first place.

Von Braun's V-2 was the world's first ballistic missile and first human artefact to achieve sub-orbital space flight. It was a terror weapon, deployed in the face of Allied advances against the German Reich, and while many rockets were misdirected and did little or no damage, their potential was terrifying: the V-2's speed and angle of attack made it invulnerable to anti-aircraft guns and fighters, as it dropped from space (it could reach a height of 109 kilometres) at up to four times the speed of sound.

Recruited by America after the war by Operation Paperclip, Braun defended his wartime achievement, claiming he was a good man caught up in a bad situation. Bad it certainly was: many more slaves died building his rockets than died in the rocket attacks. Was Braun responsible for the horrors surrounding the manufacture of the V-2s? Or was he simply less brave than we would wish him to be? Braun claimed that he turned a blind eye to the horrors around him for fear that, were he to say anything, the SS would put a bullet in his brain. It is true that he hankered after more innocent employment. Among friends, he once expressed regret that they were not working on a spaceship. That naive remark was enough to get him arrested: in 1944, the SS imprisoned him for two weeks without charge.

In April 1945, as Allied forces pushed deep into Germany, the Peenemünde team was escorted to the town of Oberammergau in the Bavarian Alps. Their SS guards had orders to shoot them if approached by the enemy. Von Braun's quick thinking may well have saved them: he persuaded the major in charge of the guard that they were an easy target for US bombers and should be dispersed to outlying villages. This bought them all a little time as the US 44th Infantry Division rolled into town. Wernher's kid brother Magnus – himself a rocket physicist – set off on his bike to orchestrate his brother's surrender. 'My name is Magnus von Braun,' he called out to an American soldier. 'My brother invented the V-2!'

Braun lived long enough to become a different, perhaps better person. In America, he enthused about the peaceful uses of rocketry and joined Disney in inspiring a generation of children with a hankering for outer space. Braun's work for Disney went far beyond his minutes on screen. *Man in Space* and the two other Disney space films were largely his creation; they in their turn were drawn from articles in the general-interest magazine *Collier's*, a hugely successful series that lifted the title's circulation to a staggering 4 million and – thirty years late – triggered rocket fever across the US.

By the time he was filming television programmes for Disney in the mid-1950s, von Braun was well on the way to finishing the US Army's Redstone rocket, which was used for America's first live nuclear ballistic-missile tests. Still he had his heart set on space travel – and in 1957 he got his chance.

On 4 October that year, the Soviet Union launched Sputnik One, the Earth's first artificial satellite or, as Congresswoman Clare Boothe Luce put it, 'an intercontinental outer-space raspberry to a decade of American pretensions that the American way of life was a gilt-edged guarantee of our national superiority.'

In other words, the US was rattled. For all their prescient recruitment of Germany's finest rocket scientists, they were falling far behind the Soviet Union in the conquest of space. Something had to be done – and Wernher von Braun knew what.

NASA was established on 29 July 1958. On 7 October it formally announced Project Mercury: a scheme to place a manned space capsule in orbital flight around the Earth. It set about building the new Marshall Space Flight Center at Redstone Arsenal in Huntsville, Alabama. Von Braun was appointed the centre's director.

On 31 January 1961 a Redstone rocket lifted a Mercury capsule carrying Ham, a chimpanzee, into space. On 5 May, another Redstone raised another capsule; only this time, Ham's place was taken by a human being: Alan Shepard, the first American in space. Von Braun would go on to lead the design effort that birthed the Saturn 5 rocket, powerful and reliable enough to send men to the Moon.

The year was 1998. Per and Rory McCarthy and I were in Morocco, waiting for the weather to improve so that we could launch one of our first attempts at circumnavigating the Earth in a balloon. While we waited, we had nothing to do but talk.

It turned into quite a gathering: Per Lindstrand, Will Whitehorn and I were joined one evening by Buzz Aldrin, the former NASA astronaut whose missions included three spacewalks, orbiting the Earth in Gemini 12, and piloting the lunar module on Apollo 11 – man's first manned landing on the Moon. Buzz is notorious for not suffering fools gladly – after the life he's led, why would he? – but there was no doubting his enthusiasm for our ballooning project (and others': that year, two other very well-prepared teams were challenging us to be first around the world). As we talked, it became obvious that Buzz understood better than we did what was really at stake, as we prepared to spend weeks at high altitude in a balloon. As far as Buzz was concerned, ballooning was a good way – a very good way – to get into space. He told us some stories.

You know those clear plastic packets you get in health food stores, which split the moment you try to open them, spilling their contents everywhere? They're made of cellophane. They are really fragile and *really annoying*. Would you be prepared to fly into the stratosphere in a balloon made of cellophane?

Professor Auguste Piccard did. On 27 May 1931, the professor and his colleague Paul Kipfer lifted off from Augsburg, Germany, beneath a hydrogen-filled cellophane balloon, wearing crash helmets of their own design – inverted wicker chicken baskets stuffed with pillows.

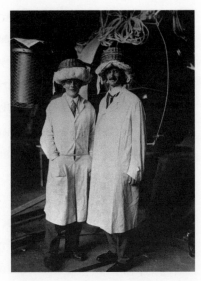

Piccard was no dummy. He understood that cellophane, for all its brittleness, is light and airtight. Equally important, he understood the mortal dangers

Some of Piccard and Kipfer's emergency gear lacked sophistication...

of a low-pressure environment: 'We must', he said, 'have a hermetically sealed cabin, carrying breathable air at ordinary pressure.' Piccard's closed-capsule system was the world's first. Carbon dioxide was scrubbed from the air by a Draeger apparatus – a piece of kit originally designed for tap beer, but which was now finding applications on early submarines and in mine rescue.

Piccard and Kipfer rose to 48,000 feet – that's more than nine miles up – and entered the stratosphere for the first time. Piccard predicted that a closed-capsule system similar to his own would one day carry a human being all the way to the Moon – and he was right. Piccard died in 1962. Three years later his widow was photographed, beaming with pride, beside a mock-up of the Apollo Command Module.

Before Apollo, before Mercury, even before NASA, men were building and testing space capsules, and achieving altitude records on the edge of space. And unlike the rocket-plane pilots made famous in Tom Wolfe's book *The Right Stuff*, these pioneers weren't just leaving the Earth's atmosphere for a couple of minutes. They were floating above the sky for hours, even days at a time. America's high-altitude ballooning programmes gathered information about conditions at high altitudes that fed directly into Mercury's preparations to put a man into space. They also amassed a wealth of experience in how to design space capsules.

The earliest and most important of these projects were the product of a rare meeting of minds. Four men – Otto Winzen, Paul Stapp, David Simons and Joe Kittinger – held Manhigh I and Manhigh II together through sheer enthusiasm and sacrifice.

The chemist Otto Winzen emigrated from Germany to the US in 1937. He spent the war in a series of internment camps and later returned to his work on plastics. His especial love was a new synthetic called 'polyethylene resin', which was being used to insulate the electrical wiring on submarines.

Winzen produced polyethylene films thinner than a human hair and set up his own company, Winzen Research, to develop applications for them. He made weather balloons, and surveillance balloons, dreamed up schemes for the US Navy and, later, for NASA. His wife Vera (to whom he was introduced by Piccard) became the finest balloon designer of her day and a world-record holder in her own right: in 1979 she set a new overland distance record of 2,003 miles in a floating art installation called *Da Vinci Transamerica*.

John Paul Stapp, the son of Baptist missionaries, was born in 1910 and grew up in the jungles of Brazil. It showed: poverty didn't trouble him at all. He went to study zoology and chemistry at Baylor University in Waco, Texas, and whenever he ran out of money he dined off guinea pigs and pigeons from the school's stock of lab animals. Stapp wanted to be an Army doctor but he kept spraining his ankle and was 'dumped' (his word) in the Army Air Corps. It was there that Stapp mastered 'bootleg research': 'unofficial projects funded on the sly at a low level of the bureaucracy.' If you could only conceal it from the 'men at the mahogany desks', you could research pretty much whatever you wanted. If it worked, you took it to your bosses, who would take the credit and turn a blind eye to whatever crazy scheme you cooked up next. If it failed, they court-martialled you.

Stapp's chief interest was high-altitude medicine. The best test pilots, flying the most expensive machines in the military's arsenal, were exposing themselves to risks that were very poorly understood. The supersonic X-planes flying out of Edwards Air Force Base kept a pilot at altitude for a couple of minutes at most, and at great cost, so there was no space or time or money on that programme for a doctor to undertake medical research. Stapp realised he would have to create his own programme: a high-altitude platform that could stay at extreme altitude for long periods, at very little cost.

Transferred to Holloman Air Force Base in New Mexico, Stapp found himself in charge of the Aeromedical Field Lab. It was there that he met Major David Simons.

Simons had spent the early 1950s at White Sands, sending fruit flies, mice, dogs and monkeys into the stratosphere aboard captured German V-2s. (Dachshunds were popular because they fitted snugly into the rocket.) At Holloman, and with no more rockets to play with, Simons switched to Otto Winzen's revolutionary polyethylene balloons. He sent animals up into the stratosphere to measure the damage caused by cosmic rays. These rays – actually radioactive particles travelling at high speed – had been discovered in 1912, and no one knew how dangerous they were. Simons's animals showed no ill effects – and one more perceived barrier to manned space exploration was cleared away.

Also at Holloman was Joe Kittinger, an ace test pilot, and slated to be Simons's first human volunteer as preparations gathered to put a man halfway into space aboard a pressurised capsule hung off a Winzen balloon.

The only problem with Joe was that he loved skydiving. He couldn't get enough of it. After high-altitude jump training over El Centro, California (a favourite military drop-zone and home of the National Parachute Test Center), making higher and higher jumps had become an obsession. If you put Joe in a capsule and took him up higher than anyone had ever been before, could he resist the temptation to jump out?

Neither Simons nor Stapp knew for sure whether Kittinger would live through such an experience, said Simons later. 'But we were dead certain that the Manhigh programme would not survive it.'

The gondola Otto Winzen designed for the project, Manhigh I, was about the size of a telephone booth, eight feet tall and three feet in diameter. Joe was to breathe an air mixture containing 20 per cent helium, ensuring that humankind's first utterances from the upper atmosphere seemed to be delivered by Donald Duck.

Manhigh was launched on 2 June 1957. The biggest safety worry on the project was the envelope. At temperatures 100 degrees below zero, even a polyethylene envelope becomes brittle. Where the air is this cold, the jet streams begin. The fear was that Joe's balloon would hit a high-altitude wind and shatter into a thousand pieces.

As it turned out, the envelope coped magnificently. The real danger lay in the capsule. Someone had installed a crucial component of the oxygen system backwards. For all the time he had been ascending, by far the greater part of Jo's oxygen had been gassing off into space.

At 96,000 feet – that's more than *eighteen miles* above the earth – Joe found himself with only a fifth of a litre of oxygen left in his tank. He doubted it was enough to get him back alive. As he hurriedly organised his descent, he stole a moment to stare through his porthole. It was frustrating beyond words to have to abandon this view: the sky was blue-black through the porthole and he could see the atmosphere making a blue band on the horizon . . .

Come And Get Me: balloonist Joe Kittinger blazed a trail for astronauts to follow.

A message clattered in over the radio ordering him to descend.

Later, Joe said his reply was just a bit of fun; that his ground crew were uptight, and should have been able to take a joke. His message read: 'COME AND GET ME'.

Divers talk about a rapture of the deep. You have only to read the transcripts from the Manhigh projects and their successors – or, more easily, get hold of Craig Ryan's superlative history *The Pre-Astronauts* – to realise that there is a rapture of the skies, too. Even with a good oxygen supply, even in a pressurised cabin, high altitude has the power to make you drunk. It's not a medical phenomenon. It's a mental one. Quite simply, it's beautiful up there.

David Simons took Manhigh II twenty miles into the air, and stayed for over a day. At this height, even dust is beautiful: 'Well above the haze layer of the Earth's atmosphere were additional faint thin bands of blue, sharply but faintly etched against the dark sky. They hovered over the Earth like a succession of halos.'

Simons saw something else, too: the curvature of the earth. Even at this height, the effect was subtle, but it was there.

X-plane pilots had spoken of a weird tint to the upper atmosphere. The Air Force had duly given Simons a paint chart so that he could pin down the colour of the sky. But the colour wasn't on any chart: 'Where the atmosphere merged with the colourless blackness of space, the sky was so heavily saturated with this blue-purple colour that it was inescapable,' Simons wrote later, 'yet its intensity was so low that it was hard to comprehend, like a musical note which is beautifully vibrant but so high that it lies almost beyond the ear's ability to hear, leaving you certain of its brilliance but unsure whether you actually heard it or dreamed of its beauty.'

*

Buzz's pride as an Apollo astronaut has never been in question; but he's old enough to understand the forces that shaped the space race and wise enough to appreciate how things might have turned out differently. That day in Morocco, he told us that lifting a spacecraft through the thickest part of the atmosphere by plane or balloon – and *then* firing its rocket engines – was a great way of getting people into space. When I asked him, innocently enough, why NASA's Apollo programme had launched its space rockets from the ground, Buzz's answer was simple: NASA had *kludged* its way to the moon.

Burdened with all the expectations of a global superpower in the middle of the Cold War, NASA adopted wartime thinking and reached for the quickest, simplest solution to every problem it confronted. As a way of accomplishing a goal, it was a good way of working – a *very* good way, placing men on the Moon decades before the technology was really ready. Even more impressive, NASA brought every moonwalker home again. But NASA's awe-inspiring Apollo programme was never going to be the shape of the future. It was too expensive. Together with the Vietnam War (which cost half as much again), Apollo virtually bankrupted the United States and triggered a global recession!

The real shape of our future in space – the sustainable, economically stable future we and our competitors are now building in the desert of New Mexico – has its roots much further back in the past.

In the 1920s, two great aviation technologies were battling for control of the skies: there were biplanes, and there were airships.

The US Navy tried to combine the two. The Skyhook project carried out extensive tests on how to create an aircraft carrier in the air. Airships, with their long range and reliability in flight, would carry deadly, manoeuvrable short-range fighters to theatres of battle and afterwards, somehow (no one was quite sure how) retrieve their planes in mid-air for refuelling and servicing. The project was shelved as seagoing aircraft carriers matured, but the central idea lived on.

It was understood – long before the first shot was fired – that victory in any future war depended upon bombing the enemy from the air. Throughout the Second World War, bomber forces depended for their protection on fighter cover. The trouble was, fighters couldn't carry much fuel. If they could follow the bombers to their target in the first place (and they rarely could), they only had reserves enough for a few minutes of combat before they had to turn back.

The solution was to re-imagine Skyhook. Never mind airships: why couldn't bombers carry their own fighters into battle? 'That way,' writes David Szondy, in his charming on-line history of unlikely technology, 'the bomber force could carry their fighter cover with them much as a small boy can tote around a jar full of wasps.'

The McDonnell XF-85 Goblin was a specially made pocket fighter, designed to be carried inside a B-36 bomber. The bomber dropped it from a hook, then gathered it back in. The Goblin was slow, underpowered, and had no range. Pilots detested it for yet another reason: some wag in the design department had decided to lighten the payload by getting rid of the undercarriage!

Again, the project was cancelled. Again, the idea of air launch lingered on. As American post-war research began on supersonic and high-altitude aircraft, it became an obvious annoyance to have to build experimental craft capable of slugging their way to 40,000 feet in order to do any interesting work. The engineers already knew how to do that bit; they wanted to know what happened *next*. What if they could carry experimental craft up to high altitude, and then launch them?

In 1945 the US Army Air Forces (it became the US Air Force in 1947) and NACA, the National Advisory Committee on Aeronautics, began the first of a series of experimental aircraft projects. NACA's X-planes were pure research craft. Some didn't even have

The XF-85 Goblin pocket fighter couldn't land. It was not popular!

wings. Some never flew. Some failed. That was and is the point: to distinguish true frontiers from dead ends.

The first X-plane – Bell Aircraft Company's X-1 – arrived at Muroc Air Field in 1946. It was a funny-looking thing – a sort of outsize bullet with stubby wings. (At the time, a 50-calibre bullet was the only shape known not to tumble at supersonic speeds.) It was powered by a rocket engine (Robert Goddard designed the fuel pump) and dropped from the belly of a B-29 bomber, and it was supposed to become the first manned vehicle to deliberately break the sound barrier.

The question was: who was going to fly it? Bell Aircraft test pilot 'Slick' Goodlin wanted $150,000 to make the attempt. NACA baulked, and instead approached a twenty-four-year-old Air Force test pilot called Chuck Yeager.

Yeager was happy to undertake the wildest mission for his regular officer's salary. He seemed to treat the whole affair as

Chuck Yeager and his X-1 rocketplane. Glennis was the name of Yeager's wife.

just part of his routine – a routine that included knocking them back in Pancho Barnes's Happy Bottom Riding Club and riding horses as though they were aircraft. (In *The Right Stuff*, a brilliant account of NASA's birth, American journalist Tom Wolfe has a lot of fun at the expense of Muroc's test pilots, who, because they were aces in the air, assumed wrongly that they were masters of every imaginable vehicle.)

Yeager's heroic drinking and hapless riding collided painfully two nights before the flight, when he rode his horse into a closed gate. The horse came off better than the test pilot. Afraid he would be bumped from the flight, Yeager had his broken ribs taped up by a vet in another town, said nothing to his bosses about the pain he was in, and smuggled a sawn off broom handle on to the flight so that he could lever the canopy of the X-1 closed with his good hand.

On 14 October 1947 Yeager climbed aboard the X-1, felt his B-52 mothership drop him into the air and started the engine: at an altitude of 45,000 feet, he broke the sound barrier.

The final flight of the North American X-15, in October 1968 – though not the end of the X-plane series (the projects continue to this day) – is generally agreed to mark the end of Muroc's golden age of the high-speed, high-altitude research. By then, the airfield had been transformed into the sprawling Edwards Air Force Base, and Pancho Barnes's Happy Bottom Riding Club, where Chuck Yeager once rubbed shoulders with future astronauts, was a burned-out shell.

Of all the X-plane programmes the X-15 is generally considered the greatest success. That's partly because bits of the X-15 ended up copied into virtually every high-performance aeroplane, spaceship and missile that came after it. The Space Shuttle owed some of the design of its main engine and many of its materials to the X-15. But the X-15 is best remembered for

A B-52 bomber launches America's first manned spaceship: the spectacular X-15.

Joe Walker flew his X-15 into space – twice! He later helped develop NASA's lunar lander.

flying like a bat out of hell. Its high speeds and altitudes made it the perfect test platform for other projects. It even carried micrometeorite collection pods and heat-shield samples for the Apollo programme. Best of all, it could carry you into space.

In 1960 the physicist and ace Second World War pilot Joe Walker took his first flight in the thing. Like most X-series aircraft, the X-15 was designed to be carried to its operating altitude under the wing of a B-52 bomber. Walker felt himself fall, and started the X-15's rocket engine. Experienced pilot though he was, he was in for a surprise. The X-15's rocket engine used ammonia and liquid oxygen for propellant and hydrogen peroxide to drive the pump that fuelled the engine. This rocket could be throttled like an aeroplane engine and was the first of its kind to be put under a pilot's control. It was simply monstrous. 'Oh my God!'

Walker screamed, as he was flung back into his seat and pinned there by the acceleration.

'Yes?' said flight control. 'You called?'

The X-1 was a rocket plane. The X-15 was a spaceship. Designed to operate in extremely thin air at high altitudes, it had small rocket engines in its nose for steering when the air ran out and its wing surfaces no longer worked. (A repeating figure in Tom Wolfe's *The Right Stuff* is that the X-plane pilots *flew* their rockets into space, while the Mercury astronauts were – against their fierce protests – merely *conveyed.*)

Before Sputnik's launch changed America's game plan, and gave birth to the Mercury project, the Air Force and NACA had plans under way to heave an X-15 into orbit on top of a Navajo missile! And though the X-15 never made orbit, it did blast into space.

There is no magical point at which the Earth's atmosphere stops and space begins. At the time of the X-15 tests, by the US Air Force's own measure space began fifty miles above the surface of the Earth. Eight pilots earned their USAF astronaut wings flying the X-15 past this imaginary line. Since the mid-fifties, the world's air sports governing body, the Fédération Aéronautique Internationale, has recognised the Theodore Von Kármán's boundary marker of 100 kilometres (62.1 miles). Of all the X-15 missions, two. in 1963, crossed this boundary. Joe Walker flew them both, making him the first ever person to visit space twice.

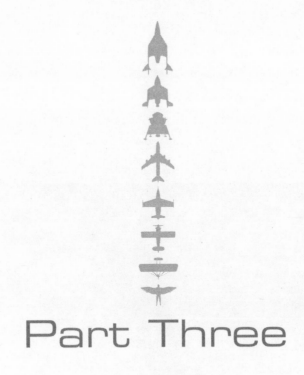

Part Three

'To Infinity and Beyond!'

The Pterodactyl Ascender: arguably my worst memory – now a design classic!

nine

Fast Glass

When I was little, I dreamed I could fly. The harder I flapped my arms, the higher I rose. I soared on imaginary thermals. I steered around imaginary trees. My first real experience of flying was with an early microlight contraption built around a Rogallo wing – a steerable triangular parachute originally designed to bring NASA's Mercury capsules back to earth, and which eventually inspired the sport of hang-gliding.

I was in my early twenties, and had never set foot aboard a plane, when I took the phone call. A chap called Richard Ellis said he had got hold of a Pterodactyl. Invented by flying enthusiast Jack McCornack in California in the mid-1970s, the Pterodactyl Ascender was what you got when you crossed a primitive hang-glider with a lawnmower. It had a wheeled undercarriage, of sorts – the wheels looked as though they had come off a kid's tricycle. It had a reclining seat, and a small engine that you operated with your teeth. (You needed both hands free to steer, so the throttle was a rubber bulb you stuck in your mouth.) Ellis wanted to be the man to bring McCornack's invention to Europe, and he wanted me to be his first airborne advocate. He offered to teach me how to fly.

Pterodactyls have been flown on many long flights. In the summer of 1979, years after my own experience, a man called Jack Peterson, Jr, flew one of these beasts from Long Beach, California, to Hilton Head, South Carolina, covering the 3,200-mile distance in 120-mile hops. His machine is on display in the Smithsonian Museum.

Ellis had assembled his own Pterodactyl from a kit. It looked a hundred years old: the sort of primitive prototype that a dashing pilot of the First World War – a Cecil Lewis or Manfred von Richthofen – might have obsessed over as a child. It looked as though it had fallen into the present from out of some earlier, more romantic, more swashbuckling time. As soon as I saw it, I knew I had to fly it.

One Friday afternoon I rode over to Oxford with some friends, full of dreams of becoming a great pioneer of the air. I imagined that Douglas Bader's spirit, looking on, might give me an approving thumbs-up as I sailed over hedges. We met Ellis at the local airfield – little more than a sun-bleached windsock and a long strip of weathered concrete – and he kindly but firmly brought me down to earth. He said it would take him about a week to get me airborne, and that we should spend the first two or three days on the ground, getting me used to the machine.

As Joan and a handful of friends looked on, Ellis sat me in the thing and handed me its peculiar throttle mechanism: a rubber bulb connected to a tube. 'Biting down on this,' he said, 'engages the throttle. Spit it out, and engine will cut out. So for starters, we'll set you rolling down the runway. Pedal like crazy to get the engine started. Bite down, and when you get near the end of the runway, spit the bulb out.'

The engine kicked into life sooner than I expected. Bare inches behind my head the propellor began chopping up the air, and I picked up speed. It felt like riding a motorbike for the first time. I grinned into the wind, savouring every one of my thirty miles per hour; and as the hedge at the far end of the field approached, I spat out the throttle.

The hedge hurled itself at me. I was going to crash. Pure reflex tightened my grip on the steering controls – and the Pterodactyl rose into the air. Far from cutting out, the engine seemed to be working harder and harder!

I opened my eyes. I was above the trees. I was flying. Except that I didn't know how to fly. Or land. Or slow down.

A tree got in my way, fear gripped me, I tightened my hold on the twist-grips, and the plane grazed the topmost branches. It was only by the grace of the gods that I was still in the air; and I knew my luck wouldn't hold out much longer. I had to get down.

The thought came to me: *Pull the wires out.* If I could disable the engine, then one of two things would happen: either the wing would glide me to earth at a safe speed or – well, it wouldn't! But killing the engine was surely safer than fooling around in mid-air, completely out of control. Of course, pulling the wires out of the engine meant letting go of the steering. A good long time seemed to pass as I tried to summon the courage to begin. Finally a looming oak tree made the decision for me. I wove drunkenly around it – I have no idea how – gritted my teeth, let go with one hand and ripped out a wire. And another. And another.

After what seemed an age, the thing eventually died on me. I yanked on the twist-grips, performed a couple of hairy turns, and landed – badly, but more or less upright – in a neighbouring field.

I opened my eyes. I was above the trees. **I was flying.**

Except that I didn't know how to fly.

Or land. Or slow down.

My friends were with me in seconds. I had visions of them on their motorbikes, weaving through the countryside in hot pursuit. It took me a few minutes, while I got my breath back, to realise I had covered barely any distance at all. All the while my friends were cheering and clapping and Joan, my girlfriend (later to become my wife), was slapping me on the back saying, 'Well done, Richard, that was amazing!' They had not heard Ellis's instructions. They had no idea I was supposed to stay firmly on the ground.

I walked away from my first flying lesson with a few bruises and with my confidence badly shaken. Maybe, I thought, I am not cut out to fly. I shook hands with Richard Ellis, wished him well with his other students, and drove away.

I never saw him again. A couple of days later, the news came through: Ellis had been killed, flying that same contraption. So that afternoon in Oxford was not just my first experience of flight; it was, looking back, my first unvarnished glimpse of what

it is to be a pioneer in the air. No one much remembers Richard
Ellis now. The man who wanted to teach Britain how to fly died
before his work could even really begin. For every adored hero of
the air, there are men like Ellis – men whose qualities will never
be truly tested because they lack that one essential possessed by
all great aviators: a barrowload of luck.

What does it feel like to really fly, the way a bird flies? The nearest
I've ever come is being dangled off a cable beneath a helicopter as
it swooped over Darling Harbour in Sydney. We were promoting
the Australian launch of Virgin Mobile and some wag in the
publicity office thought it would be a great idea to dangle me
over the city. The problem being that as you're propelled forward,
you don't just hang there in the air: you tumble. It took me some
heart-stopping moments to sort myself out: finally, I adopted the
position skydivers have learned makes them stable in the air – and
hey presto, I was flying. I felt the air sticking to me. I felt how the
wind and my flying suit became one.

In 1938, in North Africa, nineteen-year-old Leo Valentin made
his first parachute jump. It was not an elegant display. Nor was
his outfit, the French Armée de l'Air: 'All of us, and I was no
exception, jumped like sacks of flour,' he complained. 'When a
man leaves the plane he falls anyhow; he tumbles about the sky;
he twirls like a sack of potatoes.' This style of parachuting wasn't
just ugly: it was very often lethal. Valentin went in search of a
better way to dive. Unaware of Art Starnes's pioneering skydives
a generation earlier, Valentin studied acrobats, dancers, and –
naturally enough – divers. He finally found his inspiration from
his studies of birds. He imitated, as far as he could, the posture
of birds as they held themselves aloft in a breeze: spread-eagled,
with his chest thrown forward, he found that he could direct

himself through the air with careful movements of his arms and legs. It was like swimming!

Not content with perfecting modern skydiving technique, Valentin then wondered whether, with the right posture, he might be able to fly like a bird. 'A few of us want to open up the air to man on his own,' he wrote. 'When machinery reaches its limit, man feels the need to return to simplicity. There comes a time when he wants to get out of his car and walk and so, getting out of a supersonic aircraft, he wants to fly with his own wings.'

It was the old dream, and to fulfil it Valentin returned to some of the earliest works on flight. He studied Otto Lilienthal. Clearly, he understood the problems of Lilienthal's design. Somewhere along the way must have decided: 'What the hell.' After all, the higher you were, the longer you had to experiment and correct a mistake. If the early days of flight had taught aviators anything, it was that altitude was your friend. Lilienthal, though, had had no choice but to launch himself from hills. The conical hill he built himself – and from which he launched himself on his last and fatal glide – was barely seventy feet high. Maybe Lilienthal's style of gliding could be made to work, after all – provided that you started high in the air.

Valentin built a set of canvas wings, attached them to his shoulders and threw himself out of a plane to see what would happen. The results weren't pretty – he tumbled and spun – but he did manage to control his fall well enough to deploy his parachute and execute a reasonable landing. After a few days' practice, he had learned to glide and turn. Finally, in April 1950, before 30,000 spectators, he made his first public demonstration. For ever afterwards the newspapers called him 'L'Homme-Oiseau' – the Birdman.

Don Cameron's light, inexpensive *Bristol Belle* launched modern hot-air ballooning in Britain.

The *Virgin Atlantic Flyer* was the first hot-air balloon ever to cross the Atlantic. As you can see, our landing was far from smooth!

1991: Per and I prepare to launch the *Virgin Pacific Flyer* on the world's first lighter-than-air flight across the Pacific.

In 1997 Alex Ritchie (right) joined Per and me for a round-the-world balloon flight. A day later our capsule malfunctioned, and Alex saved our lives.

In 1998 Per Lindstrand, Steve Fossett and I attempted to circle the earth on board Per's rozière, the *ICO Global Challenger*.

I leapt to safety as the *ICO Global Challenger* bunny-hopped across the Pacific.

Per, Steve Fossett and I were nearing Hawaii in 1998 when our jet stream petered out, ending our dreams of ballooning around the earth.

1999: Bertrand Piccard and Brian Jones circle the earth on the *Breitling Orbiter 3*.

2005: I say goodbye to Steve Fossett as he prepares to fly around the Earth without refuelling in Burt Rutan's revolutionary all-composite plane.

A thing of beauty. And the *Virgin Atlantic GlobalFlyer* looks pretty neat, too...

Nudging their way into space: *WhiteKnightOne* and *SpaceShipOne* reach launch altitude.

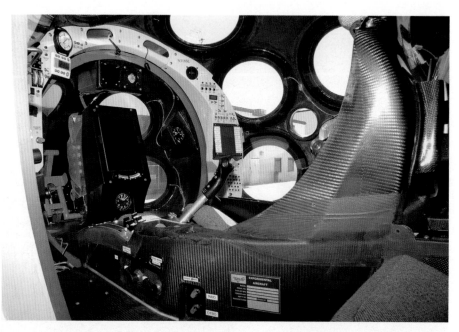

This is not a film set: it's the cockpit of *SpaceShipOne*, the first private craft ever to reach outer space.

VMS Eve in flight over Mojave. If you think it looks odd now, just wait until you see it launching the *Enterprise*!

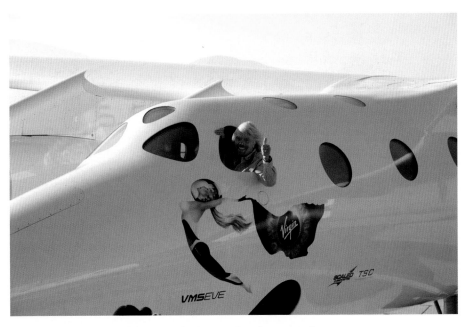

We named Virgin Galactic's launch vehicle *VMS Eve* after my mother.

My life in his hands! Aeronautical designer Burt Rutan plays with a model of Virgin Galactic's *SpaceShipTwo*.

Green air travel comes a step closer thanks to NASA's unmanned *Helios* plane, powered entirely by the sun.

By 1951, Valentin had abandoned his canvas wings for wings made of balsa wood. His progress wasn't just astonishing; it was surreal. Single-handedly, Valentin seemed to be playing out the history of aviation in reverse. Wooden wings were just the sorts of contraptions that had got daredevils killed since written records began. Yet, by 1954, here he was, jumping from 9,000 feet with wooden wings attached to his

Mission impossible: skydiver Leo Valentin learned how to fly like a bird.

shoulders – *and flying.* Granted, the moments of lift he achieved as he plummeted towards the ground were rare, but they were real enough and witnessed by plenty of independent observers.

In May 1956, before a crowd of 100,000, Valentin stepped into the air at 8,500 feet. The slipstream snatched one of his wings and smashed it against the plane's fuselage. Valentin tumbled. He opened his main parachute, but it fouled around what was left of his glider. He opened his reserve. It wrapped itself around him, mummifying him. He died on impact.

Valentin was not the only birdman of the twentieth century, but of the seventy-five who tried it, only four survived into retirement.

Yet the dream of flying like a bird is a common one. A universal one. Absurd and unobtainable as it seems in our waking hours, we cannot ignore it, and we should not belittle it. One day, the dream will be realised, in its purest form.

On 23 April 1988 the Massachusetts Institute of Technology's human-powered aircraft Daedalus, its propellor driven by a

bicycle chain, ditched into the sea just short of the island of Santorini, a staggering three hours, fifty-four minutes into its maiden flight. To this day, the Daedalus holds the record for distance and duration for human-powered aircraft.

The human-powered aeroplane Daedalus before its record-breaking flight.

Even more exciting, in 2006 Frenchman Yves Rousseau flapped his way (after 211 unsuccessful tries!) into the record books, as the first man ever to launch himself into the air using mere muscle power. The Royal Aeronautical Society reacted quickly, announcing four new prizes, including one for a human-powered flapping flight over a marathon-distance course. If birdmen aren't competing for Olympic medals in time for Rio in 2016, I have a hunch they'll be taking the podium – or hovering just above it – by 2020.

Read any average history of aviation and you'll be forgiven for thinking that after about 1950, and the dawn of the jet age, all the fun fell out of the sky. There seem to be no more daredevils to gasp at, no more single-handed battles against the elements, no more heroes.

Well, of course that's not true. In 1979 Tom Wolfe's *The Right Stuff* began to set the record straight, showing that aviation's daredevil spirit was very much alive at Edwards Air Force Base throughout the 1950s and 1960s. Still, the X-Plane and Mercury programmes were hugely expensive and exclusive, and the experiments and test flights were mostly kept top secret. What happened to the fairground spirit of the early barnstorming shows?

Valentin and the birdmen aside, what happened in the twentieth century was that flying ceased to be much of an attraction, and became much more of a sport: something people *did*. An hour's flying lesson will set you back around £100. If you can afford to join a golf club, you can afford to learn to fly and buy a share in a light plane. Now this is not exactly *cheap*, but if you've only a modest budget, there are plenty of alternatives. Hang-gliding and paragliding are mature technologies now, and well worth the punt. If you're feeling particularly brave, you can learn to free-fall in a wingsuit and fly, as Valentin once flew, through mountain passes and off cliffs and (though you'll get arrested) off tall buildings.

In this chapter I want to tell you about what happened to the barnstorming spirit of the inter-war years. Rumours of its death are greatly exaggerated. It's thrilling more people, and spinning off more new technologies and new aviation ideas, than ever before.

Barnstormers disappeared from our skies after the Second World War, not because they became unfashionable, but because so many people got in on their act. Why thrill to someone else's stunt when you can get up out of your chair and try a few stunts yourself? By the end of the war, you didn't even need a plane – or not much of one. The era of a one-size-fits-all biplane was over very quickly, as numerous light and microlight aircraft, wings, kites and parachutes took advantage of new lightweight materials.

Some of these designs, like the Rogallo wing, were brand new. Others, like the autogyro, had a venerable history. It was back in 1919 that the Spanish engineer and aeronautical enthusiast Juan de la Cierva invented an unusual and very effective safety device for aircraft: a freewheeling rotor. Not only would the rotor help keep the plane up in the air; should the plane lose power, the rotor would allow the craft to make a slow and reasonably controlled descent.

Juan's safety feature never caught on. Instead, and much later, his principle inspired a line of tiny, lightweight, personal flyers called autogyros. The Wallis autogyro, developed in England in the 1960s, became an instant icon when it starred in the James Bond film *You Only Live Twice*. Sadly the designer, Ken Wallis, held no truck with amateur aviators and never released his designs to the public, saying that his work was strictly for 'reconnaissance, research and development, surveillance and military purposes'.

The hang-glider is born! NASA's Paresev (Paraglider Research Vehicle).

Juan de la Cierva's C-30 autogyro turned heads. Sadly, no flyable models survive.

Well, never mind Wallis. Today the autogyro is a hugely popular machine among amateur aviators. If you only have £100 to spend, and take only one flying lesson in your life, give yourself that Sean Connery moment: fly an autogyro.

Meanwhile regular aeroplanes have not only got bigger and more expensive; they've also got smaller and cheaper. The era of the modern home-build aeroplane was ushered in by a French furniture manufacturer called Henri Mignet. Mignet failed to be accepted as a military pilot and decided to build his own plane instead. Between 1931 and 1933 Mignet built prototypes in Paris and tested them in a large field north-east of the city.

The proud result of his researches was the Flying Flea (Pou du Ciel) – a light aircraft first flown in 1933. Mignet claimed that anyone who could build a packing case and drive a car could fly a Flying Flea – and he published details of its construction in a book. Costing only about £100 to build, it seemed the answer to many an amateur aviator's prayers. In France at least 500 were completed. Unfortunately, a significant number crashed, owing to the spacing of the craft's wings.

The authorities of the time were very supportive: the Royal Aircraft Establishment in the United Kingdom and the French Air Ministry conducted full-scale wind-tunnel tests to isolate the problem, and later Flying Fleas were a lot safer. Though the aircraft never quite overcame its dangerous reputation, enough French enthusiasts fly Fleas today to justify an annual meeting every June.

Home-build movements have come and gone over the years, and different countries seem to foster different kinds of low-tech flying. BASE jumping – that business of flinging yourself off a tall building and paragliding to a police reception at street level – was a largely American invention, enthusiastically adopted by the British: in 1990 Russell Powell jumped from the Whispering Gallery inside St Paul's Cathedral, London – the lowest indoor BASE jump in the world.

Across the Soviet Union in the 1930s, parachuting was all the rage among high-school children, who competed in accuracy contests. Parks and playgrounds boasted steel jump towers. There were even small towers for young children, complete with cables and safety harnesses.

The Germans, on the other hand, have always excelled at flying gliders. This is largely because, between the world wars, sport aviation was virtually the only way Germany's aviation pioneers could get around the restrictions of the Treaty of Versailles. By 1931, German gliding pioneers had discovered thermals and were keeping their gliders up in the air for hours rather than mere minutes. Willy Messerschmitt, who would fill the skies with German fighter aircraft throughout the Second World War, began his career designing a light sport plane, and the Luftwaffe's brilliant pilots all earned their wings in gliders.

European gliders remained by far the world's best well into the twentieth century. Don't take my word for it. Ask the celebrated US aircraft designer Burt Rutan. Burt's love of European gliders inspired his use of lightweight composites for kit aircraft. Years later, tricks of composite construction would make a vital contribution to his X Prize attempt, and place him at the head of the grid in the race for space.

Burt was born in Dinuba, in rural California, in 1943. He and his elder brother Dick shared a room, converted from an open woodshed. They filled it with model aeroplanes, engine parts, glue, balsa and tools. Dick built the models out of kits, flew them, and broke them; Burt picked up the pieces and made new

Burt Rutan's model planes performed so well, competitions had to change their rules.

models out of them. His mother Irene would drive him into the Sierra Mountains; Burt operated his planes from the back seat while his mother drove the station wagon as a chase vehicle. In the end he began carrying off so many prizes that the model-aeroplane associations had to change their rules.

Rutan began his career at Edwards Air Force Base, writing the rule book for flying the notoriously unstable F-4 Phantom fighter-bomber. Exciting as that job was, however, it didn't compare with the pleasures of aircraft construction. What Burt really wanted to do was design and build his own plane, in his own garage. And he did: his scale-model version of a Saab fighter was as exciting to fly as a military jet, a fraction of the size, and extremely forgiving. Burt started selling the plans of his VariEZE aircraft to other home-build enthusiasts.

The VariEZE was easy and cheap to build. 'If you can chew gum and walk a straight line simultaneously,' Burt wrote, 'you won't have any trouble at all.' You didn't need to use metal in its construction. You didn't even need to mould anything. Instead you took a block of packing foam, carved it to the right shape and laid on shredded glass and epoxy. The technique – one he developed while studying imported European gliders – became his signature.

Burt's customers admired his policy of radical openness: he kept on improving his designs, read and replied to every letter, and produced little magazines detailing every glitch, problem, accident and, yes, crash. Eventually, though, he ran into a problem as old as flight itself: being sued. The selfsame thing happened to the Wright brothers. When people started building their own planes, and building them wrong, they took the brothers to court demanding compensation for their accidents. It stymied their later careers.

There has never been any doubt that a Rutan-designed VariViggen, VariEZE or LongEZE aircraft, built right, is one of the safest light aeroplanes ever designed. Nevertheless, the more plans he sold, the more Burt became exposed to lawsuits, and so, rather reluctantly, he began looking for other ways to make money. He went back to model-making, of a sort, and built small-scale versions of prototype aircraft for flight testing. This approach

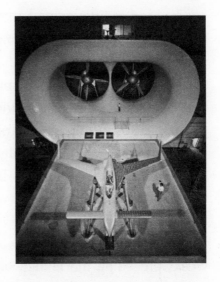

A kit plane that thinks it's a fighter jet: Burt Rutan's VariEZE.

to aircraft development – one that would have been perfectly familiar to German glider and sports-plane pioneers between the wars – turned out to be more reliable and cheaper than wind-tunnel testing, and the company Burt started to do this work, Scaled Composites, is now a world leader in aeronautical designs built around composite materials – materials the trade has nicknamed 'fast glass'.

Putting on the pressure suit and climbing into the cockpit was the easy part. The difficulty was climbing out again. 'Cramped' does not begin to express conditions aboard what was, in 2005, the world's most advanced all-composite plane.

The *Virgin Atlantic GlobalFlyer* was designed by Burt Rutan to carry one extremely brave pilot around the world on a single tank of fuel. In return, that pilot would have to spend at least eighty hours struggling to stay awake in a space no bigger than a coffin – and as I floundered my way out of the cockpit and into the dry glare of the Mojave sun, it hit me for the first time: that someone might be me.

The plane's owner and lead pilot, Steve Fossett, had made me his back-up because we were friends, and to thank me for Virgin Atlantic's sponsorship of the project – and, maybe, to tease me a little: I was approaching my fifty-fifth birthday, I owned several airlines and I held numerous ballooning world records – but I still hadn't got around to obtaining my pilot's licence. (I still haven't!)

The plan was that if Steve was struck down by illness in the weeks preceding the launch of the GlobalFlyer then I would devote the intervening time to getting my licence and almost immediately afterwards attempt to fly around the world in this most radical of experimental planes. This was taking my life philosophy of 'learning on the job' to new and scary extremes.

It never came to that: come 28 February 2005, with my feet firmly on the ground, I waved Steve farewell on his record-breaking journey. My heart was in my mouth as I watched him go. Steve had put his heart and soul into this project; now he was putting his life on the line.

Fully six years before, in the summer of 1999, Steve had been having dinner at the Flying M Ranch with his host, Barron Hilton, and Dick Rutan, a test pilot, brother of Burt Rutan, and the man who, with his partner Jeana Yeager (no relation to Chuck), had circumnavigated the world in a plane, non-stop and without refuelling, in 1986.

Dick and Jeana had spent nine days in an unpressurised cockpit three and a half feet wide by seven feet long. The flight had damaged their hearing, and the project as a whole frayed their relationship to nothing. (Plenty of people in this book paid the ultimate sacrifice for their adventures; everybody in this book paid something.)

At the dinner table, Dick's enthusiasm for record-breaking aviation – and for the materials his brother was using on new aircraft – remained boundless. He reckoned that it would now be possible to fly around the world in a fraction of the time taken by the original *Voyager*. It might even be possible to do a *solo* circumnavigation . . .

Steve listened spellbound: the last great aviation record left inside the Earth's atmosphere! The first great aviation achievement of the twenty-first century!

The following August, Steve went out to Oshkosh, for the annual Experimental Aircraft Association 'Air Venture'. This is America's largest aviation meeting, and it attracts about a million visitors each year. Steve wasn't there just to rubberneck (though knowing Steve he most likely crawled over and into anything with wings); he had a meeting planned with Burt Rutan. Burt needed seed money. There were a couple of projects he was trying to get off the ground. He offered Steve a pilot's seat on a spaceship for $7 million, and the chance to circumnavigate the world solo for $2.5 million.

Steve was awestruck. A *spaceship*?

Burt explained the X Prize: a $10 million prize for the first private company that could haul a vehicle past the Kármán line into space, twice, in the space of a fortnight.

Steve swallowed. 'And the other thing?' He later regretted not seizing both opportunities, but I think he chose well. *SpaceShipOne* needed a test pilot; the *GlobalFlyer* needed an adventurer.

There aren't many people capable of sitting in a space the size of a coffin for anything up to four days, let alone without sleep, let alone at the controls of a more or less unproven aircraft. Psychologically, Steve was the right man. He was even then attempting (six times, in the end) to be the first person to fly around the world alone non-stop in a balloon: a journey that would eventually take him fourteen days and nineteen hours. Gregarious and cheerful, he was, at the same time, perfectly content with his own company. Solitude held no terrors for him.

Not long after that his meeting with Burt, Steve took part in a sailing regatta near my home in the Virgin Islands. He called me up and invited me to join his crew for the race. (Steve always knew how to pique my interest!) Later, he showed me the plans for his plane, then called *Capricorn*. The basic design decisions had already been taken. Dick and Jeana's *Voyager* had been driven by two propellors. The new plane was powered by a single jet engine, designed by Dr Sam Williams. This in itself was very good news. (Williams is a book in himself: blind since youth, he hand-crafts what many say are the most beautiful engines ever built.) The more Steve told me, the more excited I got.

For a start, it was a terrific adventure. Even better, it could help revolutionise the air industry.

The importance of *Capricorn* – later to become the *Virgin Atlantic GlobalFlyer* – lay in its construction. The airframe was to be made entirely from composite materials.

Composites are any construction materials that are made of two or more distinct substances webbed together. When you pour concrete around a mesh of steel reinforcing rods, you're making a composite. Mix mud and straw for bricks, and you're making a composite (a good one at that; in some environments mud bricks stand up to the weather better than concrete). When you paint epoxy resin over a mat of glass shreds to fix the hole in your boat, you're creating a composite called fibreglass.

The kinds of composite Burt Rutan developed at Scaled Composites are descendants of the kinds of material regularly used by model-makers and glider manufacturers: glass, resins, foam cores and fillers. Composites like these are as strong as the strongest metals and much, much lighter. If you could build a passenger jet of composite, you would save huge amounts of fuel.

The question is: can you?

There was no way Virgin Atlantic was ever going to build its own passenger planes, of course – that particular approach to the business disappeared well before the Second World War! But we could, by our efforts and investments, encourage Airbus and Boeing to take composites seriously.

Long-haul passenger planes are the most complex machines ever constructed, and right now, Boeing and the European consortium Airbus make most of them. Being far and away the market leaders, and being very big, complex organisations, both companies tend to be very conservative. In some ways this is a good thing. We put our lives in their hands every time we step aboard one of their planes, and we expect their machines to be tried and tested. The downside, however, is that Boeing and Airbus find it difficult to innovate. They leave it up to their customers to work out precisely what they want them to make.

Well, Virgin Atlantic was their customer. As I talked to Steve Fossett, I realised that by backing his project, we could demonstrate exactly the sort of plane we wanted to fly from now on.

The *Virgin Atlantic GlobalFlyer* would carry more than four times its own weight in fuel. Its three-body layout spread the weight of the aeroplane across the wing. Sam Williams's engine was built around a conventional jet engine, computer-controlled and with a contoured, high-efficiency fan carved from a single block of titanium. The airframe was woven from glass, graphite and aramid, and bonded with epoxies and resins. Once heated, this composite material became immensely strong and far lighter than aluminium. The controls were conventional – the last thing Steve needed was some fly-by-wire malarkey sitting between him and his plane's control surfaces – but the control and communications systems were sufficient to hold Steve in the air while he grabbed the occasional two-minute nap. Computer-aided design had refined the aerodynamics of the plane, making it far superior to the 1980s-vintage design of Dick and Jeana's *Voyager*. The flight plan took advantage of the jet stream, giving *GlobalFlyer* a staggering 75 per cent more range than anything previously achieved by jet-powered aeroplanes. We reckoned that, with the angels on our side, our plane could make it around the world.

The question was, could Steve?

It was a freezing evening on Monday, 28 February when the *Virgin Atlantic GlobalFlyer* took off from Salina, Kansas. The flight did not go smoothly. What does? First, Steve's GPS navigation system packed in. Without it, he couldn't possibly meet the waymarkers required to authenticate his flight with the World Air Sports Federation (FAI), and earn his world record. I remember a strained conversation: me in the relative comfort of the chase plane, encouraging him to fly on for the sake of the project; Steve, depressed and frustrated, wondering whether he shouldn't just turn back. And just then, as if by a miracle, the GPS rebooted!

The following morning, a much more serious problem came to light. Steve's cabin, like every other pressurised aeroplane

The *Virgin Atlantic GlobalFlyer*: around the world on one tank of fuel.

cabin, was kept at an even pressure by the plane's engine. Were the engine to fail, the cabin would depressurise, and Steve would have to reach for his reserve oxygen supply. Only he didn't have one: on climbing into the craft the previous day, he'd knocked over his emergency-oxygen switch. Sam's engine not only had to get him around the world; now it had to keep him alive.

The next problem was farcical. Virgin Atlantic pilot Alex Tai, flying our chase plane, came in close to take pictures. We had been doing this without trouble since the beginning of the flight, but suddenly the backwash from Alex's plane swept over Steve's left wing and disrupted the area of low pressure that was keeping it up in the air. When a wing comes unglued from the airflow in this way, we say it has 'stalled', and a stalled plane has the aerodynamic properties of a housebrick. Steve, fighting to stay in the air, gave poor Alex a hell of a mouthful – Alex all the while capturing the exchange on film!

By now Steve was flying very confidently. Time for the next really serious problem to emerge. Over the Persian Gulf, Steve learned he had lost over 2,000 pounds of fuel. It had somehow dumped through the vents during his initial climb. Low on fuel, and with no oxygen reserve, Steve had no choice but to hold on and hope, the roar of Sam Williams's jet engine his only real companion.

At last, on 3 March 2005, Steve Fossett nursed the world's most revolutionary aircraft on to the tarmac at Salina, Kansas – the very spot from which his voyage had begun. He had not run out of fuel, and he had not needed any emergency oxygen.

Waiting on the tarmac to greet him was another amazing aircraft – the *Cayley Flyer*, shipped over from the UK and flown, that day, by Allan McWhirter, the gliding expert who had helped with the restoration and, two years earlier, had tried his level best to teach me how to fly the thing.

'Sir George Cayley was a true pioneer in his day,' I told assembled journalists, 'just as Burt Rutan is in the modern day. The technologies used in the design and development of the *Virgin Atlantic GlobalFlyer* will help shape the future design of commercial aircraft.'

At the time, few in the press appreciated the technical work that had gone into the *GlobalFlyer*, or understood its significance. But times have changed.

In 1906, the Swedish physicist Svante August Arrhenius published *Worlds in the Making*, the first account of the 'greenhouse effect'. He was the first person to predict that emissions of carbon dioxide from burning would cause global warming.

The air around us is warmed by the sun. The air is made up of water vapour and many different gases, and they all heat up at different rates. Carbon dioxide heats up quickly, but it doesn't hold on to this heat indefinitely. Some heat escapes into space, and some of it is reflected back by the earth and reabsorbed by the atmosphere. So carbon dioxide works like a blanket. The thicker the blanket, the warmer the earth.

Arrhenius thought the greenhouse effect would turn out to be a good thing. The more humans there were, the more carbon dioxide there would be in the air, the warmer the earth, the faster things would grow – which in turn would allow the increasing human population to feed itself. Arrhenius's description of a feedback loop between human activity and climate change sounds startlingly modern, except in one crucial respect. He estimated that carbon dioxide levels were doubling every 3,000 years. Today they're doubling every century.

Humans today are responsible for only 5.5 per cent of the planet's total CO_2 emissions. Humans pump 30 gigatonnes of carbon into the atmosphere every year; living things as a whole pump out a staggering 550 gigatonnes. The trouble is, the feedback loops that maintain our climate are exquisitely sensitive. Fractional changes in the amount of CO_2 in the atmosphere are enough to change our climate for ever.

We know, for sure, that human beings are changing the climate. This surely can't come as a surprise. What other species do you know that starts fires? We burn stuff. We have done so for around 1.8 million years. There are many more of us now than there were 1.8 million years ago. We burn stuff and use the energy to power our industries. Most of these industries are essential: they keep us alive. Burning stuff cleans our drinking water, it cultivates, distributes and prepares our food, it clothes and cleans us and makes our medicines.

So it's not so surprising to learn that an industry like aviation – an industry we *could* conceivably do without – generates only 2 per cent of all industrial emissions – or less than 0.5 per cent of human carbon emissions taken as a whole. Another industry we could conceivably do without is information technology. You may feel this would be harder for us to sacrifice; so you won't be surprised to hear that IT releases twice as much carbon into the air as aviation. The industries that make a huge difference to our carbon output are the ones essential to life.

I believe that industries like aviation can actually provide us with the solution to global warming, by developing the technologies that the really vital, dirty industries like agriculture and power generation can then adopt and adapt for themselves. This is why I committed to ploughing our share of the profits and dividends from Virgin's transport businesses into initiatives such as the Virgin Green Fund, which invests in and develops new forms of sustainable and renewable fuels and energy sources. The real, global benefits will come once other industries take what we have developed and make it work for them. And let's be clear about the scale of the problem: reducing the amount of carbon we release into the atmosphere may not be enough to save us. If Lovelock's right, we will actually have to take carbon out of the atmosphere!

According to Lovelock, if we want to maintain our current climate, we will have to start capturing more carbon than we emit. So the Holy Grail for us right now is a commercially viable product that takes carbon out of the atmosphere. It's essential that the product not only works, but makes good business sense. Good ideas are never enough. They have to catch on. They have to make sense, not just to you and me, but to people all over the world, regardless of whether they believe in global warming or not, regardless of whether they care, regardless of whether they know carbon from a hole in the ground.

On 9 February 2007 I announced the Virgin Earth Challenge: $25 million will go to the individual or group that demonstrates a commercially viable design which will result in the net removal of atmospheric greenhouse gases each year for at least ten years, without harmful effects. The Virgin Earth Prize is the largest purse in history.

The *GlobalFlyer*, the Green Fund and the Earth Challenge were the headline-grabbing parts of a strategy Will Whitehorn and I have been developing for the Virgin Group since the early 1990s. We didn't begin it out of a concern for the environment. Back then we were much more concerned about the survival of Virgin. The rocketing cost of aviation fuel had got us spooked; we realised that our long-term success depended on us coping with high fuel prices.

The first thing we did was calculate when the oil was going to run out. More accurately, we worked out when there would be no more cheap fuel. (There will always be fossil fuels somewhere under the ground, but they won't always be the sort that are cheap to extract.) Thanks to the work of an expert called Jeremy Leggatt, we came up with a date that, at the time, no one else believed. We put our money on 2015.

As the years have gone by, we've had more accurate figures to work with. The global recession that began in 2008 has slowed consumption slightly. But our original figure has hardy budged: by the middle of the decade, *if not before*, the oil we have left under the ground will become much more expensive to extract. Other forms of power will be cheaper.

Together with a few other companies including Stagecoach, Scottish & Southern and Arup we formed a task force to study the issues around Peak Oil and have produced two reports encouraging the Government to speed up the development of the UK's renewable energy capabilities

At Virgin we've gone all out to develop companies and infrastructure that will operate well in a low-carbon economy. The other day, for example, I proposed a £1 billion investment in the British rail system, taking to the next stage the low-carbon technology already in proven service on the UK's West Coast Main Line.

This isn't the place to go into more detail – if you're interested, my book of business advice *Business Stripped Bare* has some more information. Suffice it to say, from the middle of the decade, we're going to be living in a less-carbon economy *whether we like it or not.* The question is: what's this economy going to look like? Will our future have smart grids and wind turbines and next-generation nuclear power stations and solar panels and well-insulated houses and synthetic fuels and miracle batteries? Or will it have rising infant mortality, social decay and global water wars?

I know these are heavy matters to bring up in a book that's about adventures in aviation. But I want to show you how our industry and our brightest minds are reacting to the crisis. If this were just a matter of lighter planes and better fuels, it wouldn't make much of an adventure story. The reality is much more exciting, and much more controversial. There's a revolution going on in aviation, and a new race for space, and I think these changes and experiments may just hold the key to our future.

ten

Back to the Future

It was 1984 and I was poring over every conceivable detail of my new airline, Virgin Atlantic. We were decorating the Upper Class lounge in Heathrow, and we needed something for the walls. I decided that we'd put up pages from a comic I remembered reading as a child in the 1950s: stories of a future in which men and women flew into space on board ships not much bigger than Second World War bombers; where ordinary men and women were pioneers and explorers, and outer space offered people prosperity and freedom.

I remember walking into the lounge when it was done and being confronted with these lovely colour reproductions of my childhood hero, Dan Dare, in his boiler suit and fishbowl helmet. I remember thinking: 'This isn't enough.'

Just over a decade later, the excitement around private space was hotting up and Will Whitethorn and I wanted to know what was out there, so we set up Virgin Galactic. The company was, at this stage, little more than a formality – a way of keeping the Virgin Group paperwork straight. Virgin Galactic was Will and I wandering around the Mojave desert in our shirtsleeves, talking to a bunch of rocket nuts.

One day in March 1999 Will went off to register the name. He called me later the same day. 'Richard, you didn't tell me.'

'What?'

'Did you forget?'

'What, Will?

'You'd already registered the Virgin trademark signature logo for space!'

The first really interesting launch vehicle Will and I studied was a rocket-powered helicopter called the Roton, which was developed in the late 1990s. On paper, at least, the Roton had real charm. To understand it, take a garden hose up to the roof of your house and let one end of the hose dangle in your fishpond. Spin the other end around your head. Soon water will be gushing out all around you and your fish will be in trouble.

American inventor Bevin McKinney wanted to take a rotary pump into space. Roton was a space capsule with four rotor blades stuck on top. At the tip of each rotor was a rocket, fed from a tank at the bottom of the capsule. On lift-off, the rockets spun the blades, lifting the capsule into the sky. This is clever, because in the atmosphere, spinning a rotor is a much more efficient way of getting off the ground than merely blasting a rocket underneath you. Even better, the spin of the rotor siphons fuel from the tanks, doing away with the complicated and heavy fuel pumps that weigh down conventional rockets.

Eventually the capsule reaches heights where the rotors won't work, because there just isn't enough air to provide lift. At this point, the rotors swivel down and blast the capsule into space. A little of the thrust is used to keep the rotors spinning, and the fuel flowing, and that spin helps stabilise the capsule as it rises. Before re-entry, the blades are folded away, and deployed again once the air is thick enough to provide decent resistance.

The capsule whirls down to the ground gently, like a helicopter. Beautiful. Only it didn't work.

It was elegant and simple on paper, but horribly complicated to do. The Roton people – a company called, logically enough, Rotary Rocket – very kindly let Will take the controls of an early test capsule, to see how the thing handled in helicopter mode. One touch of the controls was enough to tell Will, an experienced and practical airman, that the project would never fly. It was very sad.

Good on paper: Rotary Rocket tried to send a helicopter into space.

Will wasn't the only interested party on Rotary Rocket's doorstep in 1999: the aeroplane designer Burt Rutan was there as well. I remember Will, Burt and me chewing over the Roton project in the Voyager Restaurant at Mojave Air and Space Port. I've known Burt since the 1990s, when he was designing the capsule for the *Earthwinds* balloon project. But Will had never met Burt before, and was doing a passable impression of Walt Disney's Tigger, scribbling these X-15-style rocketplanes on napkins and waving them under Burt's nose.

Three years later, Will and Burt got to play for real stakes, when Virgin Atlantic agreed to share with Steve Fossett the cost of developing what would become the *Virgin GlobalFlyer*. By this time Will had been joined by Alex Tai, a captain in Virgin Atlantic, and, yes, another rocket nut. On one occasion Alex and

Will looked in at Scaled Composites to see how the *GlobalFlyer* was getting along and got more than they bargained for. Much more.

Will phoned me first. 'With all due respect to Steve Fossett,' he said, 'fuck the *GlobalFlyer*.'

'I'm sorry?'

'Burt Rutan is building a spaceship.'

When I saw Neil Armstrong step on to the Moon, I thought: 'This is only the beginning.' I was nineteen years old, and had grown up imagining that everyone my age would have the chance to travel into space. Obviously, seeing that historic footfall made a deep impression on me. Over the years, the people I have been most drawn to in my life – my best friends and closest colleagues – have revealed themselves to be closet (and not-so-closet!) rocket nuts.

Word for word, this is what Will Whitehorn has said about the matter: 'The first thing I remember about space was when I was nine years old. I was sitting in front of a black-and-white television in Edinburgh watching Buzz Aldrin and Neil Armstrong on the moon, and my mum said to me, "One day you'll be flying into space, Willie."'

HERE MEN FROM THE PLANET EARTH
FIRST SET FOOT UPON THE MOON
JULY 1969, A. D.
WE CAME IN PEACE FOR ALL MANKIND

NEIL A ARMSTRONG
ASTRONAUT

MICHAEL COLLINS
ASTRONAUT

EDWIN E. ALDRIN, JR.
ASTRONAUT

RICHARD NIXON
PRESIDENT, UNITED STATES OF AMERICA

NASA astronauts placed this plaque on the Moon in 1969. Who will read it next?

Sounds familiar? Will and Alex and I are not alone. We are *far* from alone. An entire generation grew up thinking that space travel was just around the corner. Now, thanks to Peter Diamandis, it is.

In 1994, Dr Peter Diamandis got given a copy of Charles Lindbergh's book, *The Spirit of St Louis*. In it Lindbergh describes, in detail, how his team worked towards winning the Orteig Prize. Peter is another rocket nut. All his life he has dreamed of getting into space. For most of his life, his dream was just that: a fantasy – something not to make too much noise about over the dinner table, or in front of the interview panel; something slightly embarrassing. (In many quarters, it still is.) Lindbergh's book changed Peter's life. He realised that his lifelong dream of travelling into space could be made real: what he needed was a prize similar to the one Lindbergh won when he flew a plane across the Atlantic.

On 18 May 1996, under the Arch in St Louis, the first X Prize competition was announced: a $10 million purse for the first non-government organisation to launch a reusable manned spacecraft into space twice within two weeks.

Now, at this stage, the purse didn't have any actual *money* in it. Peter's innovation was to realise that anyone can fund a prize. His job – and the job of the X Prize Foundation – was to identify the best prizes: the ones that would inspire serious effort, transform or create a new industry, and change the world for the better.

The idea had legs: in May 2004, the X Prize was officially renamed the Ansari X, to reflect a whopping multimillion-dollar donation from the Iranian-American Ansari family. The Ansaris, who'd amassed their fortune through their telecommunications business, were looking to move into space. For Anousheh Ansari in particular, this was much more than a business decision: as well as backing the X Prize, in 2006 she became the first female space tourist, flying aboard a Soyuz spacecraft for an eight-day stay on the International Space Station.

Big, international, headline-grabbing prizes like the Orteig and the Ansari X create hope and inspiration. The day a prize is launched, people stop asking whether something can be done; they start asking *when* it will be done. By the time the $10 million prize was awarded, later in 2004, more than *$100 million* had been invested in new technologies in pursuit of the prize. Now that's what I call a return on investment!

Burt Rutan had been tooling around with spaceship ideas since 1994. He had already built a fighter plane in his garage, adapting Saab's 1962 Viggen design for the home-build market. From where he was standing, a spaceship didn't seem a much taller order. He remembered X-15 flights from his time at Edwards; he knew who to call to fit enough power into a light enough fuselage to get a vehicle into space. The only problem – and it was a problem that was going to take him years to solve – was how to get the blessed thing down in one piece.

Escaping the Earth's atmosphere takes speed: the X-15 flew at seven times the speed of sound. To get into orbit you need to hit Mach 25! However neatly you finesse your flight path, you're always going to be coming back into the Earth's atmosphere at a good lick – and certainly faster than the speed of sound. If your own engines don't push you past the sound barrier, gravity will. You've a long way to fall and plenty of time to pick up speed.

Now, a spaceplane that can survive a Mach 7 ascent can cope with an equally fast descent – just so long as it's pointing the right way. That, as the X-15's test pilots discovered, was the difficulty.

Once the X-15 left the Earth's atmosphere, its control surfaces no longer had any air to work against. Wiggling the flaps and the rudder could do nothing to stop it rolling or spinning or cartwheeling nose-over-tail. So that it could orient itself in the

When I saw Neil Armstrong **step on to the Moon,** I thought: **'This is only the beginning.'**

vacuum of space the X-15 was equipped with rocket nozzles. So far, so good. The difficulty for the pilot was to pitch the X-15 at exactly the right angle for the descent, so that when he *did* hit the Earth's atmosphere, his plane's control surfaces would work again. The angle of descent had to be perfect, down to fractions of a degree. If it wasn't, the plane – once it hit the air – would become unmanoeuvrable, or it would go into a spin, or worse. In November 1967 one of the X-15's test pilots, Mike Adams, confused his controls and got the angle of his descent badly wrong. He hit the Earth's atmosphere broadside on, and his plane exploded into fragments, killing him instantly.

For years, whenever Burt thought about building a spaceship, he would remember Mike Adams, he would remember the complex systems that had been developed to inject a descending spacecraft back into the Earth's atmosphere – and his heart would sink. Such automatic systems were way beyond anything he wanted to handle. Hell, they were way beyond anything NASA or the Russians wanted to handle! Whether you flew Mercury, Gemini, Soyuz or Apollo, you descended the same way: simply and crudely. You weren't, God forbid, given any kind of *plane*. Instead, you sat strapped into a capsule that descended through the atmosphere blunt-end first, picking up heat as it went. A thick, heavy metal shield absorbed the heat of re-entry. Once the craft reached a thick enough portion of the atmosphere, it released a parachute. If the parachute held, you survived. If it didn't, nor did you. In April 1967 Yuri Gagarin's friend and compatriot Vladimir Komarov died aboard *Soyuz One* when his parachute failed to open.

For all the work and design improvements that have gone into chutes over the past two hundred years and more, parachuting remains a high-risk sport. A few years ago I lost my good friend Alex Ritchie in a skydiving accident, and there was the one occasion when I damn near killed myself during a jump, when I somehow contrived to jettison my main parachute. Skydiving is a thrilling and worthwhile pastime; but you wouldn't ever expose the general public to those kinds of risks, or carry civilians into space, if parachutes were their only means of re-entry.

Burt Rutan was stuck. When Peter Diamandis announced the X Prize, in 1996, the best he could come up with on his own was a glorified capsule-and-parachute system. He did, though, build an experimental launch vehicle, called *Proteus*. This early version of a first-stage launcher – a launcher with nothing to launch! – tantalised the more far-sighted of Burt's colleagues. Among them was Scaled Composites engineer Cory Bird, who remembers he spent the year 2000 bugging Burt almost constantly about how they just *had* to build a spaceship – *somehow*.

Bird came up with design after design in an attempt to create an air brake – some 'feathery thing' that would slow a descending spaceship through the air in a way that wouldn't rip it apart. Eventually, Burt caught the bug. He too would be caught doodling 'feathery things' at every available opportunity. Shuttlecock-like air brakes covered restaurant napkins, charity-event programmes, and any scrap of paper that passed within his reach – until one night, in the middle of the night, Burt shattered his wife Tonya's sleep, shouting, 'I've got it! I've got it!'

Burt had come across the solution to the re-entry problem long before. As a kid, he used to fly model aircraft that operated without any remote controls. They just took off and flew. They had timers to bring them to earth after a few minutes' operation. The timers would lift the horizontal stabilisers on the wings to a forty-five degree angle – and the models would stop flying and float to the ground. Tilting the stabilisers turned them into massively efficient air brakes.

As I mentioned earlier, there is no point at which the Earth's atmosphere magically stops and space begins. The air simply gets thinner and thinner the higher you go. Now, if Burt could create an air brake efficient enough to slow his spaceship down when it was still at a *very* high altitude, and passing through *extremely* thin air, the slower his spacecraft would be travelling when it started hitting the atmosphere proper. To put it simply, he realised how to turn a whole spaceship into a giant shuttlecock. Overnight, Burt Rutan knew he could win the X Prize.

These days, Burt's SpaceShip series is synonymous with the Virgin brand: we share a vision of how the first commercial space operations will work (more on that in a moment), and Virgin has backed – to the tune of $100 million – the development of the *WhiteKnightTwo–SpaceShipTwo* launch system. Nevertheless, the man who first stumped up the money, some $26 million of it, to turn *SpaceShipOne* from a drawing on a napkin into a fire-breathing reality was Paul Allen, a rock guitarist and science-fiction fan who also just happens to be the co-founder of Microsoft and one of the most technology-minded philanthropists in the world. Getting somehow involved in the space race had been one of Paul's longest-held ambitions. Even before the X Prize was announced, he had fallen in love with Burt Rutan's hands-on, can-do approach, and had agreed to back his 'home-build' spaceship.

Burt Rutan's launch system came in two parts. There was the first stage: *WhiteKnight*, a carrier aircraft designed to lift a payload up to around 53,000 feet and then drop it into the air. Then there was the payload, *SpaceShipOne*, a rocket plane that, once dropped from White Knight, would blast out and up into sub-orbital space, before twirling back to earth.

SpaceShipOne's propulsion system was designed by Tim Pickens, the son of a NASA physicist who worked on the Apollo rockets. Tim's formal education is nothing to write home about, but his garage was crammed with old NASA engine parts and he knew, better than most, what plugged into what. Tim's lifelong devotion to laughing gas as a propellant was first realised in 1994, when he strapped a prototype rocket on to his bicycle. It worked quite well, so he built a new bike and a bigger rocket. That worked even better: the bike accelerated faster than a Porsche!

Tim's hybrid engine for *SpaceShipOne* combines the best elements of the two species of rocket engine first developed by Robert Goddard at the beginning of the twentieth century. It is both a liquid- *and* a solid-fuel rocket. The solid fuel lines the case of the rocket. The liquid oxidiser is sprayed into the motor and ignited. The surface of the solid fuel reacts, combusts and turns to gas. Because the propellants are stored separately, the only place they can ever mix is inside the engine. A leak cannot cause an explosion. Most serious systems failures on rockets over the years have been fatal. Tim's engines are quite different, and very failure-tolerant.

They're cheap: once all the designing and engineering has been done, cranking them out on a production line is a relatively simple business. Even better, they're not dirty. A ride on Virgin *Enterprise* (which uses the same kind of rocket motors) will generate CO_2 emissions less than those generated by a return commercial London–New York flight. Ours is a clean spaceship!

Can we do even better? I don't doubt it. We're already working with *WhiteKnightTwo*'s engine manufacturers, Pratt & Whitney, to upgrade the engines to run entirely on a renewable jet-aviation fuel; and as far as the rocketry goes, the future is very promising. There are all manner of novel propellants out there, at early stages of development. An engine called Alice, for example, developed at Purdue University in Indiana, burns aluminium powder in

A cross-section through the atmosphere (not to scale). Look how far we've travelled since the Wrights flew!

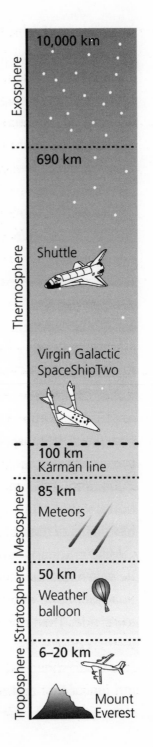

Exosphere

10,000 km

690 km

Thermosphere

Shuttle

Virgin Galactic SpaceShipTwo

100 km
Kármán line

Mesosphere

85 km
Meteors

50 km
Weather balloon

Stratosphere

6–20 km

Troposphere

Mount Everest

water ice, and promises one day to release nothing but hydrogen gas and steam in its exhaust. Imagine it: a steam-driven rocket filled with nothing more than firework powder!

The X Prize required a non-government organisation to launch a reusable manned spacecraft into space twice within two weeks. That meant that two pilots would get a stab at earning their astronaut's wings in *SpaceShipOne*.

Neither man was Burt Rutan's first choice. Scaled's pilot-engineer Pete Siebold, who'd test-flown *SpaceShipOne* to a height of thity-two kilometres, had to bow out after his spleen became so enlarged it could have ruptured during the flight. (Pete's cancer scare proved to be a false alarm. He's back in the programme, and in December 2008 he took *WhiteKnightTwo* for its maiden flight.)

With Pete out of the running it was left to Mike Melvill to board *SpaceShipOne* for its first (pre-X Prize) stab at the Kármán line – on 21 June 2004. This was no small achievement for a man prone to airsickness, and who only learned to fly in the first place because his family box-cutting business needed a travelling salesman! That, mind you, was thirty years before. By 2004, and at the age of sixty-four, Mike had logged over 7,000 hours of flying time in over a hundred kinds of aircraft, including test flights of ten Rutan planes.

Mike's friend and fellow Scaled test pilot Brian Binnie flew *WhiteKnight* to an altitude of 47,000 feet, and dropped *SpaceShipOne* into the air. *SpaceShipOne* promptly rolled on to its side. Then one of its control surfaces jammed. Then there were a couple of loud bangs. Mike hung on – and, incredibly, the spacecraft sorted itself out. After seventy-six seconds, the rocket ran out of fuel and idled down. Mike was shooting upward at over 2,000 mph. All he could do now was hang on and hope

WhiteKnightOne carries *SpaceShipOne* on an early flight.

that this was enough to get him over the Kármán line before gravity finally curved him back towards earth.

He made it – just. The internationally recognised boundary of space is 100 km, or 100,000 metres. The official altitude Mike Melvill set was 100,124 metres. Mike had travelled just 124 metres into space – less than the length of two and a half Olympic swimming pools!

On 29 September *SpaceShipOne*, tethered to its mothership *WhiteKnight*, took off from Mojave Airport's Civilian Aerospace Test Center on its first official X Prize flight. Again, Mike was at the controls as *SpaceShipOne* fell from its mothership, ignited its engines, and blasted 103 kilometres into and out of the air, well past the Kármán line this time.

For the second X Prize flight, another pilot would be given the chance to earn his astronaut wings; and Brian Binnie just could not believe his luck.

Brian's early years were spent in Aberdeen. When he was fourteen the family moved to Boston, and after college Brian spent twenty years as a naval aviator. He had always hankered to be an astronaut, and got his first taste of true rocket science when a friend hooked him up with the people at Rotary Rocket. From there, he moved next door, to Scaled Composites, became one of Burt's most trusted and well-liked test pilots, and got to take *SpaceShipOne* thirteen miles into the air on its maiden powered flight, on 17 December 2003.

Then he crashed it. It wasn't a *bad* crash – more of a hard landing – but it broke the left landing strut. This close to the X Prize flights, Brian believed he would never be trusted behind the controls again.

Mike Melvill reckoned Brian deserved another chance. He worked out a way of setting the controls of another Rutan aeroplane – the Long-EZ – in such a way as to perfectly simulate the landing behaviour of *SpaceShipOne*. Mike and Brian even cut out cardboard masks to give the Long-EZ cockpit the look and feel and restricted view of the *SpaceShipOne* cabin. Now, it was up to Brian.

Eighty-four approaches and landings later, Brian was ready, and Mike said so, long and loud. The day after Mike's successful X Prize flight, Burt announced the name of the second pilot. Brian Binnie was going to earn his wings, after all.

On 4 October 2004, Brian took *SpaceShipOne* nine kilometres further than Mike had, set a new altitude record for a rocket plane, and won the X Prize.

*

'I'm not at all embarrassed that we're opening up a new . . . multibillion-dollar industry that's focused only on fun.'

Burt Rutan

Virgin Galactic's job is to turn the incredible intellectual achievements and acts of personal heroism we've seen lighting up the skies of Mojave and elsewhere, and turn them into a business. In April 2005, Burt Rutan spoke to US lawmakers about our plans: 'I'm not at all embarrassed that we're opening up a new . . . multibillion-dollar industry that's focused only on fun,' he told a congressional committee. Every new technology goes through an early, playful phase. Personal computers started life in amusement arcades. The first helicopters were propelled by rubber bands. The first aeroplane-propulsion system was a child's fist. The first passenger plane journeys were joyrides that landed from where they took off. Right now, space's playful phase is taking two forms – and we reckon only one of them has a future.

Some companies are saving money and development time by using twentieth-century technology – rocket boosters and the like – to blast people into space at their own risk. The journey will either be astronomically expensive – the Soviets offered to take me to the International Space Station for a princely $30 million! – or it will be unsafe and uncomfortable. One Danish outfit I know of is offering to strap you inside a capsule the size and shape of a coffin, from which you will be able to squint at space through a plexiglas porthole!

The rest of us have set ourselves much more work, but our approach will, we believe, create a sustainable market, giving us a real future in space. We are developing technologies safe enough to offer passengers the same warranties as any other travel company.

Burt wrote: 'We believe a proper goal for safety is the record that was achieved during the first five years of commercial scheduled airline service which, while exposing the passengers to high risks by today's standards, was more than 100 times as safe as government manned space flight.' Doing this costs money – so no one should be too surprised by the high price tag of our initial flights, or too worried. Once we're up and running, we want to push the fare down as far and as fast as we can. Of course we do: we'll make more money that way. There's no point being an industry leader unless you put your industry within people's reach.

Burt and his team are working to hand-build our launch system. I do mean hand-build: there's a lovely clip on YouTube at the moment showing the fuselage of *Virgin Enterprise* being assembled. It's so light, when they need to move the thing, the crew simply pick it up and walk! In such a learn-as-you go endeavour, things get tried, then changed, then tried again. This is why we never put firm dates on anything. Our *WhiteKnightTwo*, christened *Eve* after my mother, has already flown, and it's likely that we'll be flying paying passengers by 2011 or 2012. We'll be the first to do so, and for a long time offering our passengers the best experience money can buy.

Our competitors are working hard and they have their own ideas about how this business will develop, which makes comparisons between us difficult, if not impossible. When Yuri Gagarin became the first man in space, NASA astronaut John Glenn said, 'Now that the Space Age has begun, there's going to be plenty of work for everybody.' Let me introduce you to a few of the hardest workers.

When their beloved Heath-Robinson space-helicopter failed them, Rotary Rocket went through an extraordinary transformation. A bunch of engineers and project heads rethought their dreams of space travel from the ground up and came up with Xcor Aerospace, a company that makes cheap, reliable engines and intends one day to use them to put a rocket plane into sub-orbital space.

People say Xcor are our closest competition. This is unfair on Xcor, since it implies that they're a kind of cut-rate Virgin Galactic. Consider: they're charging less than half the price we're charging, for a shorter flight, on a less powerful spacecraft called the Lynx, for less time, and no opportunity to float around in zero gravity . . . All this is true. But the more differences you list – Xcor's passenger gets to wear a spacesuit, Virgin Galactic's passengers don't have to; Xcor's passenger sits beside the pilot and gets a wrap-around view, Virgin Galactic's passengers float around a cabin looking out of portholes; and so on – the more you realise that comparing such unlike offerings is really rather silly.

Xcor made the difference between us explicit in February 2009 when they announced that their $95,000 tickets would *not* take you past the Kármán line – or, indeed, anywhere near it. Rather than take you into space, Xcor wants to give you a thrilling X-15 experience. They'll give you a pilot's-eye view of the Earth some forty miles up, followed by a thrilling 4G descent back to earth. A Lynx flight is not a cut-price anything, but a brilliantly conceived ride in its own right.

Is it enough to sustain them in business? We have our doubts, but the honest answer is that nobody knows. Xcor's business model is quite different from Virgin Galactic's. Xcor doesn't want to be a travel company. It's a spacecraft manufacturer. It will lease its Lynx planes to whoever wants to operate them. If rides on the Lynx fail to capture the public imagination, Xcor will take a big hit – but it will probably live to fight another day. Because Xcor concentrates on manufacturing planes, it can mix and match its technologies to build new craft to satisfy new markets as they emerge. The Lynx itself grew out of a racing jet built for a new sport-aviation venture called the Rocket Racing League. And Xcor fully intends to build an orbital spaceplane – using mostly Lynx Mark I parts – once there's an operator around who might start leasing such a vehicle.

Xcor have taken the giant leap into orbit and they've broken it down into chunks. They plan to get into orbit one small step at a time. It's a fascinating idea: a sort of privatised version of the USAF's X-Plane programme, and very much in the home-build spirit.

Xcor are taking small sensible steps into space. Elon Musk, who made a fortune from the sale of the Internet company PayPal, hasn't their patience. He set up Space Exploration Technologies (SpaceX for short) with just one aim in mind: getting to Mars.

Then he discovered that launching his beloved Mars lander would cost two and a half times more than *building* it. The penny dropped: nothing will ever come of our dreams of space until we have developed a cheap launch system. Elon has since spent around £100 million of his own money developing cheap rockets. It was money well spent. The going rate for launching a payload into orbit is currently around $40 million. SpaceX can do it for less, using their super-reliable Falcon 1 rocket.

This kind of operation sounds miles away from the home-build scene; but appearances are deceptive. When Elon went in search of a chief engineer, he went first to the Reaction Research Society. Founded in the 1940s, the RRS is America's oldest rocketry club. Some of the brightest aerospace minds in the US are members. The RRS put Elon on to Tom Mueller. After countless nights and weekends tinkering about in his garage, Mueller – a propulsion engineer at the California firm TRW – had just relocated to a friend's warehouse, where he was putting the finishing touches to his invention: the world's largest ever amateur liquid-fuelled rocket. Spacecraft don't get more home-built than this!

When Elon visited Tom and saw what he was working on, he had only one question: 'Can you build something bigger?' Today, Tom Mueller has a new job title: possibly the coolest ever conceived. He is SpaceX's vice president of propulsion.

Just before Christmas 2008, Tom and SpaceX got their big break, winning a $1.6 billion deal to resupply the International Space Station when NASA retires its Space Shuttle. It's a brave decision by NASA: if SpaceX delivers late, then only the Russians will have the ability to maintain the station. But it's the right decision. A Space Shuttle flight costs three to four times as much as a Falcon flight, and its safety record is, to say the least, poor. NASA are finally coming to grips with the fact that they're far better off putting orbital operations out to tender.

Coming up with countless small innovations in sub-orbital and near-orbital space is the sort of thing private companies, in competition with each other, can do extremely well. Like Britain's Royal Aircraft Establishment during and after the Second World War, NASA is at its best when it thinks in the long term. The nuts and bolts of its enterprise are much better left to the private sector. It's a tragedy that NASA's fascinating and valuable planetary fly-bys, mapping missions, Mars landings and all the rest have had to be conducted on the slenderest of shoestrings, while billions are swallowed by projects like the International Space Station – structures that are obsolete even before they are complete.

What of SpaceX's ultimate ambitions? It rather gave the game away when it started putting windows in its cargo capsules! SpaceX engineers reckon a crew of seven could travel comfortably into orbit aboard their new Falcon 9 rocket, due to launch in 2010. All they need is somewhere to visit.

Enter Robert Bigelow.

Robert has some unorthodox ideas about how to spend the fortune he made from his hotel chain, Budget Suites of America. In the spring of 1999 he came across an article about a radical new kind of space station called Transhab. A Transhab space station is made of inflatable modules. They're big, and they fit together: two of them boast an interior volume greater than that afforded by the International Space Station. A year later, when the US Congress killed the programme, Robert stepped in. To say that Robert's suddenly declared interest in space came as a surprise is putting it mildly. 'I didn't even tell my wife,' he remembers. 'She never knew. Because it's possible that that kind of dream would never happen.'

In July 2006, a one-third-scale test module called *Genesis I* was carried into orbit on a Russian rocket. It was filled with mementoes belonging to Bigelow Aerospace employees. It unfurled, powered up and sent video pictures back to Earth, from

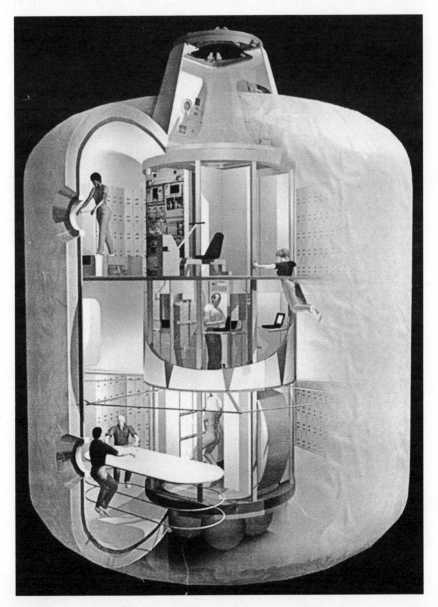

An artist's (rather earnest) impression of life aboard a Transhab module.

inside and outside the module. When I first saw these pictures, I couldn't decide which was more moving: the spectacular view of our Earth from orbit, or the photographs of children and loved ones I glimpsed spinning weightless in their new home, high above the earth. *Genesis II* was successfully launched on 28 June 2007, carrying trinkets from visitors to the company's website.

Robert's plan is to launch a fully operational, inflatable space station in orbit as a destination for space tourists by 2012. A four-week stay will set you back $15 million – that's half the price the Russians wanted to charge me to visit the ISS. Right now, what he needs most urgently is a way of getting his clients into orbit and aboard his hotel. He needs commercial orbiters. His Space Prize – announced just a month after Brian Binnie flew *SpaceShipOne* to X Prize glory – offered $50 million to anyone who could build a credible private shuttle.

The prize has yet to be claimed.

Epilogue

Joyriding

'What is the use of a newborn child?'
Benjamin Franklin, on being asked what was the
point of the Montgolfier brothers' invention

On Thursday, 16 June 1960, Joe Kittinger got his wish.

The ace American test pilot, whose love of free-falling and parachuting had put the fear of God into David Simons's Manhigh team, was finally ready to pull the ripcord on the grandest, craziest, most dangerous high-altitude experiment ever conceived.

The US Air Force project, called Excelsior, was begun in 1958, to test pressure suits and ejection systems for pilots travelling in the upper stratosphere. Without some kind of pressurised life-support system, ejecting from a plane at such heights brought you no chance of survival. Even free-falling wouldn't bring you down quickly enough into safe, breathable air. (Kittinger's own assessment: 'You're gonna be a dead son of a bitch.') So Excelsior designed and tested kit to keep pilots alive outside the Earth's atmosphere.

They developed the first space suits. Like most prototypes, they were cleverly designed, lovingly crafted, and not very reliable.

Kittinger piloted all the Excelsior flights, culminating in *Excelsior III*, which launched on 16 August 1960. The ascent – achieved, as usual, with a Winzen-designed helium balloon – was flawless. At 50,000 feet, however, Kittinger noticed that his suit had sprung a leak. When he squeezed his right hand into a fist, the glove offered no resistance. Now he could feel his hand begin to swell. He had no way of telling how serious the leak would become. Soon his hand would lose all function. Then what? He thought, quite simply, that he was going to die.

The ground crew, listening to Kittinger's reports from the edge of space, intuited that something was badly wrong. Kittinger was a joker, and here he was extemporising a sober and beautiful poetry. At 103,000 feet, with 99 per cent of the Earth's atmosphere below him, he declared: 'As you look up the sky looks beautiful but hostile. As you sit here you realise that Man will never conquer space. He will learn to live with it, but he will never conquer it.'

By now his right hand was useless: a balloon. But he was still alive, still able to conduct the experiment to which he and the Excelsior team had devoted years of their lives. What else could he do? He dragged himself to the opening of the gondola. He could see the earth curving below him, wrapped up in a thin blue trace of sky. 'Lord,' he said, too soft for anyone but the flight recorder to hear, 'take care of me now.' And he jumped.

People like Joe Kittinger make the future possible. Without Joe and people like him, there would have been no American space programme, no visits to the Moon, no space station and no Hubble telescope. There would be no space industry, and our ideas – even the modest pleasure rides of Virgin Galactic – would be mere pipe dreams.

Closer to home, the same truth applies: without the bravery and skill of *SpaceShipOne*'s test pilots Brian Binnie and Mike Melvill there would be no *Virgin Enterprise*. It's *Virgin Enterprise* that will be carrying Virgin Galactic's passengers into space and offering a view of the Earth as it really is: a living, independent thing; a ball without borders.

Those passengers, too, will be pioneers, as surely as was Amelia Earhart when she rode (like 'a sack of potatoes') across the Atlantic in 1928. At $200,000 a ticket, our astronauts are bankrolling the first ever commercial spaceliner – and then staking their lives on its safe operation.

Virgin Galactic's ticket prices will drop as the years go by. As we clock up more flights, public trust in the system – already the most thoroughly tested system in the history of commercial aerospace – will increase. At what point will our pioneers consider themselves mere 'passengers'? Not, I'd wager, in my lifetime. Space is big and empty and waiting for ideas. It is our new frontier. Those who fly with us will do so because they have a vision of what the future might hold there. Who knows which of these visions will be realised by my children's generation?

A decade hence, Virgin Galactic flights will be regular, if not commonplace. Picture it: the year is 2020 and we're coming in to land, lining up with the airstrip at Spaceport America in New Mexico. The terminal building bulges out of the desert like a great, blue, unblinking eye. It screams the future. It is beautiful, but it is not subtle. It is a building Dan Dare might recognise. Why not? This is Dan Dare's future we're building here, after all: a future in which everyone has a chance at space.

We're making our final approach now. Imagine: the plane bucks as it descends through fierce thermals rising from the desert floor. Then it steadies, cushioned by a few final feet of warm, steadily rising air.

In the beginning, virtually everyone flew here by private plane. The communications weren't great: there was no public transport and not nearly enough demand for any. This is changing. Since we dropped the ticket prices – imagine this – we're starting to carry passengers from more ordinary walks of life. People who are staking their life savings on a trip into space. These are not people who habitually charter their own aircraft. These days we pick up many of our passengers in limousines from the airport at Las Cruces.

Then there are the sightseers: people who have come from all over the world to watch our launches, as weekend vacationers once flocked to Croydon to watch film stars, dignitaries and politicians board the first ever passenger services across the Atlantic. Most of these people drive to see us, and already a handful of coach companies are operating sightseeing tours. How long before Spaceport America needs a railhead?

Our plane is still riding its warm-air cushion. Desert landings are famously drawn-out, as though the air is determined to keep us aloft. As we hurtle past the terminal building (just how long is this runway, anyway?) we catch our first glimpse of the machine that will carry us into space. Imagine two corporate jets stuck together at the wing tips. This is *WhiteKnightTwo*, Virgin Galactic's first stage. This plane will carry us to over 50,000 feet in a *SpaceShipTwo*. Then, like an eagle dropping a tortoise – it will let us go . . .

Our wheels hit tarmac at last. The aircraft shivers and trembles. Imagine it: built entirely from composite – a descendant of the

Virgin GlobalFlyer – it's lighter than planes used to be and feels every ripple in the tarmac surface. The engines cut out and the electric front wheel powers up, rolling us in virtual silence back to the terminal. There's that *WhiteKnightTwo* again. From here, against a backdrop of the desert, and with nothing familiar to compare it with, it looks impossibly small. Curiously doubled up it may be, but in essence, it still looks like a business jet.

The sleek, brash lines of Spaceport America wrap themselves around the plane as we near the gate. We come to a standstill and the door opens. The spiced, superheated smell of the desert penetrates the cabin. We'll walk to the terminal; this is not a big place (yet) and there's no need for a shuttle bus.

In the evening, we dine with our fellow astronauts. We've shared briefing sessions and we've been through the same mild medicals, but this is the moment we really bond, as we contemplate tomorrow's flight. Everyone's nervous, so there's plenty of gallows humour. Some wag reminds us of that great newspaper quip, made long before Virgin Galactic started operating: that with a propulsion system powered by rubber pellets and laughing gas, at least we'll all die laughing.

The truth is, people have died to make systems like ours possible. Tried and tested technology is exactly that: someone has tried it and someone has tested it. On 26 July 2007 Eric Blackwell, Glen May and Todd Ivens died and three others were badly injured when part of an experimental propulsion system blew up in their faces. The accident was not caused by a mistake or an oversight. It could not have been predicted or prevented. It took Scaled and the regulatory authorities months of painstaking study to even begin to understand what had gone wrong.

The bottom line is that the men and women of Scaled and other research-and-development companies test their ideas against the world. This is their job and their passion. It's what gets them up in the morning. But the world does not care about passion or goodwill, and it does not pull its punches. When an engineering experiment fails, the result is usually frustration and wasted time. Sometimes, financial trouble follows. Now and again the price is exacted in lives.

None of which makes for a comfortable night's sleep. Virgin Galactic's spaceport is a luxurious place to stay, but it will be a special person indeed who gets a full eight hours' rest tonight. Maybe you have ice-water flowing through your veins. Maybe you're like Gordo Cooper, who actually fell asleep as his Mercury 9 counted down to lift-off. More likely you'll need some kind of sedative, even if it's only hot milk. Per and I used to take sleeping tablets before our balloon flights. Even Joe Kittinger accepted sedation the night before his extreme balloon ascents.

Nothing you try seems to make any difference. After half an hour's tossing and turning you get out of bed and write some letters to your loved ones. You go over to the window. It's a

Watch this space: Spaceport America is now under construction.

full moon tonight. Picture it: for all the many robots crawling about its surface, for all the recent manned missions (China is due to make footfall again in 2020; China in 2024) the Moon remains mysterious and haunting. In October 2009, a probe called LCROSS smashed deliberately into the Moon's surface in a hunt for water ice. Amateur astronomers saw the flash through their telescopes. That flash – that instant of faltering connection – took nothing away from the Moon's mystery. If anything, the mystery was deepened. How strange, that we can cross hundreds of thousands of miles of nothing and find ourselves, at last, touching another world! One day the Moon will sparkle. Cities will etch the new moon's outline. These city lights may even be visible to the naked eye. When that happens, the Moon will seem more mysterious, not less: how strange, that men and women should be living upon the ball of rock that makes the oceans swell and the tides turn!

Moonstruck, you cease to worry about sleep. And that, of course, is the moment you drift into dreams.

Morning comes as a surprise. Today is the day. Today – after only you know how many years of dreaming and striving and saving – you will climb into *SpaceShipTwo*, and for a few precious minutes, leave the planet behind.

After a light breakfast, we dress in lightweight flight suits and prepare for take-off. The cabin of the *SpaceShipTwo* is fully pressurised throughout the flight, so you don't need to wear any heavy or cumbersome gear. All we ask is that you leave your jewellery in your room, since we don't want loose items flying around the cabin during free-fall.

On the apron, our *WhiteKnightTwo* is waiting. If it seemed small yesterday, seen from afar through a plane window, it looks gigantic now. Its wingspan is massive – about the same as a Second World War B-29 Superfortress bomber; added to which, it's acquired a payload. Between its twin fuselages hangs a *SpaceShipTwo*, a strangely bulbous sixty-foot-long spacecraft with curious, articulated wings, fully fuelled and ready to blast us into space from a height of about 53,000 feet.

If the outside of *SpaceShipTwo* looks alien and unlikely, the interior is strangely reassuring – at least, I find it so. It looks like something out of the 1960s, hovering somewhere between a *2001* film set and an Austin Powers out-take. There are portholes everywhere – in the ceiling, walls and floor. The seats are scooped and sculpted, more like shells than airline couchettes.

The interior is not quite the retro design statement it appears to be. Its shape was dictated by a hundred and one very real challenges. Among the most important: how do we give six passengers the freedom of the cabin during free-fall without having them end up in an ungainly heap on landing? How do we give everyone a decent view of the Earth, regardless of the pitch and angle of the spacecraft? How, above all, do we create a safe, comfortable, roomy interior that is, at the same time, light enough to blast into space?

Much of the design work I see being done in the commercial space sector has this retro quality, and for a very good reason: most new things draw inspiration from old ideas. The first hang-gliders would not have baffled Leonardo da Vinci. The first moon rockets would not have puzzled Robert Goddard. Long before we had the right materials to build with, we were drawing up this future for ourselves.

We have reached the *WhiteKnightTwo*'s optimum operating altitude: somewhere between 48,000 and 52,000 feet (we choose the best ceiling on the day). Without drama or fuss, and almost casually, our mothership lets us go. *SpaceShipTwo* drops through the air, a powerless, ballistic mass. A second later, a fierce roar erupts around us as our rocket ignites. Flaming nitrous oxide sprays the rubber lining of our fuel tanks, turning it to gas. The gas escapes: our rocket hurtles forward and up, right through *WhiteKnightTwo*'s flight path and into the purple spaces above the stratosphere.

The acceleration is sharp and sustained, but not painful. There's room to breathe and room to think. There's room to look through the portholes at a sky turning second by second from blue, through indescribable violets and indigoes, to black. Who will spot the first star?

There's room, too, to remember. Here, at this altitude, David Simons spent a day cramped into the world's first space capsule, watching thunderheads gather below him. Here Mike Adams's X-15 touched the edge of space, then tumbled back into the Earth's atmosphere side-on, and flew apart: poor Mike didn't stand a chance.

Here, right here, at this very height, is where Joe Kittinger jumped.

It took Joe and the 320 pounds of extra kit he was wearing nearly a quarter of an hour to fall nineteen and a half miles to earth, twenty-seven miles west of Tularosa, in New Mexico. He punched the ground and sprawled there, a horrible, dusty heap, as helicopters screamed to the scene. As the medics ran up to him, Kittinger managed a smile, dragged himself to his feet and headed over, unassisted, to the press conference. As he spoke to the waiting reporters, the swelling in his right hand gradually subsided.

Twenty-three years later, Kittinger's right hand was as hale and hearty as the rest of him (incredibly the limb, though exposed to the vacuum of space for several hours, made a complete recovery within hours). He was still flying, and he was still setting records.

He set a new gas-balloon world distance record in 1983 and, the following year, was the first to solo across the Atlantic in Rosie O'Grady's *Balloon of Peace*. In 1998 he helped Per, Steve and me plan our round-the-world attempt.

He never fulfilled his grandest ambitions. He never made it into space on a rocket, and he wasn't the first to solo around the world in a balloon. But he's not one to brood. Since retiring from the USAF, Joe Kittinger has returned to his roots and for over twenty years he's been skywriting, towing banners and flying balloons. He's been barnstorming, hurling thrill-seekers about the sky in biplanes, and he says the smiles he gets from them are the smiles he remembers from the fairs of his boyhood, as people queued up in their droves for their first taste of the air.

His preferred aeroplane is a New Standard D-25 crop duster and mail carrier. Built in 1928, it is exactly as old as he is.

It's easy to become impatient in this business, easy to complain about the slow pace of change, especially when so many changes are so desperately needed. Waiting around for synthetic fuels to be developed that are genuinely kind to the environment; hoping against hope that Virgin's airlines can one day take delivery of lightweight, all-composite jetliners – waiting for these things, year after year after year, drives me to distraction. Then I remember Joe Kittinger, born in 1928, who test-flew the first spacesuit in a twenty-mile free-fall over the New Mexico desert. I remember my own mother, doling out oxygen masks to her passengers as her Avro Lancastrian rose above the Andes. I remind myself that the entire history of powered, heavier-than-air flight is not much more than a century old: its span is not much greater than one human lifetime.

What wonders will our children live to see?

*

At an altitude of 109 kilometres, *SpaceShipTwo* tops out of its curve, above the Kármán line. The weight of Earth falls away as the ship describes its slow parabola. It is time, at last, to stop thinking. It is time to release that belt buckle. It is time to fly.

Here is the Earth – see it through that porthole. It is vast. It is not the mere marble in space that so awed the Apollo astronauts. We have barely left our mother planet's arms. We have barely dipped our toe into the ocean that awaits us. These, make no mistake, are the shallows. Enjoy them. Your next flight will take you further still. Bigelow's hotel has been open for business for years now, patiently waiting in orbit for a spaceship to dock and disgorge its first tourist. One day you will travel further still, and visit the Moon – not for pleasure, this time, but for business: you have helium 3 to mine, Mars voyagers to build, cities to survey.

Crossing the line: Brian Binnie's view of Earth from *SpaceShipOne*.

It all depends, I suppose, on how young you are. It all depends how much of a lifetime you've got left, and how you want to spend it. Because this is beyond doubt: there are wonders for the taking up here – if not for us, then for our children.

Picture a world recovering from blight and pollution, its feverish climate cooled by solar shields, its cities and industries powered by solar energy gathered by collecting-surfaces in orbit. Imagine taking heavy industry off the planet entirely and into orbit. Imagine never having to launch another rocket; imagine dangling cables from orbit instead – great ropes of artificial spider-silk, or carbon nanotubes. Imagine catching an elevator into space!

Not one of these ideas is new. Most have been around for donkey's years. Space elevators were first proposed by Konstantin Tsiolkovsky in 1895. Every one of these ideas is brought closer to realisation, year on year, by the development of new materials. Carbon nanotubes are a laboratory reality. The super-lightweight reflective material we need for our giant space mirrors has been commonplace for a while now. We currently make crisp packets out of it.

Why, anyway, do we always end up talking about the future of space? Our present uses of space are extraordinary enough, and we don't celebrate them nearly as much as we should. Following our balloon crossing of the Pacific, Per and I were incredibly lucky not to freeze to death on our lake in the Canadian Rockies (a place they've since rechristened Branson Lake!). The rescue beacon we had installed in our capsule was state-of-the-art, but back then these systems talked, not to satellites, but only to passing aircraft. If a Canadian Air Force Hercules hadn't been within range, we'd have been waiting a lot longer than eight hours to be picked up. These days, were I cast upon a desert island, I could use my mobile phone to bounce a distress message off a passing satellite, and use the same GPS function to look for water sources from space while I was waiting for my rescuers to arrive. Once back in civilisation, my phone could point me towards a decent lunch in virtually any city on earth.

Satellite communications have the most obvious, direct effect on our day-to-day lives. But industries other than telecommunications rely much more profoundly upon satellite technology. Take the always vexed business of how we feed ourselves. The world's population has tripled since I was born. There are three times as many mouths to feed now than there were at the end of the Second World War. We rely on satellite images of the earth to grow enough food for ourselves. We use good local weather forecasts to improve our yields. As agricultural land becomes ever more scarce, and our growing population does ever more damage to the planet, satellite imagery becomes ever more important. It is used to target the application of pesticides and fertilisers, reducing both costs and pollution; it is used to predict and manage changes in land use to minimise the destruction of the natural world; it is used to map the damage done by natural disasters, like Cyclone Nargis, which tore through Myanmar in May 2008, and it is used to predict the fluctuation of global food prices.

Global food supplies are managed using data from space. You hardly need me to tell you that this management is imperfect. The system is riddled with terrible inequities. Without data from space, however, things would be unimaginably worse: about one in ten of us would starve.

How did we get ourselves into this bind, where pictures from space are all that stand between us and mass starvation? The answer is in the numbers: when *2001: A Space Odyssey* hit cinema screens in 1968, there were under four billion people on the planet. Now there are nearly seven billion. When my children get to my age, the earth will be expected to feed around 10 billion people.

Images from space have helped us sustain our rising numbers for years. They have helped feed us, and they have helped us save what little of the natural world we can. Most important of all, though, they have given us – for the first time in our history – an accurate measure of just how much damage we are doing to the planet. Were it not for images from space, there would be no global green movement, no international effort (however faltering) to control greenhouse gases, and no international funding for projects to save the natural environment. We would be walking blindly into the greatest ecological crisis we have ever faced. We would have no idea how soon our way of living will be changing: for better, or for worse.

The truth is this: the earth cannot provide enough food and fresh water for 10 billion people, never mind homes, never mind roads, hospitals and schools. It's not going to happen. Space industries have sustained human beings in unrealistic numbers for years now. But soon – within our children's lifetime – there will have to be a change. Human numbers will be brought under control, one way or another. Either we do something ourselves, or we run out of food. Either way, billions of human beings *will* vanish from the Earth's books.

What can we do? First, we can minimise the damage we are doing to our world. Here, space industries have already proved their worth and will continue to do so. Information technology brings down the number of unnecessary journeys people have to make – at least, that's the theory. Unfortunately, it pumps twice the amount of carbon into the air that commercial aviation does! The good news is that we know already how to relocate the entire IT industry to orbit. Powered by twenty-four-hour, unfiltered sunlight, the world's communications systems could sustain our civilisation from space, and the climate would thank us. (Using today's rocket technology, even the environmental cost of the move would be vanishingly small compared to the long-term gains.)

The trouble is, whether you religiously recycle your cornflakes packet every week, or campaign vigorously to establish solar power stations in orbit, none of your good work is going to do anything to solve the underlying problem, which is that the planet cannot comfortably sustain more than about five billion people. Don't get me wrong: global warming is a real crisis and it needs to be addressed now. But it's nothing like as big a crisis as the one behind it: the prospect of 10 billion inhabitants who survive (and have survived, for around 1.8 million years) mostly by burning stuff.

We should begin to address this problem now. The Chinese have already tried by instituting a 'one child' policy. It has been, in some ways, a success; but it's been accused of ruining many lives and has left the state handling all manner of unexpected social problems. Anyway, getting the whole world to agree to such a policy is a pipe dream. Having children is like eating and breathing and arguing and cooking: it's one of the things we are wired to do. You can't turn human nature off at the tap.

What else might we do? Well, if this planet hasn't the energy to sustain us all, then we will have to draw our power from elsewhere: from solar panels in space, perhaps. If we can move our heavy industries into space, then we might just be able to find the room to grow enough food for ourselves – for a while, at least. Whatever we do, though, the numbers will always be at our back. Our planet is not going to grow any bigger.

Eventually, some of us may choose to live off-world altogether. Again, the idea is far older, far more serious, and far, far more topical than people generally suppose. Stephen Hawking's declared reason for joining us on Virgin Galactic is to promote the idea of space colonisation.

Business trips to the Moon may yet happen in my lifetime. Most likely they'll be to do with mining operations and the extraction of helium 3 for fusion power. NASA wanted to begin construction of its Neil A Armstrong Lunar Outpost in 2019. That programme has been put on hold, but settling the Moon is no longer a one-horse race. The odds are good that when the first NASA astronauts since 1972 finally land on the Moon, the Chinese will be there to greet them. Meanwhile the Indian Space Research Organisation's first lunar probe Chandrayaan-I was launched on 22 October 2008, stacked with helium-3-related scientific apparatus.

Another kind of off-world settlement lies much closer to home. Two-thirds of the planet's surface is covered by water, and yet we have barely begun to explore the oceans. Indeed, we have so far done little but dirty and damage this great and mysterious resource. The Chinese, Russian and American military lead the world in undersea exploration, yet their manned subs cannot descend below a depth of 20,000 feet, and their explorers can barely see out of their craft, let alone interact with the fascinating world they have entered.

A new Virgin company called Virgin Oceanic is currently looking for investment opportunities in the field of deep-sea submersible exploration. Already we've developed good relationships with the 'Burt Rutan of the sea', British inventor Graham Hawkes, whose fourth-generation reef-exploring sub Super Aviator has (as the name implies) adopted avionics for an underwater environment: it literally flies through the sea, providing its pilots with a complete wrap-around view of what surrounds them!

Graham believes a similar layout could be adapted for deep diving, and he does mean deep: the craft Graham is talking about will reach depths of 35,000 feet! Carbon fibre and metal will not stand such pressures; but glass will. Glass is, oddly enough, not a solid; it's a liquid that flows very, very slowly. This gives it extraordinary strength under high pressure. Virgin Oceanic's glass sub is, we hope, the *SpaceShipOne* of our oceanic future. On top of all that, we're is talking to Graham's fiercest competitors: his ex-wife, and her son, each of whom runs an independent company! I can't wait to see how all their efforts play out over the coming years.

Our period of weightlessness is almost up. Mother Earth begins to tug at us, urging us back into our seats. *SpaceShipTwo* prepares to whirl its way, like a sycamore seed, back down into the thick, flyable regions of the Earth's atmosphere. Set against our visions of the future, Virgin Galactic's ride seems modest indeed. But we should never be embarrassed out of our dreams. Long before planes left the ground, Henson and Stringfellow were pricing up international air routes for their civil airline. In the 1920s, biplanes carrying US mail laid the routes for today's domestic passenger services. One of Virgin Galactic's long-term goals is to fly commercial passenger vehicles from continent to continent through sub-orbital space, reducing travel times and carbon-emissions to a fraction of their present levels. To achieve anything at all in this world, your reach has to exceed your grasp.

Wherever we go in the solar system, and however far we reach into the cosmos, we will constantly be inventing new

forms of travel for ourselves and for our machines. The birth
of the Age of Space doesn't spell the end of aviation. Quite the
contrary. Every planet and every moon will set aviators of the
future unique challenges. New flying machines will be invented,
and old ones rediscovered and re-imagined. The great charm of
aviation – and I imagine this is true of other kinds of engineering,
too – is that good ideas never go out of date, and forgotten plans
can always be dusted down and repurposed.

Work has already begun to conquer the skies of Mars. Mars
has a pitifully thin atmosphere. Ordinary planes will have a hard
job riding such sparse 'air', and plans for novel aircraft include
inflatable wings and machines that imitate the flying behaviours
of insects. But existing balloon and airship designs can be made
to function just as well, especially now that their envelope fabrics
can be made photovoltaic, to gather power from sunlight. NASA
is funding a company called Global Aerospace Corporation to
research a Mars 'aerobot' – a robotic airship which will carry a
gondola of scientific equipment and a set of small probes that
can be dropped on to the Martian surface.

Venus sets aircraft designers quite different challenges. The
planet is smothered in clouds, and above this layer aircraft
manage well enough. We know this because in 1986 a joint
Soviet–French mission successfully dropped two helium
balloons into the Venusian atmosphere. The balloons settled
thirty-four miles above the planet's surface, and sent back
weather data. Since Venus is closer to the sun than we are,
we know that future aircraft might be comfortably powered
by solar cells. Designs for Venusian aeroplanes range from the
prosaic to the positively outlandish. My favourite of these is a
'solid state' aeroplane – essentially a single, photovoltaic wing
made of artificial muscle that would fly through the upper

reaches of the Venusian air like a hawk or an eagle!

Getting closer to the planet's surface is difficult. Venus's clouds are pure sulphuric acid. Most of Venus's atmosphere is carbon dioxide – and there's so much of it, the atmospheric pressure at the planet's surface is a staggering ninety-two times that of the Earth. There's so much atmosphere weighing down on you at ground level, it would flatten you to the floor and spread you out like jam. The other effect of all that carbon dioxide is heat – lots of it. On a cloudy day – and it is always a cloudy day – the planet's surface reaches 460 degrees Celsius: hotter than the surface of Mercury. Getting there – and surviving the experience – requires much new thinking. Pasadena's NASA Jet Propulsion Laboratory (JPL) is drawing up an aerobot that simply drops probes on to the surface and listens to what they have to say before the temperature and pressure put them out of action. Another idea involves a reversible-fluid balloon, filled with helium and water, that drops to the surface of Venus to pick up samples, then rises and launches the samples it has gathered aboard small rockets for pick-up by an orbiter.

Happily, most alien environments we're interested in are a lot less challenging than Venus. Titan, the largest moon of Saturn, has a nitrogen and petrochemical atmosphere twice as dense as Earth's. An airship would have no trouble negotiating the smog to study the moon's surface and search for the complex organic stuff we suspect may be hiding down there. Julian Nott – the balloonist who flew above the Nazca Plains in 1975 – reckons conditions there are perfect, enabling balloons to stay aloft for decades. This is no idle speculation, either: for the last five years, Julian's been working with JPL on the detailed design of Titan inflatables!

Titan's parent planet, Jupiter, also lends itself to airship exploration. Jovian airships will be quite unlike their Martian cousins. For one thing, Jupiter is too far away from the sun for them to rely on solar power. Instead, they'll need to gather their energy from the infrared rays emitted by the planet itself. Also, Jupiter's atmosphere is mostly hydrogen, so obviously the balloons couldn't use hydrogen or helium for lift. Jovian airships will have to be of the hot-air type. They will be *montgolfières*. How wonderful that a technology first developed in 1783 might one day prove its worth here, in the outer reaches of our solar system!

We're heading home now, falling slowly towards the earth, spinning like a sycamore seed through the stratosphere. There are no storms here – no warm fronts or cold fronts; no weather. In the stratosphere, warm air rides over cold air, and the temperature drops steadily, down to a bitter minimum of around minus 60 degrees Celsius. At this cold distance, it's easy to imagine that that life on Earth is equally calm, constant and predictable.

Between five and ten miles from the ground, however, something odd happens. The further down through the air we go, the hotter it gets. The bottom-most layers of the atmosphere are warmed by the earth. Heated from below like water on a stove, they tumble and spin. Bodies of warm air thump their way through layers of cold air, while great sinks of cold air plug-hole towards the planet's surface. The rolling winds rub against each other, charging the atmosphere. The night side of the Earth sparkles with lightning. This boisterous bottom part of the atmosphere is the troposphere. It's where the weather lives – and so, most of the time, do we. In this thick and boisterous air, our wings unfold: *SpaceShipTwo* becomes a regular glider.

We're making our final approach now.

Back in the weather, steeped in the rain, fog and ice of the uncertain, everyday world, you can't help but wonder: what will happen? Will any of our dreams come true? Will we truly map other worlds, mine asteroids, tap unlimited power from the Sun? Forecasting the future is a fool's errand. The weather itself is hard enough to fathom. The meteorologist Bob Rice can remember a time – as recently as the 1970s – when the weatherman could do little more than predict the next day's forecast. 'It took us so long to build a twenty-four-hour forecast that we almost didn't have time to do a forty-eight-hour forecast,' he remembers. 'By the time we got to the seventy-two-hour forecast we might just as well have been throwing darts at a board.'

Predicting the air has come on a little way since then. Human weather, though – for all our thought and study and science, we're no closer to understanding its workings. We remain magnificently mysterious to ourselves. Will we, in Joe Kittinger's words, learn to live with space? Will we learn to live *in* space? Or will we remain grounded, collapsing under the burgeoning weight of our own population? Will we break out of Earth's egg – or die in the shell?

The world does not pull its punches. If we get the next 100 years wrong, we will crash, as surely as this spacecraft would crash, were our pilot not clever, committed and awake; were the landing strip not laid out below us, well lit, well maintained and well prepared.

The spaceport is like a great blue unblinking eye below us. Day and night, it stares up at the stars.

In a hundred years, what will it see?

[I]n this age of inventive wonders all men have come to believe that in some genius' brain sleeps the solution of the grand problem of aerial navigation – and along with that belief is the hope that that genius will reveal his miracle before they die, and likewise a dread that he will poke off somewhere and die himself before he finds out that he has such a wonder lying dormant in his brain. We all know the air can be navigated – therefore, hurry up your sails and bladders – satisfy us – let us have peace. And then, with railroads, steamers, the ocean telegraph, the air ship – with all these in motion and secured to us for all time, we shall have only one single wonder left to work at and pry into and worry about – namely, commerce, or at least telegraphic communion with the people of Jupiter and the Moon. I am dying to see some of those fellows! We shall see what we shall see, before we die. I have faith – a world of it.

Mark Twain
Letter to the San Francisco *Alta California*, 1869

Endnotes

Chapter One

Page 18: 'Some have made flying cars...' Needham, 1965.

Page 19: 'For not only many eminent Greeks...' Gellius, 1927.

Page 29: 'We have had birds-eye views...' Vanderbilt, 2002.

Page 30: 'No imagination can paint...' Ibid.

Page 31: 'obtains...unerring tokens...' Mason, 1838.

Page 32: 'We had difficulty hearing each other...' Marion, 1874.

Chapter Two

Page 44: 'While I do not see any evidence...' Nott, 2009.

Page 45: 'Get in a supply of taffeta...' Crouch, 2003

Page 46: 'grew large even under the eyes of the spectator...' Marion, 1874.

Page 49: 'surrounded on all sides by eager multitudes...' Ibid.

Page 50: 'an immense crowd...' Ibid.

Page 50: 'a number of peasants...' Ibid.

Page 51: 'they immediately began to assail it...' Ibid.

Page 53: 'its beautiful emerald colour...' Ibid.

Page 56: 'The dead body of Rozier...' Mason, 1838.

Page 57: 'a machine furnished with oars...' Marion, 1874.

Page 57: 'For my sake, my good friend, reflect...' Ibid.

Page 59: 'The rays of the sun so heated...' Ibid.

Page 59: 'The cold became excessive...' Ibid.

Page 61: 'and in fifteen to twenty minutes I arrived...' Ibid.

Page 61: 'had fitted a sort of ventilator...' Ibid.

Page 62: 'After many vicissitudes...' Ibid.

Page 64: 'All of a sudden, however, it burst into its proper shape...' Mason, 1838.

Page 65: 'especially trained for the purpose' Ibid.

Page 65: 'In [Green's] view, the Atlantic is no more than a simple canal...' Ibid.

Page 68: 'and the wounded, almost crippled travellers' *Harper's*, 1863.

Page 75: 'quite a little airship...' The British Women's Emancipation Movement.

Chapter Three

Page 81: 'They keep telling me I should learn to fly...' *Northern Echo*, 2003.

Page 82: 'Please, Sir George...' Wintle, 2002.

Page 87: 'From the time we were little children...' Culick & Dunmore, 2001.

Page 88: 'My own active interest...' *Journal of the Western Society of Engineers*, volume 6, 1901

Page 93: 'We certainly can't complain of the place...' Crouch, 1990.

Page 95: 'I cut the crankshaft...' *New American Supplement to the Encyclopaedia Britannica*, 1897.

Page 95: 'nothing about a propellor...' Crouch, 1990.

Page 96: 'It is so simple it annoys one...' Crouch, 2003.

Chapter Four

Page 102: 'the United States to fall...' Crouch, 2006.

Page 103: 'It is not beautiful...' Ibid.

Page 105: 'I was entirely ignorant about the activities of our flying men...' Richthofen, 1917.

Page 105: 'The draught from the propellor...' Ibid.

Page 106: 'Whether you're on your back...' Lewis, 1936.

Page 107: 'When it was blowing hard...' Culick & Dunmore, 2001.

Page 112: 'Instead of having a harness...' Ryan, 1995.

Page 113: 'I do it to demonstrate what can be done...' Onkst, www.centennialofflight.gov/essay/Explorers_Record_Setters_and_Daredevils/wingwalkers/EX13.htm

Page 117: 'We know he broke some part of the Federal Aviation Act...' BBC, http://www.bbc.co.uk/dna/h2g2/A21776709

Page 118: 'Here, the crust of the earth...' Saint-Exupéry, 1939.

Page 118: 'Map-reading was not required...' Heppenheimer, 1995.

Page 124: 'I knew I had to fly' California Museum, 2008.

Page 125: 'I was just baggage...' Summerscale, 2007.

Chapter Five

Page 132: 'The distinction between combatant and noncombatant...' Vanderbilt, 2002.

Page 133: 'The brutal but inescapable conclusion...' Douhet, 1942.

Page 146: 'Beginning his workday ritual...' Armstrong, 2003.

Page 146: 'What captured me...' DeBlieu, 2006.

Chapter Six

Page 161: 'I never felt more keenly...' Lindbergh, 1974.

Page 172: 'People would make up names...' Trend, 1999.

Page 174: 'And we were having our fish and chips...' National Security Archive, at www.gwu.edu/~nsarchiv/

Page 177: 'We carried oil drums...' Ibid.

Page 178: 'I shouted and got headline treatment...' Trend, 1999.

Page 178: 'I fought, kicked, shouted...' Calder, 2006.

Page 180: 'Go has been given permission...' Ibid.

Page 186: 'We change the way people live their lives...' Ibid.

Chapter Seven

Page 192: 'As I came up to him...' Royal Air Force History (2003–5).

Page 194: 'I wanted to wipe the floor with him...' Nahum, 2004.

Chapter Eight

Page 224: 'My name is Magnus von Braun...' Bille & Lishock, 2004.

Page 225: 'an intercontinental outer-space raspberry...' Wikipedia.

Page 227: 'We must have a hermetically sealed cabin...' Ryan, 1995.

Page 229: 'unofficial projects funded on the sly...' Ibid.

Page 232: 'Well above the haze layer...' Simons, 1957.

Chapter Nine

Page 247: 'All of us, and I was no exception...' Ryan, 1995.

Page 248: 'A few of us wanted to open up the air...' Ibid.

Page 256: 'If you can chew gum and walk in a straight line...' Rollo, 1991.

Chapter Ten

Page 283: 'I'm not at all embarrassed...' David, www.msnbc.msc.com/id/7646263/

Page 284: 'We believe a proper goal...' Burt Rutan Testimony – Opening Statement. The House Committee on Science, Subcommittee on Space and Aeronautics hearing: 'Future Markets for Commercial Space'. Wednesday 20 April 2005, 9.30am.

Page 285: 'Now that the Space Age has begun...' Wolfe, 1979.

Page 288: 'I didn't even tell my wife...' Belfiore, 2007.

Epilogue

Page 292: 'As you look up the sky looks beautiful...' Ryan, 1995.

Page 311: 'It took us so long to build a twenty-four-hour forecast...' De Villiers, 2006.

Further Reading

Armstrong, W, *Just Wind,* New York: iUniverse, Inc., 2003.

Belfiore, M, *Rocketeers.* New York: Smithsonian Books, 2007.

Bille, M, & Lishock, E, *The First Space Race: Launching the World's First Satellites,* College Station: Texas A&M University Press, 2004.

The British Women's Emancipation Movement 1830–1930 (retrieved 2009) at http://www.hastingspress.co.uk/history/muriel.htm.

Calder, S, *No Frills: the Truth Behind the Low-cost Revolution in the Skies,* London: Virgin Books, 2006.

Clary, DA, *Rocket Man: Robert H. Goddard and the Birth of the Space Age,* New York: Hyperion, 2003.

Crouch, T D, *The Bishop's Boys: Life of Wilbur and Orville Wright,* London: W W Norton, 1990.

Wings: a History of Aviation from Kites to the Wright Brothers to Space Age, New York: W W Norton & the Smithsonian Institution, 2006.

Culick, F, & Dunmore, S, *On Great White Wings: the Wright Brothers and the Race for Flight* (1st US edn), New York: Hyperion, 2001.

David, L, 'Space Tourism's Next Giant Leap', MSNBC, (retrieved 13 November 2009) at http://www.msnbc.msn.com/id/7646263/.

DeBlieu, J, *Wind: How the Flow of Air Has Shaped Life, Myth,* Counterpoint, 2006.

De Villiers, M, *Windswept: the Story of Wind and Weather,* New York: Walker, 2006.

Doganis, R, *The Airline Business* (2nd edn), London & New York: Routledge, 2006.

Douhet, G, *Command of the Air,* New York: Arno Press, 1942.

Eglin, R, & Ritchie, B, *Fly Me, I'm Freddie!*, London: Weidenfeld & Nicolson, 1981.

Fortier, R, *The Balloon Era*, Ottawa: Canada Aviation Museum, 2004.

Fossett, S, *Chasing the Wind*, London: Virgin Books, 2006.

Gregory, M, *Dirty Tricks: British Airways' Secret War against Virgin Atlantic*, London: Virgin Books, 2006.

Harper's Weekly, 'The French Balloon "Le Géant"', 5 December 1863.

Heppenheimer, T A, *Flying Blind*, Invention and Technology Magazine, vol.10-4, Spring 1995.

Jones, L, *easyJet: the Story of Britain's Biggest Low-Cost Airline*, London: Aurum, 2005 and 2007.

Lewis, C, *Sagittarius Rising*, London: Penguin Books, 1936.

Lillienthal, O, *Birdflight as the Basis for Aviation*, Hummelstown, PA: Markowski International Publishers, 1891 (reprint 2001).

Lindbergh, C A, *Autobiography of Values*, New York: Harcourt Brace Jovanovich, 1974.

Marion, F, *Wonderful Balloon Ascents or The Conquest of the Skies*, Whitefish, MT: Kessinger Publishing, 2004 – first published in 1874.

Mason, M, *Aeronautica*, F C Westley, 1838.

Nahum, A, *Frank Whittle: Invention of the Jet*, London: Icon Books, 2004.

National Security Archive, at www.gwu.edu/~nsarchiv/.

Needham, Joseph, *Science and Civilisation in China*, vol. 4, Cambridge: CUP, 1965.

Northern Echo, Bid to Give George a Place in History Gets off the Ground, 7 July 2003.

Nott, J, *Julian Nott* (retrieved 2009) at http://www.nott.com/Pages/projects.php.

Onkst, D H, *Wing Walkers*, US Centennial of Flight Commission (retrieved on 11 November 2009) at http://www.centennialofflight.gov/essay/Explorers_Record_Setters_and_Daredevils/wingwalkers/EX13.htm

Orlebar, C, *The Concorde Story*, Newnes Books, 1986.

Richthofen, M, trans. J E Barker, *The Red Battle Flyer*, R M McBride, 1917. Reissued 2007, Kessinger Publishing.

Rollo, V. *Burt Rutan: Reinventing the Airplane*, Lanham, MD: Maryland Historical Press, 1991.

Royal Air Force History (2003–2005), *Frank Whittle* (retrieved 11 November 2009) at http://www.raf.mod.uk/history_old. Crown Copyright.

Ryan, C, *The Pre-Astronauts: Manned Ballooning on the Threshold of Space*, Annapolis, MD: Naval Institute Press, 1995.

Saint-Exupéry, A de, *Southern Mail/Night Flight*, Penguin, 1929. New edn, 2000.

Wind, Sand and Stars, London: Penguin, 1939. New edn, 2000.

Simons, D, 'A journey no man had taken', *Life*, 2 September 1957, Vol.43, No.10.

Simons, Lt Col. David G with Don A Schanche, *Man High*, New York: Doubleday, 1960.

Spufford, F, *Backroom Boys: the Secret Return of the British Boffin*, London: Faber & Faber, 2003.

Summerscale, K, 'Amelia Earhart: Missing in Action', *Telegraph*, 2 December 2007.

Szondy, D (2004–2009), *Tales of Future Past* (retrieved 13 November 2009) at http://davidszondy.com/

Trend, N, 'Laker Holds Court – Again', *The Sunday Telegraph*, 'Travel', 1999.

Vanderbilt, T, *Survival City: Adventures Among the Ruins of Atomic America*, New York: Princeton Architectural Press, 2002.

Wintle, J, *Makers of Nineteenth Century Culture: 1800–1914*, Oxford: Routledge, 2002.

Wolfe, T, *The Right Stuff*, New York: Farrar, Strans and Giroux, 1979.

Yaeger, J, & Rutan, D, *Voyager*, New York: Knopf, 1987.

Picture credits

Integrated images

Page vi Earth touches heavens © Mary Evans Picture Library

Page 5 Richard Branson with Steve Fossett © Getty Images

Page 14 Relief depicting Daedalus and Icarus, 1st–2nd century (stone) (b/w photo), Roman / Museo Torlonia, Rome, Italy / Alinari / The Bridgeman Art Library

Page 17 Da Vinci's Parachute © Mary Evans/Rue des Archives/Tallandier

Page 20 Children's Games (Kinderspiele): detail of left-hand section showing children making toys and blowing bubbles, 1560 (oil on panel) (detail of 68945), Breugel, Pieter the Elder 9c.1525-69) / Kunsthistorisches Museum, Vienna, Austria / Ali Meyer / The Bridgeman Art Library

Page 27 Cameron N-type envelope © Cameron Balloons Ltd, Bristol, UK, www.cameronballoons.co.uk

Page 29 Nadar (1820–1910) elevating photography to the height of art, published 1862 9litho), Daumier, Honore (1808–79) / Private Collection / The Stapleton Collection / The Bridgeman Art Library

Page 38 Branson with Per in cabin © Getty Images

Page 42 Nazca lines © Charlie & Josette Lenars / CORBIS

Page 47 Lenormand's parachute © Mary Evans Picture Library

Page 51 Peasants attacking a balloon © Mary Evans Picture Library

Page 56 The death of Francois Pilatre de Rozier (1754–85) near Boulogne on 15th June 1785 after trying to cross the Channel in a Mongolfiere balloon (gouache on paper), French School, (18th century) / Louvre, Paris, France / Archives Charmet / The Bridgeman Art Library

Page 60 The Flying Machine of Jean Pierre Blanchard (1753–1809) (coloured engraving) by Martinet, Francois Nicolas (fl. 1731-80) / The Bridgeman Art Library

Page 67 Felix Nadar's Giant Balloon in Paris, c. 1863 (b/w photo), French Photographer, (19th century) / Bibliotheque Nationale, Paris, France / Archives Charmet / The Bridgeman Art Library

Page 71 Giffard's airship © Getty Images

Page 74 The Hindenburg © Getty Images

Page 79 Breitling Orbiter 3 © Cameron Balloons Ltd, Bristol, UK, www.cameronballoons.co.uk

Page 82 Sir George Cayley's sketch of the *Cayley Flyer*. Courtesy of the Royal Aeronautical Society (National Aerospace Library)

Page 85 Aerial Steam Carriage © Science Museum/SSPL

Page 86 Avion III, 'The Bat', designed by Clement Ader (1841–1925) at the Satory military camp, October 1987 (engraving) (b/w photo) French School, (19th century) / CNAM, Conservatoire National des Arts et Metiers, Paris / The Bridgeman Art Library

Page 89 Otto Lilienthal © Getty Images

Page 92 Wing illustration © Ruth Murray

Page 93 Evolution of wing design © Nasa

Page 94 Wright brothers' kite © Library of Congress – digital via/Science Faction/Corbis

Page 96 Wright brothers' propellor © SSPL via Getty Images

Page 101 Curtiss in flight © Corbis

Page 102 Louis Blériot © Hulton-Deutsch Collection / CORBIS

Page 104 Helen Dutrieu (1877–1961) standing beside a plane, before 1914 (b/w photo) by French Photographer, (20th century), Private Collection / Archives Charmet / The Bridgeman Art Library

Page 107 Red Baron with father © Bettmann / CORBIS

Page 108 Bessie Coleman © Getty Images

Page 109 Florence Barnes © Underwood & Underwood/CORBIS

Page 111 Georgia 'Tiny' Broadwick © Bettmann / CORBIS

Page 113 Ormer Locklear © Bertram / CORBIS

Page 115 Guillamet and Mermoz © Mary Evans/Rue des Archives/ Tallandier

Page 120 A giant Sikorsky biplane, one of which bombarded the Germans in East Prussia. © Hulton Archive/Getty Images

Page 121 Lindbergh and the Spirit of St Louis at Sandpoint Airfield, Seattle © PEMCO – Webster & Stevens Collection; Museum of History and Industry, Seattle/CORBIS

Page 123 Wiley Post © Getty Images

Page 124 Amelia Earhart © Getty Images

Page 126 Howard Hughes © Bettmann / CORBIS

Page 129 Hughes at the controls in the 'Spruce Goose' © Bettmann / CORBIS

Page 132 La Guerre Infernale © Leonard de Selva / CORBIS

Page 136 Japanese fire balloon. US army photo A37180C

Page 139 The Coriolis effect © Ruth Murray

Page 140 The jet streams © Ruth Murray

Page 143 Richard Branson and Per Lindstrand © News (UK) Ltd/Rex Features

Page 151 Interior of an Avro Lancastrian. © Science Museum/Science and Society

Page 156 Interior of first class compartment of commercial passenger plane © Getty Images

Page 162 Pan Am Boeing 377 © Hulton-Deutsch Collection / CORBIS

Page 165 Juan Trippe © Time & Life Pictures / Getty Images

Page 167 Dining passengers © CORBIS

Page 169 Pan American Airways System © Smithsonian Institution / Corbis

Page 171 London Airport (Croydon) in 1925 (sepia photo) by English Photographer, (20th century) / Private Collection / The Stapleton Collection / The Bridgeman Art Library

Page 173 Freddie Laker © Getty Images

Page 175 Remembrance stamp – Berlin Airlift © Getty Images

Page 176 Berlin Airlift © Time & Life Pictures / Getty Images

Page 185 Royal Flying Doctor Service © Getty Images

Page 190 Coanda's missile-aeroplane © aviation-images.com

Page 192 Frank Whittle with turbojet engine © Bettmann / CORBIS

Page 196 Fracture in a Comet's fuselage © aviation-images.com

Page 198 Mitsubishi Zero © Roger Viollet / Getty Images

Page 199 X-15 in a supersonic tunnel © NASA

Page 204 Avro Vulcan © Popperfoto / Getty Images

Page 207 Concorde prototype © Hulton-Deutsch Collection / CORBIS

Page 208 TU-144LL © NASA Dryden Flight Research Center (NASA-DFRC)

Page 216 Ramjet model © NASA/GRC

Page 218 Skylon cutaway © Reaction Engines

Page 220 Goddard and rocket at Roswell © Bettmann / CORBIS

Page 223 V-2 missile © Science Museum/SSPL

Page 227 Piccard and Kipfer's wicker-basket helmets © Bettmann / CORBIS

Page 231 Kittinger © Time & Life Pictures

Page 235 Goblin © aviation-images.com

Page 236 Chuck Yeager/Glamorous Glennis © Time & Life Pictures / Getty Images

Page 237 X-15 drops from B-52 © NASA Dryden Flight Research Center (NASA-DFRC)

Page 238 Joe Walker © Bettmann/CORBIS

Page 242 Pterodactyl Ascender© aviation-images.com

Page 249 Leo Valentin © Getty Images

Page 250 Daedalus © NASA Dryden Flight Research Center (NASA-DFRC)

Page 252 Paresev © NASA Dryden Flight Research Center (NASA-DFRC)

Page 253 Cierva C-30 © Getty Images

Page 255 Burt Rutan with model © Burt Rutan

Page 257 variEZE plane © Courtesy of Burt Rutan

Page 263 *Virgin Atlantic GlobalFlyer* © Thierry Boccon-Gibod

Page 271 Rotary Rocket © Getty Images

Page 272 Plaque placed on the moon. © Mary Evans Picture Library / INTERFOTO AGENTUR

Page 279 © Ruth Murray, based on a drawing by the US National Oceanic and Atmospheric Administration

Page 281 *WhiteKnightOne* and *SpaceShipOne* © Jim Koepnick

Page 289 Transhab module © Time & Life Pictures / Getty Images

Page 296 New Mexico Spaceport © Jared Tarbell

Page 301 Photo of Earth as seen by Brian Binnie © Brian Binnie

Page 344 'DNA of flight' © Virgin Galactic

Plate section credits

Section One

Page 1: (top left) photograph Larry Dale Gordon, (top right) © Mary Evans Picture Library, (bottom) Blanchard and Jeffries crashing in the Channel in 1785 / The Bridgeman Art Library

Page 2: (top) SSPL via Getty Images, (bottom) © Hulton-Deutsch Collection/CORBIS.

Page 3: (top) © Rex Features, (bottom) SSPL via Getty Images

Page 4: (top) © Rex Features, (bottom) © Bettmann / CORBIS

Page 5: (top left) Cover of Le Petit Journal commemorating Roland Garros's flight across the Med, 1913 / The Bridgeman Art Library, (top right) © Getty Images, (bottom) © STR/Keystone/CORBIS

Page 6: (top) © Popperfoto/Getty Images, (bottom) © Bettman/CORBIS

Page 7: (top) © aviation-images.com, (bottom left) © Time & Life Pictures/Getty Images, (bottom right) © NASA

Page 8: (top) © NASA, (bottom) © SSPL viaGetty Images

Section Two

Page 1: (top) Courtesy of Cameron Balloons Ltd, Bristol, UK 1966, (bottom) Sipa Press/Rex Features

Page 2: (top) © Rex Features, (bottom) © Jacques Langevin/Sygma/Corbis

Page 3: (top) © Thierry Boccon-Gibod, (bottom) © US Coast Guard Service

Page 4: (top) © AFP/Getty Images, (bottom) © Fabrice Coffrini/epa/Corbis

Page 5: (top) Thierry Boccon-Gibod, (bottom) © AFP/Getty Images

Page 6: (top) © Jim Koepnick/Virgin Galactic, (bottom) © Claire Brown/ Virgin Galactic

Page 7: (top) © Mark Greenberg/Virgin Galactic, (bottom) © Mark Greenberg/Virgin Galactic

Page 8: (top) © Mark Greenberg/Virgin Galactic, (bottom) Photo by Nick Galante/PMRF © NASA

Acknowledgements

I'd like to thank my colleague and friend Will Whitehorn for his encyclopaedic knowledge of aerospace – and his terrifyingly good memory. Doug Millard at London's Science Museum and Rhidian Davis at the British Film Institute sent me tumbling down some wild and wonderful aeronautical rabbit-holes, while Simon Ings helped me pull my story out of all the other tens of thousands of others that have yet to be told about our dreams of flight. Thanks also to Ed Faulkner and Davina Russell at Virgin Books.

Copyright Acknowledgements

Every reasonable effort has been made to contact copyright holders of material reproduced in this book. If any have inadvertently been overlooked, the publishers would be glad to hear from them and make good in future editions any errors or omissions brought to their attention. For permission to reprint copyright material the author and publisher gratefully acknowledge the following: Extract from *Wind, Sand and Stars* by Antoine de Saint-Exupery, translated by William Rees (Penguin Books, 1995, first published as *Terre des Hommes*, 1939). Translation copyright © William Rees, 1995. Reproduced by kind permission.

Index

Virgin Galactic DNA of Flight

Man's ambition to take to the stars is equalled only by his determination to live this dream. Virgin Galactic is pioneering the next step in this quest, taking its place at the head of a long line of achievement before it. This genetic desire to move forward through technology is explained by the Virgin Galactic DNA of Flight. Beginning with Icarus, the story moves through time to the Wright Brothers (the first controlled plane) and all the way to the Apollo Lunar Landing and on to the Ansari X Prize-winning SS1. The DNA of Flight communicates the undeniable DNA of humankind to explore. Virgin Galactic's SS2 is the latest part of this story, but where will it end?